THE SECRET COALITION

THE SECRET COALITION

Ike, LBJ, and the Search for a Middle Way
in the 1950s

GARY A. DONALDSON

Carrel Books

Carrel Books may be purchased in bulk at special discounts for sales promotion, corporate gifts, fund-raising, or educational purposes. Special editions can also be created to specifications. For details, contact the Special Sales Department, Carrel Books, 307 West 36th Street, 11th Floor, New York, NY 10018 or carrelbooks@skyhorsepublishing.com.

Carrel Books® is a registered trademark of Skyhorse Publishing, Inc.®, a Delaware corporation.

Visit our website at www.carrelbooks.com.

10 9 8 7 6 5 4 3 2 1

Library of Congress Cataloging-in-Publication Data is available on file.

Cover photo credit: The LBJ Museum, San Marcos, TX
Cover design by David Sankey

Print ISBN: 978-1-63144-000-7
Ebook ISBN: 978-1-63144-019-9

Printed in the United States of America

Contents

Introduction

By 1950 the American people had grown tired of economic calamities and wars. The nation was hit with the Great Depression in the 1930s. That was followed by the New Deal and then the wars against Germany and Japan. When World War II ended, there seemed to be a collective sigh of relief. But the nation's leaders continued to push forward, insisting that the American people sacrifice even more. The end-of-the-war celebrations were followed by a continuation of wartime rationing, then a series of massive labor strikes that nearly shut down the nation's economy. Within just five years, the nation was at war again, this time in Korea; and the emerging Cold War with the Soviet Union brought with it an anxiety for what the future might hold for the nation and, indeed, for the entire world.

At the same time, the nation seemed on the verge of a great economic expansion. The economy was humming along, spurred by the gigantic demands of wartime production. The American worker was flush with cash. Work had been plentiful during the war, and overtime pay pushed income levels even higher. In addition, wartime rationing and shortages meant that there had been very little to purchase during the war. With the war over, Americans were ready to spend, and spend some more. A number of economists, however, saw all this as a recipe for inflation and out-of-control growth that could lead to another economic downturn and eventually a reoccurrence of the Great Depression.

Most Americans, by 1950, were also ready to get back to the way things were in those illusive golden years before the depression. Any such reversion to normalcy was, of course, impossible—just as it had been following the first great war of the century—but that was how many Americans saw themselves as the new decade of the 1950s opened.

The personification of all this was General Dwight D. Eisenhower. He seemed the perfect leader for a nation looking toward a new era. Eisenhower was often described as "above the fray," a man who refused to wallow in the mud of politics, who prided himself on his own bipartisanship, and the leader who might be able to bring together the two sides of America's divisive political tradition. Americans also saw Eisenhower as someone who could deal with the nation's problems. He was a decisive figure, a doer. He had, after all, defeated the Germans, marched Allied forces into Germany, and dealt with the churlish Soviets at the peace table. He was a calming and unifying figure; so much so that his very presence in Washington allowed the nation the luxury of apathy. America was in the good hands of the good general. By most accounts, the American people stepped back from politics and foreign policy and allowed Eisenhower to do what they thought he did best: look out for the national interest.

This, of course, made for one of the most popular figures in modern American history. Americans, it seemed, liked Ike. But Eisenhower was a long way from being universally liked. His greatest detractors were inside his own Republican Party. He was a moderate, a self-styled middle roader, and that did not sit well with the GOP conservatives who saw political moderation as a surrender to American liberalism. That group was led most aggressively in the immediate postwar by Robert A. Taft, the conservative Ohio senator, the son of a president, and the vocal leader of the Republican right since before the war. When Taft died in the summer of 1953, the conservatives lost their guiding light. The right-wing mantel fell to others, most notably California senator Bill Knowland. But it was not until 1957, when Barry Goldwater stood up and took the reins of the rapidly growing conservative wing of the Republican Party, that conservatives were again able to coalesce around a strong and vocal leader and make their voices heard.

During most of Eisenhower's two terms, these Republican conservatives pushed back at Eisenhower and his administration at nearly every turn, criticizing his fiscal policies, his handling of communism (both domestic and foreign), and for cutting defense spending at a time of an expanding Soviet threat. They often gritted their teeth and called him a liberal, and complained bitterly that they believed his objective was to expand the New Deal, increase the power of the federal government, and accept a coexistence with the Soviets. At the same time, however, these conservatives needed Eisenhower. His popularity and long election coattails often kept them in office. So, through much of the decade these conservatives held their noses and remained in the Eisenhower coalition and worked with the president whenever possible.

Eisenhower managed to make peace with Taft in the months before Taft died. In fact, Taft softened much of his rhetoric and became something of a moderating influence on Eisenhower. But after Taft's death, Eisenhower refused to be burdened by the likes of Knowland or even the upstart Goldwater. Rejected by the conservatives in his own party, he often turned to the moderates in the Democratic Party for assistance in passing his legislative agenda.

Those Democratic moderates were led by Lyndon Johnson, a whirlwind Texas senator with presidential ambitions and an astounding ability to mold the Senate into his own image and get legislation passed. Just as Eisenhower fought off the right in his own party, Johnson fought off the Democratic left, those in his party who wanted a reversion to New Deal–style liberal legislation. But they also believed strongly in a need to present an opposing agenda, a program that gave voters a choice between the Democratic Party's program and that of the administration. To those Democrats, a Democratic Party that did little more than camp onto the agenda of a popular president was a recipe for failure at the polls.

Johnson faced another issue: Eisenhower's immense popularity, particularly among American moderates of both parties. To attack Eisenhower or any of his policies threatened to alienate large segments of the national electorate. Often Johnson, and those in the Democratic Party who followed him, had to be satisfied with only partial victories—"half a loaf," as Johnson often called his strategy. To try to grab more, to push against Eisenhower's immense popularity in an attempt to pass New Deal–style liberal legislation, would be overreaching and yield nothing. To Johnson, and those who supported him and his policies, moderation and compromise with a popular president would continue to move the Democratic Party agenda forward—just slower and at a more measured pace.

Johnson and Eisenhower may have appeared to be in some sort of political harmony, but the two men truly saw the world differently. Eisenhower's priorities were directed at national defense, a balanced budget, economic prosperity, and a sound dollar. He was willing to maintain any social programs with what was left over. Johnson held just the opposite view. To avoid an unequal economic structure, he believed that the federal government had the responsibility to provide for those who needed assistance: the ill-fed, the ill-housed, and the undereducated. Eisenhower had no such concerns. He believed, in fact, in the old Republican Party principle that a strong economy would do more to help those in need than any tax-supported social programs. And that coupled with a strong national defense became the primary goals of his presidency. Despite their different perspectives, the two men (as leaders of the moderates in their respective parties) found some common ground at the center of the political spectrum, and that resulted in compromise, cooperation, and finally legislation.

Nor was this celebrated spirit of bipartisanship sparked by any real contact between these two men; there were no high-level meetings to pound out compromise legislation. Eisenhower and Johnson did not even direct their subordinates to negotiate differences and language.[1] But moderate legislation was passed. More often than not, the GOP right found the outcome too liberal, and those on the left in the Democratic Party complained that it was too conservative. However, through most of the decade, moderation prevailed, the center held, and the people's work was done.

George Reedy, one of Johnson's closest advisors and an astute observer of the political process in this period, explained the process in the simplest terms: The idea was "to approach *all* issues by amending Eisenhower's requests.... The point was to change [Eisenhower's] bill, replace Republican language with Democratic language, leaving the Eisenhower name on the bill." This, he added, had a "placating effect upon the president, which meant that he was unlikely to intervene in the debate . . . and unlikely to veto the measure." The result was simple: a bill introduced by the administration, liberalized to a degree in the Senate by the Democratic leadership, and signed by the president. What did Eisenhower get in exchange for this cooperation? Democratic support for his foreign policy—to him, his real challenges. It was not a bipartisan marriage made in heaven, but it was a means to an end, a way to produce compromise legislation that pushed the country forward. The process gave the appearance of a moderate president coming together with moderate Democrats (in opposition to extremists in both parties) to do the people's work. "It was little wonder," Reedy observed further, "that the Democratic congressional majorities increased at each election while [Johnson] was leader."

At the same time, it always frustrated Eisenhower that the nation seemed to like him ("I Like Ike") but they did not care much for his party. At his most surly, he once told a friend that he was going to form a new political party (perhaps one more popular than his own) made up of the moderates from the two parties. This, he said, would allow him to control the vital center of American politics, letting the two "radical wings" that he despised so much wither on the vine of an antiquated political system.

Through the nation's history, Americans have seldom seen such bipartisan cooperation of the type exhibited through most of the 1950s. The Constitution nearly mandates a system in which the minority is protected from the majority's juggernaut, leaving opposing sides to come to some sort of compromise in order to pass legislation. In the 1950s, the chief political conflicts were generally within the parties, between the moderates and the left among the Democrats and between the moderates and the right among the Republicans. Eisenhower and Johnson, with almost no contact or common strategy, saw common ground among moderates of both their parties and worked to build a moderate coalition that pushed through legislation. This coalition of interparty moderates was never named; indeed, it was never truly identifiable. In fact, its most apparent identifying characteristic was its vocal opposition: from the leaders of the Democratic left who kept up a constant drumbeat against Johnson's willingness to enable the administration's legislative agenda and from the leaders of the Republican right who criticized Eisenhower for his all-too-liberal unbalanced budgets and his unwillingness to confront international communism.

By the last two years of the decade, however, the political system had changed. The left inside the Democratic Party and the right among the Republicans had gained new strength and weakened the political center, pushing out the moderate political philosophies of both Eisenhower and Johnson. By the end of the decade the center had all but collapsed and extremist wings in the two parties were ascendant.

Since the 1950s, Americans have lamented the inability of their national legislature in Washington to cooperate, to work out their many differences, and get legislation through its complicated process—and then onto the president's desk. The nation often looks to the 1950s as a time when the system worked, when legislation was born from the labors of bipartisan cooperation and good intentions. In some ways that was true. But there was still plenty of old-style American political conflict—and it was crushing at times—but it was from the outlying wings (Eisenhower called them the "radical wings") of the two parties, often giving the appearance that the Republicans and Democrats were getting along.

CHAPTER ONE

Postwar Politics

With the 1944 presidential campaign on the horizon, Republicans began casting about for a candidate who might be able to unseat Franklin Roosevelt, then preparing to run for an unprecedented fourth term. They looked first to General Douglas MacArthur, the theater commander in Asia and an outspoken conservative, and then to General Dwight D. Eisenhower, the Allied commander in Europe. It had been suggested to Eisenhower by a war correspondent as early as 1943 that politics might be in his future. Eisenhower's glib response was that the correspondent had surely "been standing in the sun too long."[1] But by late 1943 and early 1944 the drumbeat quickened as the Republicans became increasingly desperate. Arthur Eisenhower counseled his younger brother to issue a statement that he was not interested in a political career, arguing that MacArthur's military reputation was being damaged because he had refused to issue such a statement immediately. Eisenhower responded that any such statement would only make him appear ridiculous and that he would not, he wrote to his brother, "tolerate the use of my name in connection with any political activity of any kind."[2] There was even some additional talk that Roosevelt might choose Eisenhower as his running mate in 1944, particularly if the Republicans nominated MacArthur.[3] But both

MacArthur and Eisenhower became consumed with the war effort, and all talk of making generals into politicians in the midst of the war quieted.

On April 12, 1945, Roosevelt died, quite unexpectedly, at his home-away-from Washington, in Warm Springs, Georgia. Vice President Harry Truman became president of the United States. The war in Europe was winding down quickly. The war against Japan, it seemed, would last much longer.

In 1945, at the Potsdam Conference in Berlin, the new president Truman and Eisenhower were bantering about the postwar world when Truman jolted the general with a suggestion that he might want to consider a political future. "General," Truman said, "there is nothing that you may want that I won't try to help you get. That definitely and specifically includes the Presidency in 1948." Eisenhower later recalled his amazement at the offer. "I doubt that any soldier of our country has ever [been] so suddenly struck in his emotional vitals by a President with such an apparently sincere and certainly astounding proposition as this. . . . [T]o have the President suddenly throw his broadside into me left no recourse except to treat it [as] a very splendid joke which I hoped it was." "Mr. President," Eisenhower replied, "I don't know who will be your opponent for the presidency, but it will not be I."[4]

When Eisenhower returned home after the war, he was asked over and over again: will you run? To an audience in his hometown of Abilene, Kansas, in 1945, he seemed to make it pretty clear. "It is silly to talk about me in politics," he said, "and so for once I'll talk about it, but only to settle this thing once [and] for all. I should like to make this as emphatic as possible. . . . In the strongest language you can command, you can state that I have no political ambitions at all, make it even stronger than that if you can. I'd like to go even further than Sherman in expressing myself on this subject."[5] He could hardly have been anymore definitive, but the 1948 campaign was still three years away, and in that time Eisenhower definitely considered making a run.

As the 1948 election approached, the nation seemed poised for a wave of Republicanism that was about to wash over Washington. The Democrats had been in power since March 1933; they had taken

the nation through the Great Depression and the war. Now, some fifteen years after the Democrats pushed their way back onto the political stage, it seemed time for a Republican resurgence and what many Americans saw as a return to normalcy—or something resembling a lifestyle away from the emergencies of the last decade and a half. If anyone doubted the Republican resurgence, there was the evidence of the 1946 midterm elections when the Republicans swept both houses of Congress for the first time since Herbert Hoover was in office. On the first day of that congressional session, Republican members of the new 80th Congress arrived on Capitol Hill carrying brooms. They refused to reveal to the press what the brooms symbolized, but to anyone who knew the mind of the GOP in 1946, they were intended to represent a sweeping away of the New Deal.

All of this assumed that Truman would be cast out two years later in the 1948 presidential election. The "Little Man from Missouri" had brought the war to a conclusion in good order, but to most Americans he had done little more than observe the giant American war machine as it did its business of finishing off Germany and Japan. He had made the decision to drop the bomb on Japan, and he was generally praised for that decisive act—and for ending the war as quickly as possible. But even that was perceived by many Americans as little more than carrying out a decision that had already been made.

‡

It is a phenomenon of the American political system that (in order to appeal to the largest possible range of voters) a presidential candidate is often bound to select a running mate who carries nearly the opposite appeal. Such was the case in 1944 when Roosevelt chose Harry Truman to run with him on the Democratic ticket. Roosevelt was urbane, urban, a wealthy patrician, a career politician who had risen to political importance in New York as a reformer, a battler against the corrupt bossism of Tammany Hall. With the Roosevelt money and Roosevelt name, he had glided through life from the social prominence of Hyde Park, to

Groton, Harvard, and on to Columbia Law. He headed to Wall Street, the New York state legislature, national politics in 1920, and finally to the White House in 1933. Truman was different. His life had been hard. He grew up on the Missouri frontier where opportunities were limited and prospects were bleak. There was no prominent family name, no family wealth, no marvelous education to carry him through life. Harry Truman was ordinary. He served in France during World War I and returned home to try his hand at business. His small haberdashery in Kansas City, Missouri, soon failed. He then tried his hand at investing in oil and mining interests, failing at that as well. At thirty, he turned to politics and found some success at the local level where he seemed destined to stay. But by allying with the Pendergast machine (a corrupt Kansas City organization named after political boss Tom Pendergast), Truman moved up the political ladder and finally into the U.S. Senate, where he made a name for himself by uncovering wasteful wartime spending and then as one of the few southerners who stood by Roosevelt and the New Deal.

After the death of FDR, Truman stepped into the White House with a convincing 87 percent approval rating, a figure that clearly owed more to his anonymity and the nation's expectations than to his popularity. By 1946, however, his approval rating had slid to a paltry 32 percent. For most of the nation, Truman's problems revolved around reconversion, the process of regulating the postwar economy that was his first real act as president. And he generally stumbled. Taking advice from economists who insisted that the immediate removal of wartime price controls would cause either debilitating inflation or depression, or both, Truman left price controls in place for nearly two years after the war ended. At the same time, organized labor pushed at the other end. Generally quiet during the war in an effort to keep production up, unions went out on strike when the war ended in numbers that were unprecedented. As labor and other production costs increased, while prices remained fixed by the federal government, production of consumer goods ground to a halt. To meet the demand, a vibrant black market emerged, embarrassing the government even more. Finally, under pressure from just about every direction, an embattled

Truman removed the price controls. It was a popular decision, but the long wait had hurt the president. His first real decision had been wrong.

Organized labor presented an additional challenge. Truman's handling of the postwar labor strikes not only brought the unions out against him, but it hurt his standing generally. Certainly, labor had done its part to win the war, but following V-J Day the American worker was taking home less real income than before the war. In addition, when the war brought an end to cutbacks in overtime, wages were dragged down even further. In 1941, the average American laborer's real wage was just over $28.00 per week. That had risen to $36.72 in 1945. But by the fall of 1946, inflation and a reduction in overtime pay had pulled real wages back to the 1941 level. The pie was expanding, but labor's share remained the same. Industry, however, argued that it was shackled with Truman's wartime price controls, plus it was stuck with the immense cost of retooling for peacetime production. Labor and management were on a collision course that would engulf the nation in the immediate postwar years. And Truman, caught in the middle, was damaged by the events.

The result was nearly inevitable. Through the summer of 1945, the nation experienced 4,600 work stoppages involving some five million workers. Following V-J Day, the situation worsened. In September, 43,000 oil refinery workers went out on strike, cutting off one-third of the nation's oil supply. Six weeks later, the United Auto Workers struck General Motors, idling some 325,000 workers. Then in January, 750,000 steelworkers walked out, followed by 200,000 electrical workers and another 200,000 meatpackers.[6] The nation seemed on the verge of paralysis, and the people looked to their president for answers. Truman responded as he often did to crises: he pulled together a blue-ribbon committee to find a solution. They had none.

In April 1946, the United Mine Workers went out on strike, and the nation's infrastructure (fueled by coal) ground to a halt. Truman responded by seizing the coal mines. It was a decisive, even popular, decision, but it alienated organized labor, whose leaders and rank-and-file began to see the president as a tool of management. Finally in May, railroad engineers and trainmen struck, which threatened to shut down the nation's commerce and industry. Truman responded by asking Congress for emergency powers to bring contempt charges against labor leaders, and then he threatened to draft striking workers into the military. Truman's threats caused labor leaders in the railroad industry to back down, and the president basked in his victory. But as the 1946 midterm elections approached, it was clear that organized labor had no friend in the White House.[7]

As Washington geared up for the 1946 election campaigns, Truman's approval ratings sank to the low thirties. And most Americans had come to see him as a sort of caretaker president, someone who would keep things going until the Democrats could nominate a strong candidate to take the reins of the party. The Democratic National Committee, in fact, had so little confidence in Truman's appeal that in several congressional campaigns that year they purchased national radio time and broadcast old Roosevelt speeches rather than send Truman out on the campaign trail.

Not surprisingly, Truman's general lack of leadership abilities caused a splintering within the Democratic Party. Through the 1930s, Roosevelt had cobbled together a fragile coalition of diverse groups that included southern conservatives, northern liberals, western farmers, organized labor, big city bosses, and minorities and immigrants in northern cities. Truman simply did not have the qualities necessary to hold these disparate groups together. Roosevelt was a born leader. He held the coalition together with well-applied charm, cajolery, and flattery. Without Roosevelt's leadership parts of this fragile coalition began to break away, each intending on building its own power base and lead a new party coalition into the next political generation.

All this became apparent in 1946 when the Democrats lost control of Congress for the first time since Hoover was in office. The losses were big, but predictable. The Democrats lost fifty-four seats in the House and twelve in the Senate. The era of Democratic dominance appeared over, and the nation seemed ready for a tidal wave of Republicanism. Truman's lack of effective leadership, followed by the 1946 Republican surge, all seemed like the natural order of things to most Americans. The political pendulum had swung back. Thus, the Republicans of the 80th Congress entered the Capitol in January 1947 carrying their brooms, ready to use their mandate to sweep away what they saw as the refuse of New Deal liberalism. Their November campaign call had been "Had enough?" And the nation, it seemed, had answered with a resounding yes.[8]

The Republicans of the 80th Congress coalesced around Ohio senator Robert A. Taft, "Mr. Republican," the austere conservative and prewar isolationist, the son of a president. It was no secret that Taft had his eye on the 1948 Republican nomination, and just about everyone agreed that whoever received that nomination would ride the Republican wave into the White House with little difficulty.

Truman, however, was not prepared to hand over power to the Republicans—at least not yet. Through the next two years, he maintained a unique relationship with the 80th Congress. On domestic issues, it was a gloves-off affair. The president vetoed seventy-five bills in the two sessions. Five of his vetoes were overridden, and very little was accomplished. On foreign affairs, however, it was a different story. A Cold War consensus was in the process of forming, and the two parties worked together to establish a foreign policy that would prevail for another forty years. In the final analysis, however, Truman used the 80th Congress to enhance his standing with several sectors of his party. By introducing and pushing liberal legislation that he probably knew would never pass, Truman was able to portray the Republicans as the political arm of big business, insensitive to the needs of the average American, and unwilling to act on much needed domestic reforms.[9]

Consequently, as the 1948 campaign approached, Truman was able to present himself as the defender of the common man, a fighter against oppression, and the real successor to the New Deal. And by opposing the Taft-Hartley Act (designed by the Republicans in the 80th Congress to curtail the powers of organized labor), Truman was able to pull many of those disgruntled organized labor leaders back into his coalition. Then on foreign affairs, he worked with congressional leaders to adopt a firm and decisive anti-Soviet stance that was generally popular. Using Congress as his foil, Truman, by the summer of 1948, had established himself as the new leader of the old New Deal coalition, the defender of the common man and organized labor, and a strong world leader.

In turn, the Republicans in the 80th Congress proceeded under the assumption that the 1946 election was a portent for the future and that in 1948 they would put one of their own into the White House with little effort. That is, they played right into Truman's hands. A Republican bill to reduce taxes in the upper income brackets was passed over Truman's veto. The Republicans excluded several groups from Social Security benefits, overriding two presidential vetoes to get the job done. They killed administration-supported bills to provide aid to education, increase the minimum wage, and provide comprehensive housing. Southern Democrats, seeing no need to support what appeared to be Truman's failing lame-duck presidency, got behind most Republican initiatives in exchange for Republican support in killing civil rights legislation. All this appeared to be an insurmountable obstacle to Truman's domestic agenda, but it worked to increase Truman's image with the American people as their representative fighting against the forces of big business and privilege.[10]

After 1946, Taft emerged as the clear leader of the Republicans in Congress, and in that position he was considered the immediate frontrunner for the 1948 Republican nomination. But he was not uncontested. Standing in the wings were at least two formidable candidates: Eisenhower, who continued to claim that politics was not in his future; and Thomas Dewey, who had lost to Roosevelt in 1944 and (it seemed to be common knowledge) would at some point make a run for the 1948 nomination.

It was Eisenhower, however, who was the true wildcard. It was clear that if he wanted the nomination—of either party—he could have it. And that was, in fact, part of his appeal. No one knew if he was a Republican or a Democrat, and he refused to reveal his affiliation, even to the point of avoiding issues that might define him. In this noncandidate role, he was able to maintain a candidate's visibility without carrying the weight of a candidate's responsibilities. With his intentions unknown, no one dared attack him, and he made no enemies. He was also not responsible to the press or the public for possessing policies on specific issues. All of this added to his growing popularity. In a 1947 poll, 22 percent believed Eisenhower was a Republican; 20 percent thought he was a Democrat. The largest group, 58 percent, confessed that they did not know his affiliation. In 1946, *Time* reported the obvious, that he could run successfully on either ticket.[11]

The boom for Eisenhower began immediately following the Republican 1946 victory when it seemed clear that the Republican tide was on the rise. *Time* referred to his "tremendous reputation, unencumbered by political liabilities, his wonderful name, his poise, and amazing popularity. . . . Ike," the article continued, "might find it hard to slap down the presidential bee." *Life* reported that Eisenhower was on the stump, despite his almost constant insistence that he was not a candidate, and discussing various issues beyond the military, "thereby starting a big boom to make him a presidential candidate." Another *Life* article announced that a "boom for Ike" was underway and included a cover shot of a pretty girl wearing a "Draft Ike" button as a monocle.[12]

Eisenhower continued to deny his candidacy, however. Finally, in June 1947, he announced that he had agreed to become the president of Columbia University. There, he told a friend, he would find "some shelter from the constant political darts that are launched in my direction by well-meaning, but I fear short sighted, friends."[13] That might have been the logical conclusion, but some saw it differently, that his acceptance of the Columbia position was an affirmation that he wanted to remain in the public eye and in public service. Journalist John Gunther wrote that Eisenhower's announcement that he would go to Columbia caused "the movement to make him President to spread like fire through dry wheat."[14]

In late 1947, Eisenhower continued to insist that he would not run, but he still toyed with the possibility. To his friend and wartime chief of staff, Walter Bedell Smith, he wrote: "I do not believe that you or I or anyone else has the right to state categorically that he will *not* perform *any* duty that his country might demand of him. . . ." To refuse to run, he told Smith, "would be almost the same thing as a soldier refusing to carry out the desires of his commander." He added that he had no taste for political life, but perhaps under the right circumstances he might reconsider. "On the other hand, if you should assume the occurrence of an American miracle of a nature that has never heretofore occurred, at least since Washington, you might have the spectacle of someone being named by common consent. . . ."[15] Eisenhower often referred to his fantasy of being drafted by acclamation. To another friend he wrote: "Since no man—at least since Washington's day—has ever gone into high political office except with his own consent, indeed with his own connivance, I feel perfectly secure in my position" of rejecting a candidacy.[16]

His decision not to run became clearer as he considered other factors. He had come to believe that the politicians stalking him were only interested because of his status as a war hero, that his only real virtue was that he was popular enough to win the presidency. It was not in Eisenhower's nature to be an ineffectual front man for a political organization—and the idea was repugnant to him. He told his brother Milton that he did not feel any sense of duty toward a political party that would, "in desperation, turn to some name that might be a bit popular around the country, in the effort to drag a political . . . organization out of a hole."[17] And then there were the rigors of the campaign itself. If he chose to run in 1948 as a Republican, he would have to fight several primary battles, and since primary victories then garnered less than half the delegates needed to win the nomination, he would almost certainly be forced into a bloody convention fight as well. Eisenhower may have been a popular national figure, but it would have taken a great effort to win a nomination in 1948. Of course, he would not be running unopposed. Other Republicans wanted the nomination. Particularly Taft and Dewey were unlikely to give up without a struggle, and their combined forces might well push Eisenhower right out of contention. He also had no real political organization, and he had raised no money. Rather than risk his reputation in a bloody battle that he might well lose, Eisenhower decided to decline.

His hand was finally forced in January 1948 when a group of his supporters entered his name in the March New Hampshire primary. Either he had to allow it to happen and be a candidate or he had to withdraw. The intentions of these Eisenhower supporters were apparently not known to Eisenhower until Leonard Finder, the publisher of the Manchester *Union*

Leader, sent him a copy of the newspaper's endorsement. Along with the column, Finder added a personal note designed to appeal to Eisenhower's desire for a draft: "While we appreciate that you are not anxious for political aspirations, we are equally confident that you will not resist or resent a genuine grass-roots movement. That is exactly what we have here in New Hampshire." In a reference to Eisenhower's long-held commitment to duty, Finder concluded, "no man should deny the will of the people in a matter such as this. All that we are attempting is to have the will of the people made so clear that it cannot be obviated by the usual politicians assembled in convention."[18]

Eisenhower apparently felt that his hand had been forced. He immediately issued a statement claiming that he had no desire to enter politics. Nine days later, on January 23, he issued a more formal response in a letter to Finder that was released to the press.[19] It was as close to William Tecumseh Sherman's statement—"If nominated I will not run; if elected, I will not serve"—as Eisenhower would get. He wrote that he was not surprised that admirers and supporters had misinterpreted or found hidden meaning in his statements, "but my failure to convince thoughtful and earnest men . . . proves that I must make some amplification. I am not available and could not accept nomination to high political office." He went on to apologize to those who had given their time on his behalf. He concluded with a statement that should have left nothing to the imagination: "My decision to remove myself completely from the political scene is definite and positive [and] I could not accept nomination even under the remote circumstances that it were tendered me."[20] That, he thought, would certainly end all the speculation. He wrote to a friend, "I feel as if I've had an abscessed tooth pulled."[21] With that, the Republicans stood down and headed off to look for other candidates. For the Democrats, however, it was a different story. They seemed to interpret the response to the Finder letter as Eisenhower's disavowal of his Republican affiliation. Thus, they concluded, he must be a Democrat.[22]

Like the Republicans, the Democrats had been trying for some time to persuade Eisenhower to cast his lot with them, and he had refused just as he had refused the Republicans. But the Democrats were more desperate in 1948 than the Republicans. They believed that Truman was a loser, and they saw no one on the horizon except Eisenhower who had enough popular support to defeat the Republicans in November. The objective of these Democrats-for-Eisenhower was little more than to keep the Democrats in Washington (and the Republicans out) for another four years. When Eisenhower wrote to Milton in October 1947 about a political party that "in desperation [would] turn to some name that might be a bit popular around the country, in the effort to drag [itself] out of a hole," he no doubt had the Democrats in mind. At the same time, the Democrats were not just infatuated with Eisenhower. They knew the situation well. Polls showed that Eisenhower-as-Democrat running against any Republican was a winner in 1948.[23]

The draft-Eisenhower Democrats were a fairly diverse group, ranging from the sons of Franklin Roosevelt to labor leaders like Walter Reuther and big-city bosses like Chicago's Jacob Arvey and Jersey City's Frank Hague. There were even southern supporters, particularly senators Lister Hill and John Sparkman, both from Alabama, and Florida senator Claude Pepper. Their only common cause was that they disliked the doomed Truman, and they wanted to keep the Democrats in power. The real force behind the movement, however, was the Americans for Democratic Action (ADA), a liberal political organization that considered itself the harbinger of New Deal liberalism that, at the same time, despised communism both at home and abroad. To the ADA, it was simple: "Anyone but Truman." He was anathema, an unworthy proponent. The ADA political philosophy in 1948 was summed up in a letter from theologian and ADA founder Reinhold Niebuhr to ADA head James Loeb: "We are sunk now" with Truman, he wrote, "and Eisenhower is the only possible candidate who [can] defeat the Republicans. I would support almost any decent man to avoid four years of Republican rule."[24]

In mid-April 1948, the executive board of the ADA met to devise a strategy to organize the diverse Eisenhower supporters under ADA leadership. They issued a statement designed to pull directly on the strings of Eisenhower's sense of responsibility to the nation: "This Nation has the right to call upon men like Dwight D. Eisenhower . . . if the people so chose. . . . No one . . . can enjoy the privilege of declaring himself unavail-able in this hour of the nation's need." Eisenhower, they added, "would stir the popular enthusiasm which will sweep progressive candidates across the country into Congress."[25] For the ADA, the Eisenhower drive was an expedient, an act of desperation. He was simply someone the ADA and other Democrats thought could win.

Eisenhower had managed to keep his distance from much of this Democratic Party activity as it developed during the early spring of 1948. By March, however, local Democratic Eisenhower-for-President organiza-tions had begun to spring up throughout the country, and many were raising money to support the Eisenhower campaign that did not exist. By April, Eisenhower realized that he would again have to deny all charges that he wanted to be a candidate—this time for the benefit of the Democrats. On the day following the ADA endorsement, Eisenhower wrote Bedell Smith, "Recently the Democrats have taken the attitude that Mr. Truman cannot be re-elected; therefore they do not want to re-nominate him. In this situation they are turning desperately to anyone that might give them a chance of winning, and they have the cockeyed notion that I might be tempted to make the effort."[26]

The ADA endorsement was reported in *Time* on April 19. In that same issue, Eisenhower was asked to respond. "I wrote a letter," he said, referring to the Finder letter of some four months earlier. "And I meant every word of it."[27] But even that did not satisfy some Democrats. Florida senator Claude Pepper and a few other Democrats continued to push for an Eisenhower nomination. In the weeks before the Democratic conven-tion, James Roosevelt sent telegrams to each party delegate inviting them to a meeting to select "the ablest and strongest man available. . . . It is our belief," the message continued, "no man in these critical days can refuse the call to duty and leadership implicit in the nomination and virtual election to the Presidency of the United States."[28] Again, Eisenhower's hand was forced. On July 5, he issued a statement: "I will not, at this time, identify myself with any political party, and could not accept nomi-nation for any public office or participate in partisan political contest."[29] But because Eisenhower had used the phrase, "at this time," the fires continued to burn. A plan was hatched to have Eisenhower's name placed in nomination at the convention without his consent. Claude Pepper sent a note to Eisenhower notifying him of the plan, then concluding the note with: "I neither expect nor desire either an acknowledgment or reply."[30] The scheme forced Eisenhower to disavow his political ambitions one last time. On July 8 and 9, he wrote letters to the leaders of the draft-Eisenhower movement. All the letters were personalized and written differently, but each letter contained the following phrase: "No matter under what terms, conditions, or premises a proposal might be couched, I would refuse to accept the nomination."[31] And with that, the 1948 draft-Eisenhower movement was finally shut down.

The Republicans went on, for a second time, to choose Thomas Dewey after he jumped into several primaries in the eleventh hour and then outmaneuvered Taft at the convention to win the nomination. Dewey had run against Roosevelt in 1944, the young fresh-face (Dewey was the first presidential candidate of either of the two primary parties to be born in the twentieth century) against the old man. He had little chance of beating Roosevelt in 1944; victories were close on both war fronts, but Dewey did better than most observers expected, and he immediately became the front runner for the next presidential campaign in 1948. To just about anyone paying attention that year, Dewey was about to become the next president. Since there seemed to be no campaign battle to win, he followed the advice of his chief advisors and barely bothered to campaign; and as the election approached, he even leaked his cabinet choices.

The Democrats split badly. Henry Wallace (perceived as the communist-sponsored candidate) formed a third party, the Progressives. Many southern conservatives became disenchanted with Truman and his concessions toward civil rights for African Americans, and at the convention they walked out. Eventually these southerners formed the States Rights Democrats, a name quickly whittled down to the "Dixiecrats" by southern newspaper editors. Their claim—as it had been the claim of southern politicians through the nation's history—was that they represented the true aspirations and beliefs of the Democratic Party; that it was the national party that had varied from the party's mainstream structure. They nominated South Carolina governor Strom Thurmond for president.

To just about everyone's surprise, Truman won the election fairly easily, carrying 49.5 percent of the popular vote to Dewey's 45 percent. The Electoral College vote was even more convincing, with Truman winning a solid 303 votes to Dewey's 189.

Thurmond won thirty-nine electoral votes in four southern states, but his most important impact was to carry the racist label. That, along with Truman's concessions to civil rights, gave the president a big turn-out of African American voters in northern urban areas. He may have lost thirty-nine electoral votes in South Carolina, Louisiana, Alabama, and Mississippi, but he won California, Illinois, and Ohio because (at least in part) African American voters turned out in big numbers in Los Angeles, Chicago, and Cleveland. It was a good trade-off for Truman, and it began a slow shift in the national party structure as conserva-tive white southerners began moving into the Republican Party and northern African Americans began deserting the party of Lincoln for the Democrats.

Wallace's impact was much the same. Republicans had wanted desperately to label Truman a communist or at least soft on communism. But Wallace had, almost eagerly, accepted support and assistance from the American Communist Party in his campaign. Any attempt to attack Truman as a communist sympathizer fell on deaf ears with Wallace in the race. Both third-party efforts aided Truman by deflecting criticisms that might well have damaged his campaign. Because of Thurmond and Wallace, the vola-tile charges of racism and communism did not stick to Truman.[32]

It was the 1948 statewide election in Illinois, however, that may have had the greatest impact on Democratic Party politics for the next decade. Two of the most important political figures in that state had jumped on the draft-Eisenhower bandwagon: Cook County political boss Jacob Arvey and the state party's chosen candidate for the Senate seat that year, Paul Douglas. Adlai Stevenson, the Democratic Party's choice to run for governor against two-time Republican incumbent, Dwight Green, refused to join the Eisenhower movement and continued to stand by Truman. Then at the convention, once the draft-Eisenhower movement collapsed, Stevenson seconded the nomination of his distant cousin (and Truman good friend) Alben Barkley for vice president.

As late as the last weeks of October, the *New York Times* followed most pundits and predicted that Green would defeat Stevenson by a wide margin. Most pollsters had by then, however, given up the polling process, declaring Dewey's victory a foregone conclusion—along with most of the other Republicans who, they thought, would ride his coattails into Washington. Green was so overconfident, in fact, that he spent much of the summer lobbying for the vice presidential nomination instead of campaigning for the job in Springfield. For his efforts, he made the short list of Dewey's perspective running mates, and he was chosen to deliver the keynote address at the Republican National Convention in Philadelphia. By then, however, Green had been tainted by what some saw as his negligence in preventing the tragic Centralia, Illinois, mine disaster a year before. Also, he was too far to the right for Dewey's taste. He was finally overlooked in favor of California governor, Earl Warren.

When the election-night numbers rolled in, it was clear that Stevenson had won an unexpected victory. He buried Green with a whopping 57 percent of the votes, the largest plurality in the state's history. His margin of victory was almost 600,000 votes, and he took half of the traditionally conservative downstate counties. In the national election, Truman won the state by a squeak of just 33,000 votes—in fact, riding Stevenson's coattails to victory. It was a crucial state and a big win. Although Truman and Stevenson had very little in common and really never connected on any level, Truman did not forget Stevenson's loyalty and his role in the 1948 campaign. In 1952, when Truman began looking for a successor, Stevenson, one of the party's fresh faces, would make the short list.[33]

Stevenson was one of several Democrats who emerged with victories in 1948, along with Hubert Humphrey in Minnesota and Lyndon Johnson in Texas. Massachusetts Representative John Kennedy won a second term.[34] The "class of 1948," as both parties called it, propelled several of the nation's future political leaders into politics

Stevenson had come up through the ranks. During the war he served in the Navy Department as the assistant to Secretary Frank Knox and was sent on several inspection tours of naval installations in the Pacific. As early as 1942, Stevenson, at age forty-two, considered an Illinois Senate run against Republican Curly Brooks, but the all-powerful Chicago Democratic Party machine overlooked Stevenson in favor of Congressman Raymond McKeough.[35]

Stevenson then turned his interests toward the state gubernatorial election in 1944. But as the campaign approached, he simply could not make the decision to run, and that indecision exposed a serious flaw in his character. Stevenson's indecisiveness became almost legendary in a profession where the ability to be quick and decisive is considered an attribute. Several times, including his decision to run in 1952, Stevenson seemed almost debilitated by apprehension, much to the frustration of his supporters. Several of his friends and cohorts have, however, disagreed with that analysis. They have argued that it was not so much indecision that plagued Stevenson as a natural lack of desire to promote himself and a central belief that the office should seek the individual and not the other way around. He was also careful and cautious about such decisions. Nevertheless, the image stuck to Stevenson throughout his political career. He was often perceived as an indecisive figure who might not be up to the job when the tough decisions had to be made. That often translated into what one of his biographers has called "a soft head," a leader who begs off toughness for a compromising and conciliatory approach. As a presidential candidate during the first decade of the Cold War, such an image was not helpful.[36]

Stevenson, however, was burdened with more than just the decision to run. His wife, Ellen, hated Washington, and in 1943 she returned to the Stevenson family home in Libertyville, Illinois. As early as 1941, Ellen had asked for a divorce, and the couple's marriage problems continued into Stevenson's 1948 gubernatorial campaign. In 1949 the couple divorced. Stevenson was also distracted by his aspiration to buy the *Chicago Daily News.* He seemed to be torn between conflicting desires to be an attorney, a politician, or a newspaper man. Consequently, he had difficulty deciding to run for governor in 1944. Finally, he demurred.

When Frank Knox died, somewhat unexpectedly in April 1944, Stevenson joined a syndicate that attempted to buy Knox's controlling interest in the *Chicago Daily News* (which had been published by Knox until 1940). But within the year, that project had collapsed. In that same year, Stevenson was eased out of the Navy Department, now under the leadership of James Forrestal, who had accepted the analysis that Stevenson was too indecisive, too soft for the position.[37] From there, Stevenson went on to the State Department to become part of the commission to establish the United Nations. Serving mostly under Archibald MacLeish, he became the senior advisor to the nation's UN delegation and was named an alternate delegate in the fall of 1946, representing the Truman administration on a number of committees.

In November 1946, when the Republicans swept both houses of Congress, Illinois Democrats managed to hold on to only six of Illinois' twenty-six congressional seats. Even most of the party machine candidates in Chicago were turned out that year. There was, however, one bright spot for the Democrats, and that seemed to awaken Stevenson. In the spring of 1947, Martin Kennelly won the election for mayor of Chicago. An honest, civic-minded Democrat, Kennelly changed the face of Chicago–Cook County Democratic Party politics from the unethical organization headed by Ed Kelly and Jake Arvey to a new appearance of honesty and good government. Stevenson took from Kennelly's victory that there was still a place in government for honesty and moderation. Stevenson wrote to a friend, "Kennelly's victory has reinvigorated the local [Democrats] and suggested the revolutionary idea that you can do better with good candidates."[38] Stevenson fit that bill—as a moderate, reliable, good-government Democrat.

By the early postwar years, Stevenson had become one of the leading lights of American postwar liberalism. He did not, however, fall in on the side of a true New Deal–style liberal. Part of his appeal may have been his willingness to attack the Republicans at a time when the rise of the Republican Party for many Democrats meant a need to find some accommodation with the new political order. While Democratic leaders (particularly southerner leaders like Richard Russell, Lyndon Johnson, and

Sam Rayburn) tried to work with Republican moderates, Stevenson often attacked Republicans as aloof, isolationist, and narrowly nationalistic. He was also an ardent internationalist and anti-fascist in the prewar years, standing against the popular isolationism of other midwestern politicians like Taft.

Stevenson's willingness to stand up to Joseph McCarthy and the Red Scare of the early 1950s, when others would not, may well have endeared him to party liberals more than anything else. As Illinois governor in 1951, Stevenson vetoed the Broyles bill, named after Illinois state senator Paul Broyles. Often called the "Little McCarthy" bill, the Broyles bill would have made it a felony to belong to a subversive group and required a loyalty oath of all Illinois public employees and candidates for office. In 1949, two years before the Broyles bill veto, Stevenson— for the first time—appeared to snub the anti-communist movement. In August 1948, Whittaker Chambers, an editor at *Time,* confessed to having been a secret courier for the Communist Party in the 1930s and accused Alger Hiss, a Democrat and an important figure in the State Department during and after the war, of being one of his accomplices. Hiss denied the charges and was indicted by a federal grand jury on two counts of perjury. To American liberals, the case became a cause célèbre at least in part because Hiss was something of a darling of the liberals and because the Republican right had begun to use the case to attack other liberals who had, over the years, been associated with Hiss. Hiss's attorneys, however, hoped to exonerate their client by parading a series of witnesses before the grand jury who would testify to Hiss's good character. In that capacity, Stevenson was asked to testify. Stevenson and Hiss had been little more than acquaintances when both worked at the Agricultural Adjustment Administration in the 1930s.[39]

At first, Stevenson refused to testify, citing the burden of his work in Springfield. But he finally agreed to give a deposition under oath. He explained that he had known Hiss only briefly, and when asked if he could testify to the level of Hiss's integrity, loyalty, and veracity, Stevenson responded "good."[40] The testimony, as insignificant as it was, would be used against Stevenson for the remainder of his political career as an example of his "soft" stand on communism. But to American liberals it made Stevenson a pillar of integrity when many in the political and entertainment worlds were denouncing others to save their own skins and careers.

Stevenson also did not shy away from attacking McCarthy and McCarthyism. In June 1950, he told a group of supporters in Chicago: "We are behaving like nutty neurotics. We . . . are nervously looking for subversive enemies under the bed and behind the curtains. We exchange frenzied, irresponsible accusations of disloyalty. 'Guilt by association' has been added to our language. The slander is honored. The shadow of a nameless fear slopes across the land. There is talk of thought control among Jefferson's people."[41] A year later, in a commencement address at the University of Illinois, he lashed out at McCarthyism, calling it an "hysterical form of putrid slander."[42]

In hindsight, neither the Broyles bill veto nor the testimony in the Hiss case can be counted as powerful stances against McCarthyism or the Red Scare. Stevenson's message in vetoing the Broyles bill was based mostly on his belief that the bill would be ineffective in stopping the spread of communism, and that, as he asked, "Does anyone seriously think that a real traitor will hesitate to sign a loyalty oath?"[43] And the Hiss deposition was little more than a statement of recollection about a man he had known only casually. But together, for American liberals looking for a standard bearer, they made Stevenson a champion in the face of America's growing anti-communist movement.

Stevenson also fit the liberal bill as an intellectual—or at least he appeared to be one. Most liberals had seen FDR as a genuine intellectual, mostly because he sounded like one, gathered intellectuals around him, and was willing to accept and implement new ideas. Liberals wanted Stevenson to capture that image again. If he was not an intellectual his oratorical style seemed to perk the ears of many liberals because in some ways he was like their beloved Roosevelt in his delivery. He was eloquent, quick, and sharp witted. He was also perceived as charming—a word often used to describe Roosevelt.[44]

Stevenson was, in fact, a fairly conservative patrician attorney, an elitist who spent most of his political life courting downstate Illinois conservatives and independents, and well outside most liberal circles. According to George Ball, one of Stevenson's closest advisors, Stevenson was "never a real liberal."[45] And John Kenneth Galbraith once said of Stevenson that "[h]e ran for President not to rescue the downtrodden but to resume the responsibilities properly belonging to the privileged."[46] In that way he may well have been much like Roosevelt.

One aspect of Stevenson's political life that continued to bother liberals was his refusal to join the ADA, the postwar liberal organization devoted to both liberal causes and anti-communism. ADA leaders like Walter Reuther, Hubert Humphrey, James Carey, Eleanor Roosevelt, and its chairman James Loeb would one day be Stevenson's most ardent supporters, but when the ADA was forming in the years right after the war, Stevenson refused to attend their organizational meeting or even to address ADA dinners. Almost certainly he saw the ADA as too radical for his blood and possibly detrimental to his political future.[47] In 1952, in an outburst that must have caused the ADA leadership to wince, Stevenson said that "I don't agree with your program." He added that he did not see eye to eye with the ADA's support of public housing, he had no interest in repealing Taft-Hartley, did not support federal aid to education, and disliked what he called "socialized medicine." He added that he believed that civil rights was a concern of the states and not the federal government and that he had no intention of putting "the South completely over a barrel" over the issue. "You know," he continued, "I've got southern blood in me."[48] On the economy, he took his most conservative stance by insisting that he could not abide the rising national debt. In a speech in early 1950, he warned that "beneath the heavy hand" of "the monster state . . . the only thing worse than neglect and too little government is paternalism and too much government."[49] Carl McGowan, a close Stevenson associate, recalled later that "[t]hose who said they were for Eisenhower solely for reasons of fiscal responsibility knew not whereof they spoke. They voted against the man who was . . . their dream candidate."[50]

Stevenson may, in fact, have been more in tune politically to the early-twentieth-century progressives than midcentury liberals—that is, he may have had more in common with Theodore Roosevelt than with Teddy's cousin Franklin. Like the progressives, he saw government (both state and federal) as the nation's moral center, both efficient and honest. As Illinois governor, he went a long way toward cleaning up the corruption in the state government and ending the influence on Illinois state government by the successors to Al Capone's crime syndicate. He defended states' rights because he believed, like the progressives, that state governments could serve as laboratories of social experimentation while solving local social problems. At the same time, he fought for a state employment practices commission that would monitor the hiring of minorities, although the Illinois state legislature refused to support it. He thought that the nation's budget should be balanced, and he did not believe in the gross expansion of federal powers. "If we can't balance our national budget now, when will we?" he asked a crowd of Democrats in early 1950. "And I hope and pray that history will never record that the Democratic Party foundered on the rocks of fiscal responsibility after leading America boldly, wisely, courageously, through two world wars and the most extensive social revolution in the short period of time in history."[51] All of this does not mean that Stevenson was, necessarily, out of step with national politics in postwar America; but for most liberals a call for a balanced budget was cut from the cloth of conservative economic policy.

Not unlike most Americans, Stevenson's foreign policy opinions were formed from the lessons of World War II and the developing postwar conflict with the Soviets. During the war he seemed to hold hope, as did many in government, including the president, that the end of the war would bring a healthy relationship between the United States and the Soviet Union. When the war ended, and Stevenson began his tenure as one of the U.S. representatives at the UN organizational meetings in San Francisco, he quickly saw that the United States and the Soviets were headed down a path of distrust and power politics, and he hoped that the United States would work to avoid alienating and isolating Moscow. Unlike George Kennan and others at the Pentagon, Stevenson refused to concede that the Soviets were innately expansionist, arguing instead that if Stalin and the Moscow leadership could be allowed to develop what they considered a satisfactory level of security, and then be convinced of the West's peaceful intentions, that any impending East-West conflict could be avoided. He expressed, for instance, a fear that a combination of Western nations might continually outvote the Soviets in the UN General Assembly, resulting in an isolated, cornered, and eventually combative Moscow.[52]

But like most diplomats in this period, much of Stevenson's optimism faded as the Cold War hardened into a clash at various hot and cold points throughout the globe. By early 1947 his voice began to harmonize with much of the rest of the West's diplomatic leadership and he started calling for the containment of Soviet power. As Truman hardened his stance, Stevenson followed. He decried any appeasement of Soviet aggressions and threw his support to the two pillars of containment, the Truman Doctrine and the Marshall Plan.[53] Stevenson willingly joined the Cold War consensus that included leaders from both parties, and he became to the Democrats what John Foster Dulles was to the Republicans, their leader on most foreign policy issues.

Stevenson's one-term tenure as Illinois governor revealed mostly a marked fiscal conservatism combined with a strong reformist tendency—a decidedly progressive-type outlook that was undoubtedly designed to keep the conservative down-staters in line. His most liberal initiatives, a constitutional convention to rewrite Illinois's antiquated constitution, and the implementation of a fair employment practices commission, both died at the hands of a hostile state legislature. He did, however, support labor legislation to increase workman's compensation and unemployment compensation and to increase cost-of-living payments for old-age pensioners and the blind. Most of his political failures came from his unwillingness to compromise; he too often held his ground and then lost the fight. As his biographer John Bartlow Martin has written, "His record of legislative achievement was neither really outstanding nor really poor."[54]

In 1951 a series of scandals rocked his administration while threatening to blemish his good government reputation. A Stevenson aide got involved in an illegal gambling-stock deal that had originated with the old Capone gang. In July, it was found that a Stevenson appointee at the state Department of Agriculture had been allowing horsemeat to be ground in with hamburger in exchange for kickbacks. The ever-hostile *Chicago Tribune* began referring to "Adlaiburgers."[55] Stevenson weathered the Illinois scandals, and they did not filter into the 1952 national campaign, but several of his friends and political acquaintances insisted that the events of the summer of 1951 bothered him throughout much of is life.[56]

The coming 1952 campaign held great promise and expectations for both parties. It would be the first election that would break from the Roosevelt-Truman liberalism—no matter who won. Would it be a time for a Republican resurgence? Or would the Democrats continue their hold on the White House and Congress?

CHAPTER TWO

The 1952 Presidential Campaign: Awaiting the New Order

In his 1956 study *Revolt of the Moderates*, Samuel Lubell wrote of American politics at midcentury: "The 1952 election may well have been our most emotional campaign since the McKinley-Bryan or Hoover-Smith contests." He called Eisenhower's victory a "crucial turn" in American political history and further compared it to Andrew Jackson's electoral victory in 1828, Lincoln's victory in 1860, and Roosevelt's victory in 1932.[1]

The 1952 campaign had added significance because of the Korean War and the accompanying fear that it was just the beginning of a major conflict between the United States and the Soviet Union, in fact, the origins of what some feared might become World War III. In the summer of 1950, the North Korean army unexpectedly attacked south, across the 38th parallel and pushed the South Korean army back, nearly off the peninsula. In an almost impulsive decision, President Truman launched a counterattack of U.S., South Korean, and UN forces that pushed the North Korean army back north, nearly to the Yalu River. By mid-October, China intervened in the conflict to aid the North Koreans and to protect their own frontier.

In October 1950, just as Chinese troops entered the war in Korea, Truman summoned Eisenhower to the White House, recalled him to active duty, and then ordered the general to take command of NATO, the newly formed North Atlantic Treaty Organization, the instrument designed mostly as a means of defending Europe against a Soviet attack, an attack that many saw as imminent. The general accepted the post, and again Eisenhower became the nation's greatest soldier at the center of great events.

As the world situation appeared to worsen, Eisenhower began to believe what his friends had been telling him for years—that he was the only man who could lead the nation in crisis. In his diary, he wrote of his disenchantment with Truman. Poor Truman, he wrote, "a fine man who, in the middle of a stormy lake, knows nothing of swimming. . . . If his wisdom could only equal his good intent."[2] At the same time, he was convinced that another Democratic presidential victory (following five consecutive victories) might end the nation's two-party system—and he was not convinced that Taft, the Republican frontrunner, could defeat all Democratic comers in 1952. Eisenhower was particularly bothered by Taft's stance on foreign affairs. Taft had voted against the NATO treaty and made it clear that he opposed U.S. involvement in any type of collective security. Eisenhower was steeped in internationalism, the belief that an American nation interconnected and engaged in world events was more of a military deterrent than the isolationism of Taft and the GOP right; and he believed strongly in NATO, the United Nations, and collective security against international communist aggressions.

Before he left for Europe, Eisenhower decided to meet with Taft, to get his support for NATO, and then remove himself from politics by taking his name out of contention for the 1952 campaign. It seemed like a fair trade: if Taft agreed to support NATO and collective security, Eisenhower would support him and the nomination would almost certainly be his.

Before the meeting, Eisenhower wrote out a statement that would, unequivocally, remove him from the nominating process. "Having been called back to military duty," he wrote, "I want to announce that my name may not be used by anyone as a candidate for President—and if they do I will repudiate such efforts."[3] Gone were the little equivocations, the carefully chosen words that left the nation wondering whether he really wanted the job or not. But the meeting with Taft did little more than produce further animosity between the general and the politician. Taft made it clear that he would not support NATO and that he did not believe that Truman had the authority to send troops to Europe in peacetime without the consent of Congress. Eisenhower argued that the president did, indeed, have that power, and that he was immediately requesting several divisions. He recalled in his memoir that he "insisted on an answer regarding support of the collective principle. I failed to get an assurance. . . . My disappointment was acute," he continued. "I was resentful toward those who seemed to me to be playing politics in matters I thought vital to America and the Free World." Taft left—taking with him the only chance he would ever have to become president of the United States. Eisenhower commented to an aide that it "might be more effective to keep some aura of mystery around my future personal plans. For the moment," he added, "I decided to remain silent, not to declare myself out as a potential political factor. . . . The statement I had drafted was so unequivocal that if I had carried out my intention of publicizing it, my political life would have ended without ever starting. The paper was destroyed."[4] One of Eisenhower's last acts before he left for Europe on January 1, 1951, was to add one last vague statement to his diary on his possible future as a presidential candidate: "I hope always to do my duty to my country; but I cannot even conceive of circumstances as of this moment that could convince me I had a duty to enter politics."[5] That note could be stacked with the countless other statements that the nation was now getting used to hearing from Eisenhower, which all seemed to say the same thing: "I'll run if you want me to."

The New Hampshire primary was, in those days, characteristically the first flushing of the American political season. One of its most important functions was to determine who could attract voters and who could not, who was an appealing candidate and which candidates simply did not have appeal. The New Hampshire primary was also about expectations. If a candidate did better than expected, then the primary was a victory whether or not the candidate actually won in the vote count. At the same time, a candidate may have won votes and finally all the delegates, but if the margin of victory was below expectations, the results would be billed as a disaster for the candidate's campaign. The 1952 New Hampshire primary, perhaps more than most primaries, brought some clarity to the Republican campaign, while for the Democrats it seemed to raise more questions than answers.

Eisenhower's problem was clear. Army regulations stated that "members of the regular army, while on active duty, may accept nomination for public office, provided such nomination is tendered without direct or indirect activity or solicitation on their part." But Eisenhower also worried that partisan politics would destroy his usefulness at NATO. Consequently, through the first half of 1951, he chose to allow the political fires to burn without his direct encouragement, and he would allow others to work on his behalf.[6]

By May 1951, the man pushing hardest for an Eisenhower candidacy was General Lucius Clay. Clay and Eisenhower had been friends at least since the 1930s, when both men served under MacArthur in the Philippines. During the war, Clay had served in Washington under James Byrnes in the office of war mobilization, and then after the war he replaced Eisenhower as the military governor in the American zone in Germany when Eisenhower became Army Chief of Staff. On May 18, Clay insisted the time was right, that Eisenhower should make known his intentions to run. Eisenhower shot back that he had no intention of seeking "anything" unless a "larger duty compels me to do so." Unless his supporters could "visualize a situation that would obviously represent a higher call to duty than does even my present job," he was not interested.[7] Like most of Eisenhower's other supporters, Clay, however, was not deterred.

In September, Dewey (by now a Republican Party leader, a moderate, and an avid Eisenhower supporter) approached Clay to put more pressure on Eisenhower to make a run. Clay agreed. He wanted Eisenhower to run at least in part because he believed that Taft might win the Republican nomination, but lose the election.[8] In mid-October 1951, General Edwin Clark convinced Eisenhower that his supporters (mostly Republican moderates) needed some word that he would run—that at least he would make a run under the right circumstances. On October 14, Ike's birthday, Clark and Eisenhower penned a secret letter to Pennsylvania senator James Duff. The letter was designed to be sent to a number of Eisenhower's supporters through Duff. Duff was one of Eisenhower's strongest supporters, and he had been organizing for Eisenhower in several parts of the country. This secret "Duff letter" said that Eisenhower was willing to resign from the army and accept the Republican nomination if it was offered. It concluded with a promise to conduct an aggressive campaign if nominated.[9]

In November, Clay met with a group of Eisenhower supporters including Herbert Brownell, Duff, and Massachusetts senator Henry Cabot Lodge. Their purpose was to coordinate an Eisenhower campaign that really did not yet exist. Their first order was to name a leader who would promote Eisenhower's campaign. It was determined that it would be Lodge. "Every pimple has a head," Lodge said. "And so I became the head of this group." But Clay remained the key, the liaison between Eisenhower in Europe and the campaign committee.[10]

Eisenhower continued his reticence. But in early January 1952, there was a break. Lodge entered Eisenhower's name in the New Hampshire primary, and when questioned about it at NATO command in Paris, Eisenhower issued a public statement that did not repudiate Lodge's actions.[11] The next month, Eisenhower was shown a film of an Eisenhower-for-president rally at Madison Square Garden. The rally was organized by a group of Eisenhower supporters, including John Hay ("Jock") Whitney, a wealthy venture capitalist. The film itself was flown to Paris by celebrated aviator, Jacqueline Cochran. Eisenhower told Clay that he was "deeply touched, not to say moved."[12] But it was not until February 16, in England, that Eisenhower finally told Clay, confidentially, that he would make the run.[13]

Taft tried to dodge the New Hampshire primary. He had concluded that a victory over Eisenhower there would be of little significance, and if he lost it could end his campaign. There were, in fact, only fourteen delegates at stake. But Taft's advisors told him he could win in New Hampshire, and Eisenhower's people had placed rumors that Taft was afraid to take on Eisenhower—even in Eisenhower's absence from the campaign. With that, Taft decided to jump in.[14]

The results in New Hampshire were encouraging for Eisenhower. Without even an appearance by the candidate in the state, the Eisenhower machine destroyed all comers, including Taft. The Eisenhower campaign was run by New Hampshire governor Sherman Adams, who coordinated speeches by Eisenhower supporters all over the state. The *New York Times* described the campaign as a "buzz saw."[15]

Eisenhower's victory showed, for the first time, that he could attract voters. MacArthur ran that year in New Hampshire and received just a little over 3,000 write-in votes, and to most observers that showed he was not an attractive candidate. Taft took only about 39 percent of the vote to Eisenhower's 50.4 percent, a significant victory for Eisenhower. Eisenhower won more votes than all the other candidates combined, and he carried every city in the state except Manchester. "It may be argued," the *New York Times* reported, "that General Eisenhower's bare majority constituted something less than an overwhelming sweep, but who can doubt that the vote would have been far heavier in his favor if his sense of duty had permitted him to be present and personally take the stump."[16]

Taft had few bright spots. He did carry Manchester, giving him hope that he might be appealing to voters in the industrialized Northeast. But the *New York Times* reported that he actually did better in the areas of New Hampshire where he *did not* campaign.[17] *Time* identified Taft's biggest problem: He is "abrupt and cold in greeting local leaders. . . . [He] brushed off autograph hunters and hand shakers [and he] cut short or stopped questioners."[18] Taft advisor David Ingalls delivered the usual spin. He insisted that New Hampshire was Eisenhower country and that Eisenhower should have won by a bigger margin. It was, he said, "no smashing victory."[19]

The Taft campaign was nasty. Literature from the Taft camp alluded to Eisenhower's call for universal military training: "Draft Ike, and he will draft you." There were also reports of Taft people spreading rumors of Eisenhower's supposed wartime affair with Kay Summersby, that he had asked for a divorce from his wife, Mamie, and that Mamie drank heavily.[20]

Elsewhere, Eisenhower had other primary victories, including a strong showing in a Minnesota write-in campaign that was wholly unexpected—all without his presence. But in 1952, primary victories showed little more than strength and support; few primaries specifically pledged convention delegates to the winning candidate. In March, Truman announced that he would not run, and that lifted the possibility that Eisenhower would have to run against an incumbent president. On April 2, he sent a letter to Truman announcing that he believed his work at NATO was complete and that he intended to return to the United States to seek political office. He requested that the president not announce his resignation until April 11. The next day, on April 12, he announced to the press that he would resign from NATO, return to the United States as a private citizen, and make a run for the Republican nomination.[21]

For the Democrats, the March 11 New Hampshire primary seemed only to muddy the waters. Estes Kefauver, a fairly obscure senator from Tennessee with liberal credentials, beat President Truman. Kefauver made an exceptional showing, but his biggest problem was that he was not very popular in his own party. *Time* reported that "[i]n Congress he has few friends or even admirers. He's rated one of the dullest, most fumbling speakers in the Senate. . . . He flashes no sharp edge of wit, nor has he even much sense of humor to lighten his heavy sense of destiny."[22] Truman was pushed to enter the New Hampshire primary by Democratic National Committee chairman Frank McKinney, who hoped the president's sharp elbows would push Kefauver out of the campaign. Truman allowed his name to stay on the New Hampshire ballot, but he insisted that he saw little significance in the entire primary electoral system, in fact, stating famously that he believed primaries were little more than "eyewash."[23] Kefauver's victory, however, was a surprise. He took 55 percent of the vote state-wide, and he won a majority of the votes in all three cities in the state (Portsmouth, Manchester, and Nashua), and that was seen as Truman's growing weakness with organized labor. *Time* reported that Truman could still take the nomination if he wanted it, but the defeat in New Hampshire was a political body blow.[24]

From a constitutional standpoint, Truman could have run in 1952. He had only served one complete term, which made him eligible to run again, and the Twenty-second Amendment to the Constitution (which limited presidents to two terms) did not apply to his presidency. In early 1950, it looked like he would make the run. The country was at peace and prosperous, Soviet communism seemed mostly contained, and his domestic program had been a moderate success. But the Korean War, which broke out in June 1950, along with a corruption scandal close to his administration, made him think twice about the run. Then, as Eisenhower slowly made his way into the arena (and then faced with the embarrassing defeat in New Hampshire) a run seemed even more remote. But he decided he would run, win the election, and vindicate himself and his administration. Then finally, in late March, he decided he would not.

Perhaps Truman's biggest challenge was to find a suitable successor, someone he could support to take the reins of his presidency. Truman had mentioned more than once that he was interested in Adlai Stevenson, the fresh face of the party, but his first choice had always been Fred Vinson. Vinson was chief justice of the Supreme Court, appointed by Truman, and a personal friend. In mid-1950, the president asked Vinson to run. He refused.[25]

Kefauver was never an option for Truman. He simply could not stand him or much of anything about him. He often referred to him as "Cowfever," although that word does not seem to get to the heart of Truman's deep dislike for the man.[26]

Truman considered others: Georgia senator Richard Russell, Oklahoma senator Robert Kerr, Vice President Alben Barkley, and even Averell Harriman, who was then a Wall Street banker and a chief U.S. diplomat. But none fit the bill. In January 1952, Truman met with Stevenson in Washington. Stevenson's victory in the 1948 Illinois governor's race had carried Truman to victory in that state. In addition, Truman liked Stevenson and was impressed with his skills as a politician and by the

Tennessee Senator Estes Kefauver played an important role in Democratic Party politics in the early 1950s. (State Archives of Florida)

support he had garnered from the liberal community. But the two men were different. Truman was a plain man from a modest background, self-educated and simple. Stevenson was a true patrician, from an old family and old money. He was educated at Princeton, Harvard, and Northwestern. What Truman had learned to dislike about the Roosevelts and the Kennedys, he probably disliked about Stevenson. Still, Truman asked Stevenson to run and told him that the nomination would be his. But Stevenson, as Truman recalled it later, said no. Others close to Stevenson recalled that he said he would think about it.[27] Whatever the response, and however it was perceived, Truman continued to consider Stevenson the party's best hope.

But Truman refused to let go. "I felt in Stevenson I had found the man to whom I could safely turn over the responsibilities of party leadership. Here was the kind of man the Democratic party needed and, while I would not pressure him, I felt certain that he would see it as his duty to seek the nomination."[28] On March 17, Stevenson wrote to Charles S. Murphy, a White House counselor who had been pushing Stevenson to reconsider. He was not interested in his party's nomination. "I donot[sic] want to be a candidate for the nomination," he wrote. "I do not want to run for President, and I donot[sic] want to be President at this time." But then he opened the door: "[I]f my party should nominate me anyway I would accept proudly and prayerfully. . . ."[29]

Truman must have realized that the only thing standing between Stevenson and a run for the nomination was his own indecision. On March 29, after consulting with his closest advisors and his wife, Bess, Truman finally announced that he would not be a candidate for reelection.[30]

Georgia Democrat, Senator Richard Russell, however, would run. Russell had always contemplated a run for the presidency. In 1948 he allowed his name to be placed in nomination at the convention, and ever since he was considered the leading southerner for president. He knew, however, what most everyone else knew, that because of the civil rights issue a southerner stood little chance of getting nominated. But in 1952, the party was in trouble. Truman was unacceptable to most factions in the party, and there was no one in the wings prepared to take the mantle. For Russell, 1952 was the year.

The biggest push came from his fellow southerners, particularly governors Herman Talmadge of Georgia and James Byrnes of South Carolina; and senators Harry Byrd of Virginia, John Stennis of Mississippi, and Burnet Maybank of South Carolina.[31] These were some of the most powerful men in Washington and the nation, but they were all southerners and strong segregationists, signifying Russell as the candidate of the South.

Most likely, Russell's initial motive was to increase the South's bargaining power at the convention, or perhaps to place himself in a position to gain the second spot on the ticket. He would take with him to the convention at least three hundred southern delegates, certainly enough to demand attention, impact the nominations, and influence the party platform for the South.

On February 28, Russell announced his candidacy, describing himself as a "Jeffersonian Democrat" who believed in local self-government and

opposed the centralization of federal authority. Following his formal announcement, he told reporters that he would continue to oppose civil rights and any manifestation of a Federal Employment Practices Commission (FEPC) that sought to give minorities equal rights in the workplace.[32]

Russell was widely considered intelligent, capable, and generally in the mainstream on most issues. But his unqualified stance on civil rights kept him from acquiring much support outside the South. Through the campaign, up to the Democratic convention, he tried to present himself as a moderate and willing to make compromises on civil rights as long as the rights of the states were honored. He argued over and over that he was not a sectional candidate, and he continued to try to push civil rights into the background of his campaign, but he could not shake the regional image.

At the convention, Stevenson won the Democratic nomination on the third ballot, after momentum swung his way and Kefauver finally released his delegates. Russell finally threw his support to Stevenson. Stevenson chose as his running mate Senator John Sparkman of Alabama.[33]

For the Republicans, the nominating decision was much less complicated. Taft had an early lead in the delegate count, but Lodge and other Eisenhower supporters accused Taft and his people of stealing delegates in several southern states. They argued that Taft's people had unfairly denied delegate spots to Eisenhower supporters and placed Taft supporters in their place. Eisenhower's people at the convention proposed to evict the disputed Taft delegates and replace them with Eisenhower delegates. They called this proposal "Fair Play." Fair Play passed a convention-wide vote when the California delegation, led by Richard Nixon, pushed the vote over the top. With that, Nixon insured his spot on the Republican Party ticket, and American politics took a turn. On July 11, Eisenhower appeared before the convention and promised to lead another crusade, this one for the freedom of the United States.[34] He chose Nixon as his running mate.

Throughout the campaign Eisenhower and the Republicans hit hard at the Democrats for "creeping socialism" and what they called K_1C_2, an acronym for Korea, communism, and corruption. Eisenhower told voters

*Illinois Governor Adlai Stevenson (and his running mate Alabama Senator John Sparkman)
receiving the Democratic nomination in 1952.   (AP)*

that his campaign (and then his administration) would be as "clean as a
hound's tooth," in the face of what was being perceived as an atmosphere
of corruption in Washington. That image was threatened when sources
in the press uncovered a Nixon secret slush fund given to him by some
California businessmen to meet his campaign expenses. Nixon had tried
to present to voters an image of an average guy just trying to make it in a
world ruined by the Democrats. But average guys seldom had $20,000 at
their disposal in 1952. Although such a fund was not illegal, it presented
an image of impropriety, an image that Eisenhower refused to tolerate.[35]

Nixon had turned the tide toward Eisenhower's favor at the convention, but he was placed on the ticket mostly to appease the Republican

right. Nixon had made a name for himself as an aggressive communist hunter in his years on the House Committee on Un-American Activities (HUAC). Elected senator from his home state of California in 1948, Nixon had immediately moved to the front of the Republican anti-communist crusade. That position was quickly usurped by Wisconsin senator Joseph McCarthy, but Nixon remained a significant figure in the movement—and certainly a more presentable candidate than the gruff McCarthy. Nixon, at age thirty-nine, brought youth to the ticket. He was an internationalist, like Eisenhower. And he had a reputation as a hard-hitter. Eisenhower certainly hoped that Nixon would do the dirty work of assaulting the Democrats, while he carried the high ground.

The slush fund accusations pushed Eisenhower to consider dumping Nixon from the ticket, but most of his advisors insisted that Nixon should be allowed to present his side of the story to the American people.[36] Nixon jumped at the chance by taking advantage of the new medium of television. On September 23, in a widely watched speech, known famously as the "Checkers speech," Nixon told America about his wife's "respectable Republican cloth coat" and their dog, Checkers, the only personal gift he had ever accepted from supporters. "And you know the kids love that dog and I just want to say this right now, that regardless of what they say about it, we're going to keep it." He went on to explain the purpose of the slush fund, and he managed to convince most of those watching that he had, really, done nothing wrong. The next day, Eisenhower agreed to keep him on the ticket.[37]

If the election was ever in doubt, the doubt faded quickly when, on October 24, just two weeks before election day, Eisenhower announced that if elected, he would go to Korea. It was a tactic he had been saving for the last moment. And it worked. Eisenhower would again serve the nation at war, and by most accounts his statement was perceived as a promise to bring the war to a quick end. Stevenson could not answer. Eisenhower won the election by a comfortable margin of over 55 percent of the popular vote, 442 electoral votes out of a total of 531, and he brought in a Republican Congress on his coattails. He also broke into the Solid South, grabbing fifty-seven electoral votes in Virginia, Tennessee,

By most accounts, Eisenhower used Richard Nixon to keep the Republican right in line through the 1950s.   (Eisenhower Presidential Library and Museum, Abilene, Kansas)

Florida, and Texas. He also took Oklahoma, Truman's Missouri, Maryland, and Delaware.

For most Americans a new age had dawned. The era of depression, war, and partisan conflict was over. A time of increased national security, bipartisanship, and economic prosperity was beginning.

CHAPTER THREE

Shared Objectives: Bipartisanship in the 83rd Congress

Dwight Eisenhower was a moderate Republican. No matter how that phrase is defined, he would probably have agreed that he fit into that category. He insisted later in life that he had always been a Republican and that the members of his family had always been Republicans. But there is some evidence that, at least in his youth, he flirted with the Democrats, Franklin Roosevelt, and the liberal philosophy of the New Deal. On foreign policy issues, he helped formulate the strategy of internationalism that drove the Allied fight in World War II. He supported the Truman administration's postwar policy of containment, and he had supported the Korean War from its beginning.

Eisenhower may have been a Republican, even a staunch Republican, but as a moderate he was repulsed by the Republican right, the Old Guard conservatives, many of whom were prewar isolationists or the political descendants of isolationists. To Eisenhower, those very Republican isolationists had kept the United States from entering the war when a strong stance against international tyranny might have checked Nazi and Japanese aggressions in Europe and Asia. Some isolationists, like Michigan senator Arthur Vandenburg, had seen the light after Pearl Harbor, abandoned their prewar isolationism, and joined the ranks of the internationalists. Others, like Taft, continued their isolationist ways after the war, but they usually collected themselves under the banner of "unilateralism," or "go-it-alone-ism," as it was often called.

Eisenhower was an internationalist. He had spent most of the war trying desperately to unite the Allied armies and their leaders to get them to overcome their differences and to fight as a unified force against the Nazi war machine. He was, of course, successful. To Eisenhower, the future of the United States and the free world revolved around collective security—internationalism, NATO, the United Nations, and other such organizations and instruments.

On domestic issues, Eisenhower saw himself as a liberal when it came to human affairs and a conservative on fiscal matters. He was not always eloquent in making this point—or any other point for that matter. I am a "conservative when it comes to money and a liberal when it comes to human beings," he once said.[1] Early in his political career, he tried to give this idea a name, and he settled on "dynamic conservatism," a phrase that he never really defined. He intended that the phrase would distinguish him from the Old Guard conservatives in his party and eventually to undermine their influence.

Another concept often lumped with Eisenhower's notion of dynamic conservatism is "the Middle Way." Eisenhower was repelled both by the far right in his own party and by the far left among the Democrats. He rejected the concepts of both extremes (often referring to them as "radical") and worked to place himself directly in the middle of the road, or "the Middle Way." He made this point as early as 1949, telling members of the American Bar Association that the future of the nation "lies down the middle of the road between concentrated wealth on one flank, and the unbridled power of statism on the other." The fundamental principles of American life, he added, "still dictate progress down the center, even though there the contest is hottest [and], the progress is somewhat discouragingly slow." The speech was interrupted nine times by applause.[2] At the end of his administration, his opinion had not really changed. In February 1959, an increasingly powerful GOP right mounted an attack against him, complaining that his leadership was weak. He responded that anyone trying to steer down the middle of the road has "got to take it from both sides."[3]

Eisenhower felt so strongly about this that he occasionally flirted with the idea of forming a new party, a Republican Party that would be free of the GOP right *and* the Democratic left and hold the political center. As early as 1953, William Robinson, one of Eisenhower's good friends, recorded Eisenhower's words in his diary: "if the die-hard Republicans [meaning the Old Guard conservatives] fight this program too hard, [we] may have to organize a third party."[4] A year later he told his press secretary, James Hagerty, that he wanted "to build a strong progressive Republican Party. . . . If the right wing wants to fight, they're going to get it. If they want to leave the Republican Party and form a third party, that's their business, but before I end up, either this Republican Party will reflect progressivism or I won't be with them anymore."[5] By most accounts, however, Eisenhower's dalliances with a third-party movement (or of a Republican Party purged of both the left and the right) were little more than a venting of frustrations at the members of his own party who opposed his basic ideas.

In his second term, Eisenhower would pull these ideas together, give them the new name of "Modern Republicanism," and attempt to hold on to the political center. Those on the Republican right, however, found themselves increasingly isolated and conflicted. They generally opposed Eisenhower and his moderate policies, but they were faced with his popularity and vote-getting skills. Quite simply, they needed the president's coattails to stay in office.

Outside of Washington, however, the Republican right was beginning to gather steam, at least in part as a reaction to Eisenhower's moderate policies. This development on the right (led by young eastern establishment right-wingers like William F. Buckley Jr. and western libertarian-types like Barry Goldwater) continued to grow through the next two decades. In its nascent form, however, it put pressure on Eisenhower to abandon his moderation and move to the right. Eisenhower, however, continued to resist.

From the left, again toward the end of the decade, liberals in the Democratic Party rejected Eisenhower's fiscal conservatism, marked by his insistence on balancing the federal budget. By 1960, Eisenhower's Middle Way had become antiquated and old-fashioned to a growing number in both parties—both on the left and the right.

‡

The primary theme of the new 83rd Congress was bipartisanship—a spirit of compromise and even friendship. Most Americans saw the Truman administration as both unnecessarily tumultuous (at least in part because of the president's conflicts with organized labor) and politically divisive. The nation had been through a lot: the Great Depression, World War II and postwar recovery, and then Korea. Eisenhower's election seemed to represent stability, moderation, bipartisanship, and compromise. Americans considered it a matter of course when Eisenhower, just after his State of the Union message, called a foreign-policy briefing at the White House that included both Democratic and Republican congressional leaders. Bipartisanship also reflected the situation in Congress. The Republican majority was so thin that the president realized that working with Democrats was essential to accomplishing just about anything.

One of Eisenhower's biggest problems was his relationship with Taft and the other GOP conservatives in Congress. They disagreed with the president on a number of crucial issues. And it was on foreign policy that the divisions were the greatest. Many on the GOP right, including Taft, had their roots in prewar midwestern isolationism. America's run up to World War II, Pearl Harbor, and the war itself had pulled many of the isolationists away from that philosophy, but most still counted themselves as unilateralists, generally opposed to the internationalism that Eisenhower believed had won the war in Europe—and kept the Soviet Union contained since the war's end. Yet the GOP right was also strongly anti-communist and wanted desperately to blame the Democrats for allowing the advances of world communism, particularly the fall of China into the communist camp in 1949. Consequently, they opposed Eisenhower's willingness to seek a negotiated end to the war in Korea, calling it an act of appeasement. Many on the Republican right also claimed that a Korean armistice was tantamount to an acceptance by Eisenhower of Truman's firing of Douglas McArthur. McArthur, himself an ally of the Republican right, had wanted to take the war to the Chinese, and even to the Soviets if necessary, to win in Korea. Truman, however, intended to contain the war on the Korean peninsula. In the spring of 1951, the two men clashed over how the war was to be fought, and Truman fired McArthur. To the GOP right, McArthur became a martyr. When Eisenhower ended the war in July 1953, he seemed to them to be taking Truman's side in the conflict. Senate conservatives like William Jenner of Indiana and George Malone of Nevada insisted that the armistice was a victory for international communism and a defeat for the Free World. William Knowland of California argued that the armistice would cause the United States to "lose the balance in Asia."[6]

Eisenhower was a fiscal conservative, and a major tenant of that economic philosophy was a balanced budget. But the president's first budget, presented to Congress for fiscal 1955, was not balanced—primarily because of the cost of the war in Korea. At the 1952 Republican convention, Taft and the GOP right had sought a plank calling for reduced government spending and a lowering of taxes. But in April 1953, in a budget briefing, Eisenhower admitted that his first budget would have a deficit of nearly $5.5 billion. Taft was furious. He jumped up and pounded the table. "The primary thing we promised the American people," he told the group, "was reduction of expenditures. With a [budget] like this, we'll never elect a Republican Congress in 1954." Then he hit at Eisenhower hard: "You're taking us down the same road Truman traveled." Both Taft and Eisenhower had notorious tempers, and a left-right split in the Republican Party might have occurred right there, but the president remained calm and explained to Taft the need for certain expenditures, particularly military expenditures to maintain U.S. strength abroad. He promised to balance his next budget, presumably after the war in Korea was brought to an end. Taft backed off, and the situation cooled. Eisenhower, however, was mad. He wrote in his diary, "I think that everyone present was astonished at the demagogic nature of [Taft's] tirade. . . . He simply wanted expenditures reduced regardless."[7]

Eisenhower and Taft never worked well together. Taft thought Eisenhower was much too liberal, even to the point of telling a friend that the result of his presidency would be "another New Deal administration which will be a good deal harder to fight than the Democrats."[8] Still, Taft expected to be the driving force behind the Republican-dominated 83rd Congress, and he could not succeed without support from the White House and the Republican moderates in the Senate. So, he worked to heal the wounds and bridge the breach. At the same time, Eisenhower knew that without support from Taft and his followers on the right his programs would have a difficult time on Capitol Hill, even though the Republicans were in the majority. So, despite their animosity toward each other, the two titans of the Republican Party in the early years of the 1950s began working together. Just before the senator died of cancer in July 1953, in fact, the two men had become downright friends. "In some things," Eisenhower wrote in his memoir, "I found him unexpectedly 'liberal,' specifically in his attitude toward old-age pensions, school aid, and public housing—attitudes incidentally, which were miles away from those of some self-described 'Taft stalwarts.'"[9]

Taft's death dealt a blow to the conservatives in Congress. Taft had built an extraordinary power. He was, in fact, powerful enough to demand the president's ear; and through Taft, conservatives could be sure that their side was at least being heard. His death reduced conservative power on Capitol Hill, and without strong leadership, Eisenhower and the Republican moderates overwhelmed the GOP right. By 1956, Eisenhower loyalists controlled two-thirds of the Republican National Committee and forty-one state chairmanships. By that time, most of the GOP right in Congress was voting the moderate Republican line on most issues. *The National Review* complained bitterly that those who refused to support Eisenhower were being "consigned to outer darkness. . . . With such skill have [Eisenhower] and his associates conducted the movement [that] it has become quite clear what the Republican Party is not: It is not the Party of Senator Taft."[10]

Taft's successor as the GOP leader in the Senate was William Knowland, a man well below Taft's abilities. Eisenhower never warmed up to Knowland, and he often derided him in private. "It's a pity that his wisdom, his judgment, his tact, and his sense of humor lag so far behind his ambition," Eisenhower told an advisor.[11] And, he added in his diary, "Knowland means to be helpful and loyal, but he is cumbersome. He does not command the respect in the Senate that Senator Taft enjoyed."[12] Without strong Republican leadership in the Senate, Eisenhower was more willing to look to the moderate Democrats and Lyndon Johnson for leadership on a number of bills. The president quickly learned that with a few compromises and Johnson's leadership, legislation could get passed in the Senate.

‡

Not surprisingly, the Democrats were in disarray following the 1952 election. They are, *Time* wrote, "a party which is looking to fly to pieces."[13] They had just been trounced in the presidential election and lost control of Congress, and it even seemed that parts of the old reliable South had begun shifting into the Republican Party. The greatest conflict was between the northern liberals, led by Hubert Humphrey of Minnesota and Paul Douglas of Illinois, and the southern conservatives, led by Harry Byrd of Virginia and Richard Russell of Georgia. It was a division that had plagued the party since Reconstruction. It had been just five years since several southern states split from the national party and ran their own presidential candidate, and the party had really not united since then. Just after the 1952 election, Russell, speaking at his party's annual Jefferson-Jackson Day dinner in Raleigh, North Carolina, said that the South would no longer tolerate a party led by northern liberals who continued to blast the South's devotion to states' rights. "There are those," he said, "who would have us drink from the fatal potion of national state socialism." He added that he believed the northern liberals were trying to force the South out of the party. *Time* commented that "Russell's speech was an embarrassing reminder to the Democrats that the North-South feud [is] still going on."[14]

Politics from both sides of the aisle often came together in compromise legislation.   *(AP)*

The Democrats needed to unite. By most accounts, it was their lack of unity that had caused their defeats in 1952. George Reedy, one of Lyndon Johnson's chief advisors and strategists, said later that the defeat was so extreme that "it was generally thought that nobody could pull the Democrats together" again.[15]

Stepping into the breach was Lyndon Johnson. Johnson had worked his way up through the Democratic Party infrastructure carrying the mantle of the New Deal. He even became something of a Franklin Roosevelt protégé. In his youth, in the mid-1930s, he had made use of his father's friendship with Texas congressman Sam Rayburn to become head of the National Youth Administration in Texas. From there he won a seat in Congress in 1937, where he was a loyal New Dealer. In 1941, he decided to run for the Senate, but lost to Texas radio personality "Pappy" O'Daniel. He ran again in 1948, and amidst some questionable voting practices and charges of ballot box stuffing, Johnson became the junior senator from Texas.

From there he climbed the party ladder quickly. In 1952, when the Democratic Party leader in the Senate, Arizona's Ernest McFarland, was defeated, all eyes turned to Senator Richard Russell, one of the most senior members of the Senate and one of the most powerful figures in the Democratic Party. By most accounts, Russell could have taken the job of Senate minority leader. But in that role it would have been necessary to moderate his stances on race and civil rights—and work with northern liberals. He decided not to run. Immediately, Hubert Humphrey announced that he would throw his hat into the ring. Party members, however, realized that Humphrey, a northern liberal with a strong record on civil rights, would actually engage the same inner-party quarrel, only from the other side of the conflict. Russell saw the need for a compromise candidate, a consensus builder, and he threw his support to Johnson. Party liberals put up a token response, but with Russell's organizing muscle, Johnson won the election and became Senate Democratic Party Minority Leader.[16]

The Democratic Party leadership position was truly a job no one wanted—or at least it was a job that had been political suicide in the past. Illinois senator Scott Lucas was chosen in 1949, but he lost his Senate seat in the 1950 campaigns. He was followed by McFarland, but he lost his seat to Barry Goldwater in 1952. Neither man had managed to serve for an entire year, nor were they able to pull the party together in any significant way. Johnson had been party whip under McFarland, and when McFarland was defeated, Johnson seemed a logical successor. At age forty-four, he became the youngest party leader in the history of the Senate.

In many ways, Johnson was perfect for the job—at least in part because he had support from Russell. One of Johnson's greatest attributes was that he was not really a southerner and never really considered himself a southerner. "He wasn't quite southern," Hubert Humphrey recalled. "He was a different cut."[17] In fact, one of Johnson's problems was that neither southern conservatives nor northern liberals trusted him. "[O]ur little group of twenty-five or so liberal senators were very suspicious of Johnson," Humphrey remembered, "very suspicious of him."[18] That was, in fact, a reflection of Johnson's ability to walk a thin line between the two sides.

The issue, of course, was civil rights. One of Johnson's aims was to see that the issue was not brought before the Democrats. Unity on most issues, in fact, could be achieved only if civil rights was taken off the table. House Democratic leader Sam Rayburn insisted that there had been such division within the party only because Roosevelt and Truman had supported civil rights, and now that they were both out of the political picture, the party could unite again. "Some Democrats who hated Presidents Roosevelt and Truman because of [their] civil rights proposals," he said, "will now start hating President Eisenhower for the same reason. I think we are going to be more united than ever before," he added.[19]

Time noted, however, that the Democratic Party leadership was in crisis, that the party was, in fact, looking for new leadership. Stevenson, now a defeated candidate, had decided to go on a travel junket around the world, and Truman had stepped away from any real leadership role. "Into this . . . vacuum," the magazine added, "has blown a tornado from the Southwest, a Texas-sized hunk of perpetual motion named Lyndon Johnson." He "is a political operator. He senses political situations, understands individual motivations and moves swiftly to organize party positions by reasoning with individuals on an individual basis."[20] Johnson's legendary maneuverings and strategies were apparent as early as 1953.

The position of party leader in the Senate is powerful, but has no official powers. The position is, in fact, what the leader makes of it. He "has no authority, really," George Reedy recalled. He "only has the power that he can exert as an individual."[21] Years later, at the end of his Senate tenure, Johnson noted that "the only real power available to the leader is the power of persuasion. There is no patronage, no power to discipline, no authority to fire Senators like the president can fire his members of Cabinet."[22] As leader, Johnson was chairman of the Senate Steering Committee, a powerful position that allowed him to control committee appointments. In that role, he set out to change the balance of power in the Senate—not to remove the presiding southerners like Russell and Byrd, but to disseminate their power. The problem was that party southerners (returned to Washington over and over again by their constituents) were the most senior, and thus they controlled the most important committees. No Democrats from the East, Midwest, or the West Coast presided over any permanent committees; and southern control generally meant conservative control. In order to keep the party united, Johnson believed he needed to allow all voices to be heard. Otherwise, factions out of power might well split from those in power. To make this work, Johnson modified the Senate's rules on seniority, which gave the most power to those senators who had served the longest. However, to make his plan work, he needed key Democratic senators to go along. When Russell did, the doors seemed to swing open.

One of Johnson's first moves as minority leader was to fill three of the six vacant seats on the Steering Committee with liberals, giving some balance there. Then he invoked what became known as the "Johnson Rule," an unofficial pronouncement that no senator would serve on more than one of the five most desirable committees (until all the other Democrats had their first choices filled). This allowed Johnson to give plum appointments to young senators. Humphrey, for instance, went to the Senate Foreign Relations Committee; John Kennedy of Massachusetts and Price Daniels of Texas were both placed on Finance. The most important result of these maneuvers was that Johnson broke the hold of Democratic conservatives in the Senate. At the same time, he often made appointments that muted a senator's enthusiasm—enthusiasm that might damage the party. Humphrey had been on Labor and Public Welfare. By pulling Humphrey from that committee and placing him on Foreign Relations, Johnson muted Humphrey's domestic liberalism, policies that often offended the South. By removing Al Gore of Tennessee from the Senate Judiciary Committee, a committee that often dealt with civil rights issues, and placing him on Public Works, Johnson quieted Gore's civil rights activism and thereby suppressed confrontations in the party over civil rights.[23]

As leader, Johnson also controlled the Policy Committee, a mostly dead entity created in the late 1930s to determine general party policy and the manner in which individual bills would be handled in the Senate. Johnson used the committee for a number of things, but mostly to work out the compromises within the Democratic Party that were necessary to get bills enacted. He wanted all factions and opinions represented, thus he named to the committee four conservatives, two moderates, and three liberals. There was, however, no question that it was Johnson who dominated the committee.[24]

Johnson's strategy as leader revolved around two basic objectives. In a broad sense, he wanted to support legislation for a strong national defense—that is, he meant to maintain U.S. strength against Soviet expansions and aggressions. In the domestic arena, he believed that the American people wanted programs that eased the problems of a growing industrial society. In order to avoid an unequal and unfair economic structure in the nation, Johnson believed that the federal government had the responsibility to provide for those who needed assistance: the ill-fed, the ill-housed, the undereducated. To Johnson, a nation of economic equals (or near equals) was a better nation.

Eisenhower's own basic objectives were for a strong national defense and fiscal conservatism. He was willing to create and maintain most social programs if it was politically and economically expedient. To that end, he agreed to keep many of the New Deal reforms in place, most importantly those programs perceived as "safety nets" that maintained a decent quality of life for those Americans who needed assistance. The key to understanding Eisenhower was that he also cared more about foreign affairs and foreign policy than he did about blocking domestic reform legislation. Johnson seemed to understand this; as long as the domestic reform bills were not too liberal or too expensive, Eisenhower would generally play along. All this worked, with Johnson and the moderate Democrats appearing united and standing shoulder-to-shoulder with a very popular president against the naysayers on the Republican far right. Neither man was above taking potshots at the other or supporting legislation that the other opposed. But at the very basic level, both Johnson and Eisenhower were willing to work together to get moderate legislation passed.

All of this was done, not through collaboration or discussion, but as a result of a willingness of both men to accept the other's contributions and then compromise on the final result. The idea, George Reedy later wrote, was "to approach *all* issues by amending Eisenhower's requests. . . . The point was to change the [Republican] bill, replace Republican

language with Democratic language, leaving the Eisenhower name on the bill." This, he added, had a "placating effect upon the president, which meant that he was unlikely to intervene in the debate . . . and unlikely to veto the measure." Thus, "the picture before the public was that of the Republican president and a Democratic Senate cooperating in the service of the nation while a small group of GOP partisans were trying to throw sand in the gears." And it was mostly a successful strategy, at least until the later part of the decade.[25]

Johnson's objective, then, was to keep Democratic legislation in the realm of moderation. With some very significant exceptions, the Eisenhower Republicans and the Johnson Democrats often met somewhere in the middle. Republican conservatives like Barry Goldwater and Democratic liberals like Hubert Humphrey often complained bitterly, insisting that the moderate cooperation of Johnson and Eisenhower kept their parties from distinguishing themselves from each other, of not giving the American people a true choice between liberal and conservative political and economic philosophies.[26] Other party leaders, like Truman, wanted to come out swinging at Eisenhower, to do all they could to destroy the new administration as a way of keeping Republicans out of power in the future. That, Reedy told Johnson, "would [be] a terrible mistake." "The only real hope," Reedy added in another memo, "is to sit back and capitalize on Republican mistakes."[27]

Johnson and the Democratic moderates would work with the president as often as possible (particularly on foreign affairs), try to maintain as many of the New Deal–Fair Deal liberal policies as possible, often in exchange for support in other areas, and join the administration in its fight against the GOP right. That would give the Democrats an air of bipartisan responsibility in their efforts to work with a popular president and perhaps make Eisenhower appear to be more of a Democrat than a Republican.

A good example of the cooperation between Eisenhower and Johnson was the Bricker amendment. John Bricker, a conservative Republican senator from Ohio, had led a charge to stop what he and other conservative Republicans saw as an unconstitutional growth of presidential power

in foreign affairs. During World War II and immediately afterward, the presidents (Roosevelt and Truman) had made a series of executive agreements with foreign powers that had determined the fate of the nation and much of the world. These executive agreements, Bricker and others argued, had put too much power into the hands of the executive branch, and in many cases they had come to replace treaties as instruments of foreign policy. These executive agreements had gone into effect without congressional approval and, Bricker and others believed, had thus circumvented the Constitution, which requires that all treaties be approved by the Senate. Bricker's amendment to the Constitution would prohibit executive agreements in place of treaties and require that all executive agreements receive congressional approval before going into effect. The amendment also prohibited the negotiation of any treaty or executive agreement that abridged any specific individual right spelled out in the Constitution.[28]

Much of this reflected the Republican Party's disdain for the Yalta and Potsdam agreements, as a result of which, they argued, large sections of Eastern Europe had been handed over to the Soviet government without any input from Congress or the American people. They also feared that the collective security of the United Nations might mean that the United States, as a founding member of the UN, would be required to accept various UN initiatives and resolutions that would negate individual rights in the U.S. Constitution. These UN initiatives, they argued further, would also cause the federal government to expand to an unprecedented size and power. An example often given was the UN's Covenant on Human Rights, written at least in part by Eleanor Roosevelt. The covenant incorporated a series of rights to be claimed by all of the world's humanity, including some form of social security or state-sponsored old-age pension, adequate housing, health care, education, legalized membership in trade unions, and "an adequate standard of living." To Bricker and his supporters, this meant that UN members must institute broad social programs—programs that would vastly expand the powers of the federal government.[29]

In his first State of the Union message, Eisenhower criticized Democrats for treaties that led to the "enslavement" of Eastern Europeans. And he

added that he would ask for "an appropriate resolution" to deal with secret agreements.[30] He refused, however, to repudiate Yalta specifically, and he did not call for a constitutional amendment to curtail the president's executive or treaty-making powers. In fact, when the amendment was proposed it became immediately clear that Eisenhower opposed it, insisting that it would restrict the power of the president to make agreements with foreign powers. To his brother Edgar, who supported the Bricker amendment, the president argued that he believed the plan would "cripple the executive power to the point that we [would] become helpless in world affairs."[31] And in his diaries he called Bricker "psychopathetic," and made it clear that he agreed with his advisors "that the effect of the amendment would be to damage the United States materially. . . ."[32] In addition, those around the president opposed it and counseled him to work against it. Secretary of State John Foster Dulles claimed that the amendment "would subject the current day-to-day conduct of foreign affairs to impediment which would be stifling." And Attorney General Herbert Brownell insisted that the amendment might invalidate "a host of agreements" already concluded.[33]

All this reflected Eisenhower's dilemma. He could not repudiate Yalta and Potsdam, as those on the right would have him do, without implying deceit on the part of Roosevelt and Truman. That would alienate the vast majority of congressional Democrats, whose support he needed to advance his foreign policy. At the same time, Bricker's own proposed constitutional amendment was cosponsored by all but three Republicans. So, to support it was to alienate Democrats; to oppose it was to go against his own party. It was, wrote *Time*, "a time bomb threat to both G.O.P. unity and White House-congressional relations."[34]

In a series of press conferences, Eisenhower avoided questions about the Bricker amendment, explaining often that Dulles had advised him that the amendment would restrict the power of the presidency, thereby deflecting criticism away from him and toward Dulles and the State Department. This Eisenhower strategy of redirecting attention and blame has usually been considered effective in maintaining the president's popularity and integrity throughout his time in office, but in this case—as

in several others—Eisenhower's irresolute demeanor caused amendment supporters to continue their efforts to win him over. Consequently, the fight dragged on for years.[35]

The administration's first strategy was to try to delay Bricker's efforts by appealing to his party loyalty. Such a controversial issue, Brownell and others told Bricker, proposed so early in the new administration, might cause irreparable damage, even split the party. But Bricker refused to stand down or even to wait for a more appropriate time. The president saw Bricker's stubbornness as a reflection of the inability of "a party that has been in the minority for twenty years to take up the burdens of responsibility for the operation of the government. . . . [F]or so long," he added, "the Republican party has been opposed to, and often a deadly enemy of, the individual in the White House." The president's advisors also suggested that Bricker might set up a committee to investigate the need for such an amendment, a committee that might meet for months, even years. But Bricker again refused to go along.[36]

The administration then moved to push Bricker into a compromise. Eisenhower was opposed to the amendment's encroachment on his powers, but he had been sympathetic to a concern that the Constitution might be altered in someway through international agreements or that an agreement with the United Nations might expand the powers of the federal government and destroy individual rights. To most of those involved in the process, the president's willingness to consider one primary aspect of the amendment was enough to forge some sort of middle ground compromise. By the summer of 1953, a compromise seemed in place, which stated merely that any treaty that violated the Constitution was invalid. But again Bricker continued to stand firm, even strengthening his original proposal.

On July 1, Eisenhower ended all equivocation and simply came out against the amendment. By early January 1954, however, it appeared again that some sort of compromise would finally settle the issue.[37] All parties agreed that treaties would not be allowed to interfere with state and local matters. But for a third time, Bricker backtracked and repudiated the

compromise. He also publicly criticized Eisenhower by sending a letter to all senators stating that the president had been "misinformed" about the amendment and had given "wide circulation to erroneous charges." Bricker's tactic only strengthened the president's resolve to defeat the amendment. He responded by writing to Bill Knowland, the Senate Republican leader: "Adoption of the Bricker Amendment by the Senate would be notice to our friends as well as our enemies abroad that our country intends to withdraw from its leadership in world affairs."[38] Also by this time, Eisenhower's increasing opposition to the amendment had pushed several moderate Republicans in the Senate to abandon Bricker and his amendment.

With that, the president turned to the Democrats for help. The result was a much less strident substitute amendment encouraged by Johnson and proposed by Senator Walter George of Georgia. George was the ranking Democrat on the Senate Foreign Relations Committee and a well-respected internationalist. Johnson intended that the George amendment would be defeated, but only by a few votes.[39] On February 25, 1954, the Bricker amendment was voted down in the Senate, 50-42. Two days later, George's substitute amendment came up for a vote, at 60 to 30—exactly the two-thirds needed for passage. Harley Kilgore (D-WV) entered the Senate chamber late and voted "nay," defeating the measure by just one vote. The *New York Times* insisted that "The Administration's position . . . was saved by a coalition of all-out Eisenhower Republicans and liberal Democrats."[40]

The Bricker amendment did not die, however; Bricker continued his efforts to curtail the treaty-making powers of the president. In the 1954 election, several of his supporters went down to defeat, and then Bricker himself was defeated in 1958.[41]

The Bricker Amendment was an example of how the two wings of the Republican Party were at each other's throats over several issues. Here, the Republican right wanted to curtail the power of the executive branch. The president, however, would not relinquish his power—or his potential power. It nearly split the party. "The Bricker Amendment," George Reedy later said, "was probably the most divisive political proposal of the mid-50s." "I don't know of any other single issue . . . that has aroused such intense emotion."[42]

‡

In March 1947, Truman, in response to Republican charges that the Democrats were "soft" on communism, had issued Executive Order 9835, mandating a loyalty investigation of all federal job applicants, and requiring all agency heads to be responsible for the loyalty of their employees. The concern over communism grew into hysteria when Nationalist China fell to the communists in 1949, the Soviets detonated an atomic bomb just a few months before, and the Korean War broke out in June 1950. Added to that were a series of spectacular spy cases, including the Alger Hiss case; and by the time Eisenhower came to office in January 1953, anti-communism had become a national concern. All this set the stage for the rise of Joseph McCarthy, a fairly inconsequential Republican senator from Wisconsin who, by most accounts, latched onto the issue because his political fortunes were on the wane. The issue would dominate the first half of the decade.

McCarthy was elected to the Senate in 1946, but he gained real power when the Republicans gained control of Congress after the 1952 elections. He was named head of the Senate Committee on Government Operations, and that gave him the authority to place himself in charge of the Permanent Committee on Investigations, a position that included the power to subpoena witnesses. Within a year, McCarthy's long arm had reached into most federal agencies, American industry, the media, the entertainment industries, and colleges and universities. For four years, his investigations, accusations, and innuendo destroyed reputations and careers while uncovering almost no communist infiltration of the nation's primary institutions.

McCarthy was a problem for both political parties, but more so for the Republicans than the Democrats. Johnson and the Democrats had concluded early on that confronting McCarthy would probably result in political suicide. Polls showed that the American people were on McCarthy's side, and it seemed pretty clear that trying to stand up to McCarthy could, for a politician, result in being labeled "soft" on communism, sympathetic to communism, or a "fellow traveler."[43] During these McCarthy years, Johnson was being bombarded by demands from liberals to confront McCarthy and cut him down.[44] But he realized his position. He told William S. White of the *New York Times*, "I am not about to commit the Democratic party to a high school debate on the subject 'Resolved, that communism is good for the United States,' with my party taking the affirmative."[45] So, Johnson decided to bide his time and allow McCarthy to self-destruct. Hubert Humphrey recalled, "Lyndon kept saying that we had to wait until McCarthy began attacking the more conservative, the respected, the Senators of what you might call the old school."[46]

Eisenhower at first took much the same sort of stand. In his diary entry of April 1, 1953, the president wrote, "I really believe that nothing will be so effective in combating his particular kind of troublemaking as to ignore him."[47] Eisenhower clearly disliked McCarthy, but he was most upset by his methods, along with his far-right-wing stances on most issues and his willingness to divide the Republicans for his own benefit. Yet, it was Eisenhower, more than anyone else, who could have crushed McCarthy—and he probably could have done it without suffering much political damage as a result. But Eisenhower was, at least to some degree, sympathetic to the anti-communist cause. In his first State of the Union address, he said that it was the responsibility of the executive branch of government to cleanse the federal payroll of the "disloyal and the dangerous" and to keep unsuitable applicants from getting government jobs.[48] In April 1953, he signed an executive order authorizing heads of all federal departments to fire anyone they deemed disloyal, unreliable, or who lacked "good conduct and character." This executive order (and two others that followed) stripped away all legal protection against summary dismissal, appeals, and the constitutional right to invoke the Fifth Amendment against self-incrimination. These actions were taken without hearings to determine the accuracy of charges or even the revelation of charges. Eisenhower told Dulles that the action was necessary because he believed that the State Department was plagued with subversives, employees loyal to the previous Democratic administrations, and "devoted to the socialist doctrine . . . practiced over the past two decades."[49] Eisenhower also supported legislation to strip citizenship from those convicted under the Smith Act of attempting to overthrow the government, to compel witnesses to testify in national security investigations, to legalize wiretaps in internal security cases, and to broaden espionage and sabotage laws. He also ordered Robert Oppenheimer's security clearance revoked. Oppenheimer had headed the Manhattan Project during the war, but in 1949 he testified before the House Committee on Un-American Activities that he had been associated with communists in the 1930s.[50]

Just after Eisenhower became president in 1953, he learned that McCarthy would try to block two of his appointments: his good friend and Army Chief of Staff during the war, Walter Bedell Smith, as Undersecretary of State; and Harvard president James Conant as the U.S. High Commissioner to Germany. Conant had once said that there were no communists at Harvard, a statement that seemed to stick in McCarthy's craw. Smith had come to the defense of China expert and accused communist John Patton Davis, one of McCarthy's favorite targets in the State Department. In an attempt to moderate McCarthy a bit, Eisenhower sent Vice President Nixon to McCarthy with a message to tone down his attacks. McCarthy told Nixon that he would not end his anti-communist crusade, but that he would end his attacks on the administration's appointees. Eisenhower seemed satisfied and began to look toward McCarthy as at least willing to cooperate with the administration and its policies. But McCarthy then turned his attention to the United States Information Agency (USIA), the Voice of America, and the Overseas Library Program.[51]

These attacks intensified Eisenhower's dislike for McCarthy and his aggressive methods, and he wanted him out of the way. At the same time, a strategy of direct confrontation seemed out of the question. In a letter to Swede Hazlett in the summer of 1953, Eisenhower explained that "I disagree completely with the 'crack down' theory." Here, Eisenhower uses the phrase "crack down" to refer to a direct attack on McCarthy.

"I believe in the positive approach," he added. "I believe that we should earnestly support the practice of American principles in trials and investigations," something that he clearly believed McCarthy was not doing. "We should support . . . whom we know to be unjustly attacked, whether they are public servants or private citizens." Then he concluded that he would generally stay out of the fray: "Of course, the indirect defense accomplished through condemnation of unfair methods is always applicable."[52] But more directly, "I just won't get into a pissing contest with that skunk."[53]

Eisenhower clearly did not want to get mixed up with McCarthy, and he believed that if he did his presidency (or even the office of the president) might be damaged. He found it repugnant that Truman often dragged the presidency through the mud to the point, he thought, that it damaged the office. To Lucius Clay he wrote, "I don't intend to advertise this guy."[54] And he saved his most ardent criticism for those who, he believed, were causing the entire mess, the national press corps: "I was rather resentful that the very agencies who had made McCarthy were [the] loudest in their demands that I be the one to cut him down to size."[55] In addition, the advice Eisenhower was receiving from those around him was to take a conciliatory approach. The argument was that the Republican majority in Congress was razor thin and to confront McCarthy might easily upset that delicate balance.[56]

As was the case with the Bricker amendment and, later, civil rights, then the *Brown* decision, and finally the 1957 Civil Rights Act, Eisenhower had a strong opinion, but he refused to throw his considerable weight into the fight. He did deny information to McCarthy whenever possible, and by most accounts that did restrict the fuel McCarthy needed to build his fires.[57] Eisenhower also spoke out privately against him and his methods and manners, but he refused to confront McCarthy directly.

As the 1954 midterm elections approached, McCarthy set out on a speaking tour that he entitled "Twenty Years of Treason," designed as an attack on the Democrats. In his several speeches, he said that "[t]he label 'Democrat' is stitched with the idiocy of a Truman, rotted by the deceit of an Acheson, [and] corrupted by the red slime of a [Harry Dexter]

White."[58] Eisenhower immediately asked all Republicans to tone down their attacks on the Democrats, insisting that the times were too serious for such extreme partisanship. James Reston at the *New York Times* wrote that "[t]he President seemed to apply this principle to all windmill orators, name-callers and professional Democrat-baiters."[59] Nixon, who was campaigning in Connecticut, immediately cooled his rhetoric. "We should," he said, "leave the door open for all, regardless of party, to support our President and his program." Even Knowland claimed to oppose a "blanket indictment" of the entire Democratic Party.[60] Johnson responded by saying that "[t]he President's attitude is one of a gentleman and an American."[61] But McCarthy soldiered on, and Eisenhower did nothing to stop his tirades. C. D. Jackson, one of Eisenhower's chief advisors and speechwriters, accused the president of continuing a "Three Little Monkeys act" and accused the president of appeasing McCarthy—a very bad word among Republicans. But Eisenhower still refused to confront McCarthy.[62]

Johnson and the Democrats continued to hold their tongues. "It's a Republican problem," Reedy told Johnson, "because they built Senator McCarthy to his present position of power."[63] And generally Johnson agreed. In addition, he expected that McCarthy would cause an eventual split among Republicans—between the Eisenhower moderates and the party's right wing. Johnson also feared handing the Republicans a campaign issue by attacking McCarthy—giving Republicans the ammunition they would most certainly use to claim that Democratic candidates were soft on communism. By election time, however, House Speaker Sam Rayburn had had enough of the attacks, and he let go: "I can stand charges of crime and corruption," he said. "But charges implying treason are unforgivable, and my back is getting pretty sore." Then he added, these attacks are "mean, untrue and dastardly. They should be stopped by somebody."[64]

‡

For the Democrats, it was civil rights for African Americans and the issue of race that threatened to divide their party—much as it had for nearly a century. In 1948, the Democrats had split over the civil rights issue, an event that probably should have led to a Republican victory. Instead, Truman won the election by consolidating his power in the northern urban areas, among African American voters and labor. The message was clear: the white South was losing its importance in the Democratic Party, and in response it was also becoming estranged from the national Democratic leadership. Were white southern conservatives looking for a new home? Republicans thought so, and through the 1950s, Eisenhower led the Republican Party in a thinly veiled courtship of the white South.

All of this put the Democrats in a bind. They had won in 1948 *despite* the defection of the South. But it was fairly clear that an outright rejection of white southern voters (as part of an embrace of northern black voters) was probably not a good trade-off for the future. Black voters had voted for Truman mostly because of Strom Thurmond's run on the overtly segregationist Dixiecrat ticket, a political perfect storm that was unlikely to fall into place in future elections. In addition, it was powerful southern politicians like Russell, Rayburn, Louisiana's Allen Ellender, Mississippi's James Eastland, and others who headed the important committees in Congress, and thus held the keys to the governmental mechanisms. They were all strong segregationists; to alienate politicians with such power would do little more than bring an end to the Democratic Party's liberal programs and reform legislation.

Consequently, the Democrats in the 1950s found themselves trying to straddle the fence when it came to civil rights issues. To avoid a 1948-type split, the Democrats worked hard for compromise and reconciliation. In the 1952 campaign, Democrats believed that if they had any chance at beating Eisenhower they would need to conciliate the South. Governor Paul A. Dever of Massachusetts, in an address to the nation in the spring of 1952, spoke of compromise on civil rights and a need to avoid the harshness of the 1948 Democratic Party convention.[65] Four years later, at the 1956 convention, party liberals like Eleanor Roosevelt, Reinhold Niebuhr, and Hubert Humphrey sided with Stevenson, a moderate on civil rights, rather than with Averell Harriman, whose civil rights stance generally rejected southern interests.[66] Alienating the white South was, for

Democrats, simply not a viable political option in the 1950s. The nation, however, was changing.

The Supreme Court decision *Brown v. Board of Education of Topeka Kansas* of May 1954 (which served to desegregate the nation's school systems) was perhaps the most significant Supreme Court decision of the twentieth century. It proclaimed that the era of separate-but-equal was over, that the American way of racial segregation had ended. Over 70 percent of northern whites supported the decision; 80 percent of southerners opposed it.[67] It seemed fairly clear that conflicts would erupt over the issue—conflicts in the streets, conflicts in the courts, and conflicts in Congress. The *Brown* decision pitted the North and South against each other like no other time since the end of Reconstruction.

A little over a year later, in August 1955, Emmett Till, a fourteen-year-old African American from Chicago, was murdered in Money, Mississippi, for reportedly flirting with a local white woman. In standard form, the suspects were acquitted by a jury of all white men. The murder (and the acquittal) outraged many Americans, and the incident received national coverage when Till's mother insisted that the disfigured body of her son be returned to Chicago and that the child's casket be opened for public viewing. In a famous statement, she told a friend, "I want the world to see what they did to my baby." As many as 50,000 people viewed the body, and news photos of the mutilated corpse were circulated freely around the country. Perhaps most notably, a photo of Till was published in *Jet* magazine, a weekly magazine aimed at African Americans that had been founded a few years earlier.

The *Brown* decision, followed by Till's murder, seemed to awaken Americans to a need to change old patterns. But change was coming in other ways as well. The nature of the Cold War had also made it clear that the United States needed to make changes. The Cold War was, at least in part, a competition between the United States and the Soviets for the hearts and minds of the peoples of the "Third World," those regions not aligned with either the United States or the Soviets. The vast majority of the inhabitants of the Third World were dark skinned, or they were racially different from the majority white Americans.

The Soviets exploited America's overt racism by pointing out to the dark-skinned peoples of the Third World that white Americans discriminated against African Americans, segregated the two races, and occasionally murdered its own dark-skinned citizens without fear of reprisal or prosecution.[68]

All of these events pushed hard on Eisenhower. He was a moderate on race, as he was a moderate on most issues. He was a gradualist, a states' righter, a man who believed in equality before the law. But he had no use for the basic concepts of social equality. In two famous statements, often used to explain his attitudes toward race, Eisenhower said, "If you go too far too fast . . . you are making a mistake."[69] And, "the fellow who tries to tell me that you can do these things by *force* is just plain nuts."[70] But Eisenhower had a fairly good record on civil rights—certainly for the time, and certainly within his own belief system. He argued that the federal government's role in protecting civil rights should come only in areas where it has direct jurisdiction. To that end, he desegregated the Washington, DC, school system; he continued the policy begun by Truman to desegregate the military, and he mandated that all public schools operated by the federal government (those on or near military bases) be desegregated.[71] And, during the invasion of Europe, he famously ordered black laborers to fill gaps in several all-white units during the Battle of Bulge. At the same time, he never questioned the prevailing policy of discrimination in the military during the war.[72]

One popular approach to the problem of black civil rights was to see that African Americans in the South received the vote. The idea was simple: if African Americans were allowed to vote, all the rights and privileges of first-class U.S. citizenship would follow. It was a reasonable assumption. Poll taxes, literacy tests, and intimidation had kept as many as 80 percent of African Americans from voting in the South. In some counties in Mississippi, no blacks voted at all.[73] Eisenhower believed strongly in this argument. He made the point during a press conference in 1957: "If in every locality every person otherwise qualified . . . to vote, is permitted to vote, he has got the means of . . . getting what he wants in a democratic government. . . ."[74] The solution seemed simple. Laws needed to be enacted giving all Americans the most basic of all constitutional rights, the right to vote. At the same time, proponents believed that any opposition was truly indefensible.

For Eisenhower, however, the *Brown* decision went well beyond these modest convictions. Thus, his response was little more than indifference and inaction. He was not a segregationist, but he did understand the concerns of southern whites. He often spoke of his many southern friends, and he had spent the majority of his life on segregated army bases, often in the South. He wanted gradualism and patience. "Perhaps," he suggested in his diary, the courts, rather than insisting on prompt desegregation, might have instead "demanded that segregation be eliminated in graduate schools, later in colleges, [and] later in high schools, as a means of overcoming the passionate and inbred attitudes" that have developed over generations.[75] The abruptness of the *Brown* decision, and the demands of the nation's civil rights leaders for immediate federal action, disrupted his senses, putting his back against the wall as president of the United States. His response was simple: he would refuse to endorse of the court's decision, and he would agree only to enforce the ruling as law. "The Supreme Court has spoken," he said in a press conference, "and I am sworn to uphold the constitutional process of this country; and I will obey."[76]

All of this caused a delay in the desegregation process through the Eisenhower years. Many regions of the upper South had seen the writing on the wall and had begun to comply with the *Brown* ruling, and it appeared that much of the South would eventually come around. But when it became clear that the president would not put his massive power and popularity behind *Brown*, the call went out for "massive resistance." By one count, 568 organizations were specifically dedicated to resisting *Brown* and the federal government. Georgia, Mississippi, and Virginia evoked the spirit of the pro-slavery politician John C. Calhoun and passed resolutions of interposition. States passed laws specifically to obstruct *Brown*. Some teachers in some southern school districts had their state teaching licenses revoked for teaching mixed-race classes. Several states allocated funds to pay the tuition for white public school students to attend all-white private schools. Entire public school systems were declared private by state governments to avoid desegregation. And some school systems were finally shut down altogether.[77]

All of this played out in the political arena. Eisenhower's middle-of-the-road stance on race and states' rights (a stance that southerners clearly saw as sympathetic) brought the president a surprising number of southern white votes. In 1952 he had done well in the South, winning the electoral votes of Texas, Oklahoma, Missouri, Florida, Tennessee, Virginia, Maryland, and Delaware. He even received the endorsements of Texas governor Allan Shivers and South Carolina governor James Byrnes, both Democrats. In 1956, he picked up Kentucky, West Virginia, and Louisiana—although he lost Missouri.

‡

The 83rd Congress was what William S. White of the *New York Times* called a "middle of the road session."[78] Eisenhower was able to cut taxes, mostly as he had planned. He granted about $1.3 billion in tax relief to corporations, stockholders, and individuals. He was also responsible for greatly expanding the Social Security system, a goal he had mentioned in his first State of the Union message. The program now covered an additional ten million American workers, including hotel and agricultural workers, as well as state and local government employees. "[S]hould any political party attempt to abolish Social Security," he told his brother, "you would not hear of that party again in our political history."[79]

In housing, the president wanted to pass a comprehensive bill, but he was attacked by his party's right wing. He requested funding for 140,000 units to be built over four years, insisting that the program would be "a sustaining force for the entire economy."[80] The number of planned housing unit starts was compromised in conference committee down to a maximum of 35,000 units per year. However, restrictions made it impossible to fill even that quota, and only 142 housing units were started in the ten months after passage of the bill.[81] It was hardly a success, but the president signed the bill on August 2, 1954, insisting that "[w]e shall continue our public housing program until the needs can be met by private industry."[82]

Housing in the next session would be more successful for the administration and the Democrats.

One of Eisenhower's primary goals when he came to office was to reduce farm subsidies and encourage the growth of the free market in agriculture. The nation's system of farm subsidies had been adopted during the Depression and expanded during the postwar years. Eisenhower saw this plan as wasteful, but he also believed that it caused farmers, who were generally conservative, to vote Democratic. The system paid farmers a rigid price support on basic commodities, particularly cotton, corn, and wheat. This support payment was set at 90 percent of parity, a calculation used to ensure that farmers received a fair income for their yield. Eisenhower argued that the results of these payments were huge farm surpluses and falling commodity prices. Subsidies allowed farmers to prosper, as the president saw it, but it weakened the nation's agricultural system—certainly for the long run. Eisenhower also saw this plan as government management of the economy, something he detested. His plan was to scale down support payments, replacing the rigid system with a sliding scale ranging from 75 to 90 percent of parity. This, he said, would restore market forces to the nation's agricultural economy. Following a major revolt by farm state Republicans, a compromise was passed that placed subsidies on a scale ranging from 82.5 to 90 percent of parity.[83]

Public power was one of the most controversial political topics of the 1950s. But despite some of Eisenhower's statements that seemed to the contrary, the president always supported public power as a means to help the development and growth of private enterprise and farming. He supported the Upper Colorado Basin project, which eventually built dams and reservoirs on the Colorado River and its tributaries in Arizona, Colorado, and Utah. He supported water development in the Hell's Canyon and Snake River Basin. He understood the necessity of the Tennessee Valley Authority (TVA), although he opposed any expansion of the project. In 1954, he authorized a private firm, Dixon-Yates, to deliver power to Memphis, Tennessee. The result was a barrage of criticism accusing the president of trying to kill off the TVA. The conflict ended when Memphis decided to build its own power plant and distribution system.[84]

The only public power project that did not cause a public furor was the St. Lawrence Seaway Project (dedicated in 1959 as the St. Lawrence International Seaway, and constructed jointly with Canada). Originally proposed by Truman, the project had died in Congress because of the high cost of developing hydroelectric facilities along the river. In order to push the bill through Congress, Eisenhower compromised considerably. He removed the hydroelectric projects from the bill and then insisted that the American side of the development be a cooperative effort between the federal government and the states. The cost of the entire project was kept down through user fees. Finally, the president was able to convince the nation of the potential military uses of the seaway and the bill passed Congress.[85]

‡

By early 1954, Joe McCarthy had had his day in the sun. As chairman of the Government Operations Committee and its Permanent Sub-committee on Investigations, McCarthy had attacked General George Marshall (like Eisenhower, one of the nation's most revered military figures) and then the army. At least in part due to Johnson's insistence, the resulting Army-McCarthy hearings were televised.[86] Johnson believed that McCarthy's popularity would quickly vanish once the nation observed his aggressive, even repugnant, manner. Through the early summer of 1954, America watched as McCarthy bullied his opponents into submission with underhanded tactics, accusations, and innuendo. Finally, on June 9, McCarthy met his match in Joseph Welch, the army's special counsel. McCarthy accused Welch's assistant, Fred Fisher, of having communist connections as a one-time member of the National Lawyers Guild, an organization that McCarthy had asserted was a communist front organization. Welch, famously mild mannered, hit back at McCarthy, calling him reckless and cruel, and following with the well-known "Have you no sense of decency, sir, at long last?" The statement drew applause from the observers in the Senate hearing room, most of whom clearly approved of Welsh's retort and disapproved of McCarthy's tactics.[87] The event was caught on television. Almost immediately McCarthy's approval ratings collapsed, and he quickly became a liability to the Republicans.[88]

Wisconsin Senator Joseph McCarthy was a dilemma for both the Democrats and the Republicans in the early 1950s.   (Eisenhower Presidential Library and Museum, Abilene, Kansas)

Within two days, one of McCarthy's arch foes in the Senate, Vermont Republican Ralph Flanders, introduced a motion to have McCarthy removed from his chairmanships. Senate Republicans pushed Flanders to moderate his demand, and on June 30 he substituted a censure resolution for his original motion. In the first week of August, the Senate voted to establish a bipartisan six-man select committee, headed by Republican Arthur Watkins of Utah, to determine McCarthy's fate. Johnson made certain that only conservative Democrats were appointed to the committee: John Stennis of Mississippi, Sam Ervin of North Carolina, and Ed Johnson of Colorado. The other two Republicans were Francis Case of South Dakota and Frank Carlson of Kansas. McCarthy warned anyone who would stand against him. They would, he said, "either indict themselves for perjury," or prove "what consummate liars they are."[89]

Johnson continued to stay away from the controversy. He convened a meeting of the Policy Planning Committee and concluded that any significant Democratic role in the coming events would play directly into McCarthy's hands. The committee announced the party's neutrality, making it clear that it was a Republican problem.[90] "[T]he Democratic leadership [has] assumed a completely inert attitude toward the whole issue" of McCarthy's censure, the *New York Times* reported. "Senator Lyndon Johnson of Texas, the Democratic leader, never uttered a word in the debate. . . ."[91] But not everyone approved. Party liberals pushed Johnson to hit hard at McCarthy, and when he refused (insisting that it was a problem for the Republicans to solve) they criticized him severely. Joseph Rauh, the head of the ADA was a constant critic. "Johnson was awful on Joe McCarthy, he was absolutely dreadful." He "never said a word on McCarthy until the censure came through." Rauh added, "Bullies are always scared of bullies."[92]

Eisenhower found himself with many of the same problems as Johnson. He also kept clear of the events, mostly to avoid offending his party's right wing. He often told those around him, however, that he wanted McCarthy out.[93] In March, before the Army-McCarthy hearings began, Adlai Stevenson made a speech in Miami that seemed to put the Eisenhower administration on notice and may well have forced the administration to act. Stevenson said, "A political party divided against itself, half McCarthy and half Eisenhower, cannot produce national unity—cannot govern with confidence and purpose."[94] The *New York Times* criticized the administration for not taking the lead in confronting McCarthy. It was Nixon, however, who finally responded. He went on television and told the nation that "men who have in the past done effective work exposing communists in the country have, by reckless talk and questionable means, made themselves the issue rather than the cause they believe in so deeply."[95] It was, finally, a slap at McCarthy. The administration was beginning to distance itself from McCarthy as the 1954 midterm elections approached.

After some wrangling between GOP conservatives and moderates over the severity of McCarthy's actions, the Senate committee recommended censure, and on December 2, following the election, the Senate (now

Texas Senator and Majority Leader Lyndon Johnson at the height of his powers in the 1950s. (AP)

in the hands of the Democrats) voted 67 to 22 to censure McCarthy.[96] Truly, one of the nation's most dangerous periods had come to an end. Eisenhower was delighted to see McCarthy go. Most of McCarthy's efforts had been in direct opposition to what Eisenhower was trying to accomplish as president. Eisenhower wanted to hold the political center, while McCarthy, out on the radical right, was critical of the president for his moderate stances on most domestic issues. The conflict had split the party.

Eisenhower's stance on McCarthy was characteristic: avoid the fight and allow it to run its course. He did establish a counterforce to McCarthyism, in which he sought to eliminate "security risks" from the federal government; and he famously refused to allow McCarthy access to confidential documents on the grounds of national security.[97] Formidable gestures, to be sure. But McCarthy's actions and behavior were not fed by government documents. Even Eisenhower understood that publicity had kept him going and that publicity had given him his power.[98] Eisenhower always despised Truman's political methods that he believed demeaned the office of the presidency. But Eisenhower never seemed to understand the weight he carried with the American people or the raw power of the presidency. Johnson and the Democrats believed they could only bide their time and wait for McCarthy to self-destruct. But Eisenhower could have denounced McCarthy and almost certainly ended the nightmare—or at least blunted its progression and severity.[99]

The vote to censure McCarthy burdened Eisenhower. The only Republican Party leader to support censure was Massachusetts Senator Leverett Saltonstall, an administration stalwart. Other important party members in the Senate, William Knowland of California, Everett Dirksen of Illinois, Stiles Bridges of New Hampshire, and Eugene Millikin of Colorado, all supported McCarthy against the censure motion.[100] It was an indication of the growing strength of the party's right wing.

McCarthy never recovered from the act of censure, and the whole episode seemed to destroy him. "I would see him lurch down the halls in the morning," Harry McPherson recalled, "and he had a kind of bloated face with heavy jowls, he looked really terrible. And he would make those long, incomprehensible speeches, seconded by other Republican drunks."[101] *Time* concluded his career by writing: "Now McCarthy [has] receded to a mere smudge on the political landscape." He died in 1957 at age forty-eight of liver disease, most likely brought on by alcoholism.[102]

‡

With the 1954 elections on the horizon, the parties began openly attacking each other, leaving all pretense of bipartisanship behind. At a Jefferson-Jackson Day dinner in Washington in early May, Johnson unleashed an attack on the Republicans that caused the *New York Times* to call Johnson's remarks "An all-out . . . attack on the Eisenhower Administration's foreign policy, the first such attack since the President took office. . . ." "Heretofore, [Johnson] had supported the Administration on all world issues and had been a force in restraining proposed severe criticisms of the Administration by other Democrats."[103] At least for the election season, Johnson would not be a conciliatory force.

Eisenhower, in his true fashion, refused to do much campaigning (at least at first), insisting on staying above the fight. He told Dewey that he saw Truman's whistle-stop tours in 1948 as a denigration of the presidency. Truman's antics, he wrote, "shocked my sense of the fitting and appropriate."[104] He also wanted bipartisan support for his foreign policy agenda, so attacking the Democrats was certainly the wrong strategy. Democratic support was one thing; a Democratic victory was quite another. When it looked like the Democrats would win—and win big—the president hit the campaign trail. He traveled 10,000 miles and made over forty speeches, almost all for moderate Republican candidates. He told voters that he had ended the war in Korea, lowered taxes and cut the budget, and he warned that a Democratic victory would lead to a lack of accountability and ultimately stalemate.[105]

Eisenhower may also have feared that a Democratic victory in November would allow the Republican right to take control of the Republican Party. That had been the pattern in past elections: a defeat of the moderates at the hands of the Democrats had led to a surge in power by the GOP right, mostly as a result of the argument that Republican moderates failed to build a conservative agenda that would give voters a legitimate choice over the Democrats.

In the week before election day, the president saturated the media with speeches: 123 television and 471 radio stations ran his spots. He then hit four states in a last-minute whirlwind tour.[106]

It was not enough. The Democrats picked up twenty seats in the House for a thirty-vote margin; and two seats in the Senate for a one-vote margin. Democrats also won the mayoral races in New York City, Columbus, and Toledo. They took the gubernatorial race in New Jersey and several important district races in the Northeast.[107] Immediately, Republican fingers began to point. Eisenhower blamed McCarthy, Bricker, and the GOP right.[108] The GOP right blamed Eisenhower, mostly for not taking a more active role in the campaign and for working too eagerly with the Democrats.[109]

It was a common argument that the nation liked Ike, but not the Republicans. Others said it was McCarthy and the Republican right who had fought the administration, while the moderate Democrats, under Johnson's leadership, had worked closely with Eisenhower to move the nation forward and get things done. Actually, it was a fairly common occurrence (certainly since World War II) for the party in the White House to lose seats in Congress in the first congressional elections. In 1982, Republicans lost twenty-seven seats in the House, losing a majority there. In 1992, Democrats lost fifty-four seats in the House and eighteen seats in the Senate. In 2010, the Democrats lost over sixty seats in the House and lost control of that body, although they retained control of the Senate. It is the nature of American politics that the sheen of a popular president wears off within his first two years in office. Such was the case in 1954.

The Republican losses were, however, not really that bad considering the deteriorating economic situation and compared with other midterm elections. The nation was in a recession, and McCarthy's antics were beginning to grate on the nation's nerves. As James Hagerty recalled, "[T]he revulsion against [McCarthy] was just tremendous." Perhaps the *lack* of a Democratic Party landslide is owed to Eisenhower and his continued (even growing) popularity.[110]

After the election, much of the partisan bickering during the campaign calmed considerably, if for no other reason than Democratic moderates saw a continued need to work closely with Eisenhower. During a campaign speech, however, the president had said that a Democratic victory would lead to a "cold war of partisan politics." Johnson and Rayburn complained bitterly about the statement in a letter to the president: "We assure you that there will be no cold war conducted against you by the Democrats. . . ." After the election Eisenhower apologized, saying that the phrase had been too strong and pledging his cooperation with the new Democratic Congress.[111] And Johnson, now poised to become the majority leader, said: "The thing I am most proud of is that we were a responsible, united party when we were in the minority and no one, from the President down, has been able to point the finger of shame at the performance of this Democratic minority. We . . . are going to approach the country's problems in a spirit of cooperation. We are going to meet the President more than half way. . . . The desirable features of the President's program will be much more readily enacted by this new Democratic Congress than they would have been by the Republican Congress he wanted."[112]

CHAPTER FOUR

"I Like Ike," But Not the Republicans: Johnson and the Democrats in the Majority

The election of the new Democratic Congress in 1954 turned Lyndon Johnson from minority leader to majority leader, and returned Sam Rayburn to the speakership of the House. The government seemed set for a clash: a Republican president going head-to-head against a Democratic Congress. But despite what seemed inevitable, and despite the verbal clashes during the campaign, the leadership of both parties did not come out swinging after the election. The mood was again bipartisan; both sides realized that a clash of wills would not grease the wheels of government.

Almost immediately following the election, Eisenhower said that "[i]f there are any roadblocks thrown in the way of cooperation, I'm not going to be responsible."[1] A week later, the president hosted a well-publicized bipartisan function at the White House. The meeting lasted almost three hours, and the press reported that the topic was mostly world affairs and foreign policy. The Democratic leadership agreed that if they were consulted first, they would support the president on most foreign policy issues. It seemed to be implied that the president would support Congress on most domestic issues if he, too, were consulted.[2] Then, just after Christmas, the president sent a message to the Democratic Party leadership that he wanted a bipartisan relationship. "I want you to know, Mr. Rayburn and Mr. Johnson, that I am available for consultation at any time, if you want to come and talk to me about the welfare of the country."[3]

The Senate Democratic majority was paper thin, a situation that might seem dire for Johnson. Often, however, the opposite was true. The smaller majority made his job easier because he could make a strong appeal to party loyalty to get votes. In fact, he had his greatest successes by threatening a loss of Democratic Party–sponsored legislation if Democratic senators did not get into line on a vote. Had the majority been larger, senators might easily walk off the line, vote to please their local constituents, or even vote to go on record for an upcoming election. The Johnson way was to see that the legislation before the Senate was always moderate and had something for everyone, so that every Senate Democratic vote could be controlled—or cajoled if necessary.

In addition, the national economic situation had changed, and that changed the direction of the party and the party-sponsored legislation. The economy, which had fallen into recession during the last half of 1954, was showing signs of recovery into the first half of 1955. For Democrats that meant there was no pressing need for aggressive social legislation to help those suffering from the downturn.

Johnson had three objectives as majority leader in the 84th Congress. First, he had to avoid a strained relationship with the White House at all costs. Eisenhower was still a very popular figure—and thus a powerful president—and Johnson understood that he would be a formidable foe if confronted. Working with Eisenhower would be more advantageous than working against him. Even though Eisenhower and Johnson saw the world differently, their views on domestic policy were often similar—or at least they could find common ground. Second, Johnson could not work too closely with the administration. That would antagonize northern liberals, a small but powerful and vocal group within his party. And third, Johnson could not be seen as an obstructionist. The 80th Congress, the "do-nothing Congress," as Truman so successfully labeled that Republican-led session in 1947 and 1948, had done little more than stand in the way of most Democratic Party objectives, and they suffered badly for it in the 1948 general elections. The repercussions from that event were still fresh in the minds of both parties. Coming to office just after the 1946 congressional elections, the Republican-led 80th Congress achieved very little, mostly because they were biding their time in anticipation of a 1948 presidential victory. But Truman turned their inaction against them, and the voters kept him in the White House. A "do-nothing," obstructionist Congress, Johnson realized, would not help the Democrats as the 1956 general election approached.

All of this had to be managed. Johnson had to cooperate with Eisenhower, but he was also responsible for generating a legislative record that could be incorporated into a Democratic Party platform that the 1956 Democratic presidential candidate could support. He understood that a candidate whose party did little more than support the legislative agenda of the other party would be vulnerable. Johnson's strategy was to continue his support for the president in his battles with the GOP right. Then he expected the Democratic candidates in 1956 to run against the policies of Republican Party's right wing. If Eisenhower chose not to run in 1956 (and he had said several times that he might not) the Democrats would be in a strong position to take back both the White House and Congress.

‡

In the midst of the first session of the 84th Congress, Lyndon Johnson, in early July 1955, had a heart attack at the age of forty-six. By the end of September, the sixty-four-year-old Eisenhower had suffered the same fate. Both men were consigned to their beds. While they recovered, the two parties were essentially leaderless and scrambling for replacements in case either man died or decided to retire.

Johnson's health had been an issue for some time. In early 1955 (just months before his heart attack) he suffered from a severe case of kidney stones. He was in serious pain during Eisenhower's 1955 State of the Union speech and was finally persuaded to travel to the Mayo Clinic in Rochester, Minnesota, to deal with the problem. He had an operation and recuperated at his ranch in Texas for several weeks. He returned to Washington in mid-February and to the Senate on March 9.

While he was away, Rayburn nearly destroyed Johnson's efforts at holding the Democratic Party together. Although Rayburn and Johnson often prescribed to many of the same objectives, here they did not. Ever the populist, Rayburn introduced a bill in the House for an across-the-board tax cut of $20 for every U.S. citizen. "It would," he said, "give the little fella a break." Rayburn was undoubtedly trying to make the point that the administration, in the previous session, had pushed a tax cut through Congress that favored primarily big business and wealthy Americans.

At the very least, Rayburn's proposal made Eisenhower mad. By anyone's account, the tax cut would cost too much and probably lead to a debilitating inflation. The issue seemed minor, but the political ramifications turned out to be great. One of Johnson's primary objectives was to break up the old conservative coalition that had controlled congressional legislation for decades. Rayburn's proposal threatened to reunite that coalition in opposition to his plan; GOP conservatives and southern Democrats came together to denounce the proposal, and they were joined by Eisenhower moderates. Eisenhower called Rayburn's bill "some kind of height in fiscal irresponsibility."[4] Johnson, in pain and shuttling back and forth between the Mayo Clinic and his ranch in Texas, was left out of the negotiations. Once he recovered, he was able to forge a compromise that included a $20 tax cut for heads of households, $10 for each dependant, and nothing for dependant spouses. In the final vote, five conservative Democrats, including Walter George and Harry Byrd, voted with the Republican opposition to pass the Johnson compromise bill.

That inauspicious beginning was followed by a session of successes. One of Johnson's biggest victories was a three-year extension of the Reciprocal Trade Act, a bill that GOP conservatives hated because it allowed the federal government to negotiate trade policies without the consent of Congress. Following an almost notorious set of circumstances, Johnson pushed the bill through with little debate, using a series of obscure Senate rules.[5] He also pushed through a minimum wage increase, also opposed by the Republican right. In an almost sleight-of-hand gimmick, he called for a vote on the bill while several of its opponents were not present on the Senate floor.

Johnson also succeeded in passing a public housing bill. The 83rd Congress, under Republican control, had put an end to federally financed housing, and it was clear that the administration had little interest in picking up the issue. Johnson seemed to support the administration's indifference. However, from behind the scenes he pushed the Senate Banking Committee to report a bill that authorized 135,000 housing units per year up to 800,000. Indiana Republican Homer Capehart, speaking for the administration, offered an amendment to the bill that would authorize only 70,000 units over two years, really a pittance compared with the need for public housing in the nation's urban areas in the 1950s. Journalists Rowland Evans and Robert Novak, observing these events, wrote of Johnson's feigned defeatism: "Johnson . . . arranged that long face of his, brooded in self-pity, and sadly bemoaned to reporters the hopelessness of his cause." All the while, he counted votes and prepared to strike.[6] The debate moved as if a Republican victory were a forgone conclusion. Capehart even bothered to approach Johnson: "Lyndon," he said, "this is one time I've really got you. I'm going to rub your nose in shit."[7] Capehart had counted on the votes of conservative southerners, who had historically opposed funding for public housing. But Johnson had worked the phones and twisted their arms. He convinced the southerners that they should vote against Capehart's amendment because it still authorized 35,000 housing units and that they might have difficulty back home defending their support for any public housing. Johnson's argument swayed the southern Senators, and they voted against Capehart's amendment. "I was sitting up in the gallery," George Reedy recalled, "And Capehart's chin almost bounced off the desk. He turned around, and sure enough they went down bing, bing, bing, bing, bing, bing—every southern Democrat, even the most conservative." Reedy added that the press corps had already written their stories predicting Johnson's defeat. Johnson held a victory party in his office after the vote. The attendees included the coalition he had forged: a large group of southern conservatives intermingled with Hubert Humphrey, Paul Douglas, and the party's most liberal members. The amendment was defeated, 44 to 38.[8]

Johnson had phenomenal success in the Senate, a success that had a great deal to do with his abilities to cajole, build coalitions, compromise, and make deals. His objective was to get legislation passed, and he was good at it. In 1955, at age forty-six, he was at the height of his powers. And not surprisingly, he was being considered as his party's presidential candidate in 1956 or more likely down the road in 1960.

But Johnson was overweight, at about 225 pounds. He drank a fifth of Cutty Sark scotch a day, he ate badly, and he smoked. Added to that was the extreme stress and the workload of being a United States senator and his party's majority leader. Johnson's heart attack came in July 1955, just a couple of months or so before Eisenhower was struck. The president's attack was described as moderate, and by most accounts he recovered easily and quickly. Johnson, however, nearly died. His blood pressure dropped to dangerous levels, and for two days at Bethesda Naval Hospital in Washington his chances of dying seemed about as good as living. When he recovered enough to issue orders, he told Reedy to hand over the reigns of leadership in the Senate to Majority Whip Earle Clements of Kentucky, and then he told Reedy to inform the press that he would be resigning his Senate seat. Reedy ignored the order and said nothing to the press about Johnson's intention to resign. Reedy knew his boss. Johnson never mentioned it again.[9] Clements announced to the Senate that Johnson's attack was moderate, that he was recovering, and that he would return to work in January 1956, at the beginning of the next session.[10]

Several of Johnson's immediate advisors and family members believed that he should retire, that continuing on under the stress of a United States senator and his party's majority leader would shorten his life. But Johnson's family physician, Dr. James C. Cain, saw immediately what others did not: Johnson's natural state of motion was politics, and being forced to retire from the political stage might be more damaging to his health than continuing on with the work he loved. Dr. Cain said that if Lyndon were forced to sit on his porch and whittle toothpicks, "he'd have to whittle more toothpicks than anybody else in the country."[11]

In late September, Rayburn and Stevenson made a well-publicized pilgrimage to the Johnson ranch. The press referred to "The Big Three," and a "Democratic Party Summit." Other party leaders followed, all paying tribute to their leader. By that time, Eisenhower was recuperating in Denver from his own heart attack, and the Democratic leaders issued a statement that they would not take any political advantage of the president's incapacities. Johnson even sent a note to Eisenhower, letting the president know that his own recovery had been so complete that he had been dove hunting.[12]

Johnson had considered making a presidential run in 1956, and several of his supporters wanted him to run.[13] It was in this period that Joseph Kennedy approached Johnson with a deal: Lyndon would run for president in the upcoming 1956 campaign and choose Kennedy's son, John, as his running mate. In exchange, Kennedy money and influence would support the campaign. Kennedy's plan was that (whether Johnson won or lost) the young Kennedy would be in a position to take the party's nomination in 1960 or later in 1964. If Eisenhower chose not to run in 1956, the Johnson-Kennedy ticket might actually win, at least in part because the Republicans had no other candidates on the horizon. Johnson, apparently, did not take the offer seriously. He said he was not interested, that he would not run for the 1956 nomination. By some accounts, John's younger brother, Robert, considered Johnson's denial a snub of the Kennedy family's generosity, and that may have ignited a personal feud between Johnson and the younger Kennedy brother that played out through the next decade.[14]

Johnson's heart attack seemed to change his entire demeanor. He stopped smoking and drinking. He dropped excess pounds, weighing in at about 182 pounds, and he tried to get sufficient sleep. He walked a mile every day and counted calories. He built a swimming pool at his ranch and seemed to relax. He read more, and he began to reconnect with his family. Just like everything else he did, Johnson put all he had into his recovery.

Johnson's doctors insisted he cancel all his appearances and speeches for the remainder of the year. He agreed, but he insisted on participating in a tribute to Sam Rayburn at the Texas State Fair, and he wanted to make a speech at Whitney, Texas, at the dedication of a new dam there. Whitney was a small town off the main highway south of Dallas. "It was," Reedy recalled, "the most illogical place in the world to [deliver] a major speech."[15] Word got out that Johnson would be speaking, and his supporters flocked to the little armory in Whitney.

Johnson used his speech at Whitney to step forward and offer an alternative to the Republican agenda—while at the same time deflecting the anti-southern bias that had kept him from becoming a national leader and perhaps even his party's presidential nominee. He called the speech a "Program with a Heart," a proposal that included some thirteen initiatives that would connect him to the New Deal–Fair Deal agenda. Some said it would make him the heir apparent to Roosevelt. George Reedy, who wrote the speech, later recalled that it "established [Johnson] without any doubt whatsoever as *the* leading Democrat that year. . . . [I]t not only indicated that he was coming back to lead the Senate, but it also gave him a national position. This was the first time he had ever stated a program that sounded presidential."[16]

Johnson's "Program with a Heart" called for increased federal subsidies for roads, housing, schools, and hospitals; an expansion of Social Security coverage, a guarantee of 90 percent parity for farmers, the elimination of the poll tax, relief to depressed areas, tax breaks for those below the poverty line, a liberalization of immigration laws, and federal regulation of interstate natural gas prices.[17]

Johnson had been accused of giving in to the conservatism of Texas and the South, of being an instrument of big business and big oil, and of working with Eisenhower and the Republicans to squelch liberal reform. Here, at Whitney, Texas, Johnson took a political turn—not only toward a more liberal stance, but also toward his place as a national leader. He returned to his liberal roots of protecting the poorly housed, the poorly fed, and the undereducated. Those around him came to see his illness and long recovery as a turning point.

‡

In September 1955, about a year before the 1956 election, Eisenhower suffered his heart attack while visiting his in-laws, and it appeared that American politics might change dramatically as a result. "Our Republican friends are in a state of panic as of today," wrote Bobby Baker, one of Johnson's chief political advisors, in early October 1955.[18] Without Eisenhower, the power of the Republican moderates would certainly diminish swiftly, possibly leading to a GOP split. In fact, as the president lay ill in a Denver hospital, a struggle developed between the party's two wings that revealed much about the nature of the Republican Party. The struggle was more over who would lead while the president recuperated (and who would be nominated in the 1956 campaign if Eisenhower decided not to run) than who would lead if the president died. The *New York Times* reported on the morning after Eisenhower entered the hospital that Nixon was positioned to take the Republican nomination—under the assumption that Eisenhower would not run. As the person who would take the reigns of power if the president died, Nixon was in a good position to win that nomination. Nixon had come to see the light of Eisenhower's moderation, but those on the Republican right still saw him as one of their own, if not their leader. Sherman Adams, the White House chief of staff and something of a leader among party moderates, disliked Nixon; and he was not about to allow him to take over as long as the president was still alive. Adams had allies in Secretary of State John Foster Dulles, Secretary of the Treasury George Humphrey, and Press Secretary James Hagerty. All feared that Nixon would take advantage of the situation to win the party's nomination. Then, they feared, he would lose the election to Stevenson in November. In addition, Adams saw himself as the president's spokesman, and in that role he intended to become the liaison between Eisenhower and the world.[19] Several press stories reported that Adams and the party moderates were trying to push Nixon out of the picture—away from Eisenhower and away from the party's nomination.[20] At the same time, those on the right were encouraging Nixon to exert his power and lead—in anticipation either of Eisenhower's death or his decision not to run in November. Eisenhower had some understanding of Woodrow Wilson's stroke in 1919 that left him incapacitated and unable to govern. Mrs. Wilson insisted that her husband fire Secretary of State Robert Lansing for calling cabinet meetings without the president's knowledge or consent. To make certain there was no question about who had the authority to convene meetings at the White House, Eisenhower sent out a message that all cabinet and National Security Council meetings be held under the chairmanship of the vice president. But even then Dulles insisted on controlling those meetings, and Adams remained at the president's bedside in Denver.[21]

Eisenhower realized that Nixon was the one to run the government (as it was stated clearly in the Constitution) while he recuperated, but quickly he began to consider the possibility that he might not be able to run for reelection in November. A Gallup poll showed that Nixon would not win, that in fact, Supreme Court Chief Justice Earl Warren had a better shot of beating Stevenson, the probable Democratic Party candidate.[22] Consequently, the president began looking elsewhere, considering other possible candidates. His sway was toward Republican moderates and away from party right-wingers. He suggested to Hagerty that Dewey might be the right person. "He represents my way of thinking," the president told his press secretary. Hagerty told Eisenhower what he must have already known, that Dewey was anathema to the Republican right, that the conservatives would revolt, perhaps even split the party. "I guess you're right," Eisenhower relented. The discussion turned to Nixon, but both men agreed that Nixon was not up to the job. Nelson Rockefeller was considered as a possibility, then George Humphrey, then the president's younger brother, Milton.[23]

At he same time, the GOP right saw an opportunity in Eisenhower's heart attack. If the president decided not to run in 1956 (and there was speculation even before his heart attack that he might not), then the conservatives intended to place one of their own into play. The problem was that they had no real candidate beyond Nixon. Since Taft's death, no one had stepped forward to fill his sizable shoes, and there was certainly no replacement for someone of Eisenhower's popularity and stature. California senator Bill Knowland had taken the role as the leader of the right (and the party leader in the Senate), but Knowland was hardly presidential timber. Nevertheless, while the president recuperated and refused to make known his own plans, Knowland took a step toward a run for the 1956 nomination. He made his intentions known in an article in the *National Review*. In the magazine's first issue, Knowland berated the president for seeking peaceful coexistence with the Soviets. It was hardly a grab for power, but Knowland had made it clear that he was available.[24]

Eisenhower considered not running in 1956. In fact, he had often told his friends and family that he would not run. In 1953 he wrote to his brother, Milton, that "if ever for a second time I should show any signs of yielding to persuasion, please call in a psychiatrist." Then, just a few days later, he sent a note to his friend Swede Hazlett that concluded, "I shall never again be a candidate for anything."[25] Then, just a few weeks before his heart attack, Eisenhower told the Republican National Committee (RNC) that "you [should] never pin your flag so tightly on one mast that if a ship sinks you cannot rip it off and nail up another." When asked if the president would run in 1956, the RNC chairman Leonard Hall said, "When I get to that bridge, I'll jump off."[26] Such talk had always made party leaders nervous; they had come to realize that without Eisenhower on the ticket in 1956, their chances were not good. Still, they realized that Eisenhower had been making I-will-not-run statements since at least 1946.

According to Sherman Adams, it was not difficult to convince Eisenhower to make another run in 1956. Those closest to him simply convinced the president that if he left the arena, everything he had worked for would be lost and all he hoped to accomplish would never get done. In addition, it was possible that a candidate like Knowland might win the nomination, and Eisenhower simply would not accept Knowland as the Republican candidate. As Adams recalled, "The Republicans were isolationist. He looked at the people that ran the Congress . . . and he saw a bunch of isolationists."[27] In fact, if Eisenhower had ever seriously considered stepping aside in 1956, it may have been the heart attack itself that pushed him to change his mind and run. Eisenhower refused to accept that his health had defeated him, that a heart condition had kept him out of the arena. Sherman Adams recalled, "To let it be said that [the job of being president] had worn him out, that the burden of leadership had become too much for him, seemed more and more repugnant. [I]t would [have seemed] like accepting a personal defeat."[28]

‡

Just after the 1954 elections, Stephen Mitchell stepped down as chairman of the Democratic National Committee. He was succeeded by Paul Butler, a militantly partisan party leader from Indiana, a liberal who found it absurd that party policy was being set by two conservative Texans. Butler rejected Johnson's conciliatory politics in favor of a Democratic agenda that challenged the administration on all levels. His objective was clear: damage the Eisenhower administration as much as possible and build an agenda to take into the 1956 campaign. Butler had been Stevenson's choice.

Butler and Johnson had different objectives. Johnson saw the need to get legislation through the Senate. He often admitted that the legislation he sponsored was not perfect, and he often used the "half-a-loaf" analogy, arguing that he would attempt to get the other half at a later date. Butler and the Democrats who opposed Johnson were willing to concede that Johnson had succeeded in uniting an unruly Senate and that he had ended nearly two decades of unproductive disorder. But they also argued that his strategy had actually produced very little in the process. For liberals in the Democratic Party, Johnson had failed to support the trailblazing social legislation that they believed was necessary to boost the sagging economy. They intended to resume the ambitious goals of the New Deal era, with federal aid to education, federally funded health insurance, an extension of minimum wage coverage, and permanent federal programs to aid economically depressed areas. Johnson had achieved none of these. His long list of accomplishments had, in fact, produced very little that could be considered milestones.

Paul Butler intended to change that. He immediately called for a specific legislative program that was an obvious rebuke of Johnson and his moderate agenda. From 1955 until 1960, Butler led the liberals in the Democratic Party against Johnson's policies and strategies. It was perhaps the first time in Johnson's life that he was unable to pacify a rival with social amenities or compromises.

Butler was often described in the press as a Stevenson "man," and since Stevenson was poised to take the 1956 Democratic nomination, Butler carried a great deal of weight with Stevenson's supporters in the Democratic Party. In fact, Butler was perceived by some in the party as the de facto party leader until Stevenson could declare his candidacy and get into the campaign. For Butler and Stevenson's supporters, mostly on the left, a Johnson-style legislative program that was steeped in moderation and often in league with the president's agenda gave their candidate very little to run on.[29] William S. White wrote in the *New York Times* that Johnson "feels that Mr. Butler would have done well not to begin attacking the Administration and the President. . . ." And "Senator Johnson is aware that some in his party are impatient, and will be restive under a leadership policy of going very slowly."[30] Johnson was, of course, still faced with a potentially divided party (between conservative southerners and liberal northerners) and an extremely popular president. For him, at least, the only route to success was to compromise in an effort to try to hold the political center.

While Johnson battled his party's left wing, Eisenhower battled his party's right. In the mid-1950s, the Eisenhower-Johnson center continued to hold, but as the decade headed toward its end, the center would begin to deteriorate severely, and the extremists in both parties would begin to increase their power. American politics would go from conciliation and compromise to partisan bickering and political deadlock.

‡

Johnson's greatest failure in the second session of the 84th Congress was the natural gas bill. He hoped that by deregulating gas he could aid his Texas constituents and win votes in other areas of the Southwest. The bill itself was not particularly unusual; it had been steered through the House by Rayburn the year before, and leaders on both sides of the aisle wanted a quick passage. But the legislation got bogged down with charges of improper lobbying. Representatives from the oil and gas industry swarmed into Washington in an attempt to sway legislators and push the bill through. When South Dakota senator Francis Case complained that he had been offered a bribe for his vote, the situation changed quickly.[31] Reedy and others tried to convince Johnson to delay the bill until an investigation could clear the air, but on February 6 Johnson drove the bill through the Senate.[32]

Eisenhower, in response, hated the bill, and he hated the manner in which it was passed. "[T]he natural gas business," he wrote in his diary, "must be classed as a 'public utility' and is therefore subject to the regulations of the state in which the consumption of the gas takes place." However, he added, "Into this situation stepped certain of the oil and gas interests with the most flagrant kind of lobbying that has been brought to my attention in three years." He then complained of "a great stench around the passing of the bill. . . ."[33] On those grounds, he vetoed it. Johnson had appeared to confront the president over the bill—and lost. Eisenhower emerged as a national leader, working in the interest of the nation. Johnson's image suffered.

Eisenhower's greatest success in the 84th Congress was the Federal Highway Act. Eisenhower saw the bill as an example of his ability to solve the nation's problems—both for the present and the future. In the months following the war, he had passed through Germany on its modern autobahn system. He was impressed by the four-lane, high speed superhighways with accessible ramps. When he returned to the states, he was appalled by the conditions of the nation's roads.[34] By the time he became president, the number of cars in the United States had grown rapidly, the nation was moving to the suburbs, and the national car culture was at its beginning. He had come to the conclusion that a massive superhighway system would improve the economy by encouraging the development of new residential areas, allowing industry to spread out beyond its common centers of activity, and speed the movement of troops and materiel in the case of a military event. He named General Lucius D. Clay to head a blue-ribbon committee to explore the idea.[35]

Clay's committee recommended a system of 40,000 miles of four-lane highways to be built at a cost of $101 billion to be spent over ten years. The system would be financed through bonds, making it the largest public works undertaking in U.S. history. Based on the recommendation from Clay's committee, Eisenhower sent legislation to Congress in February 1955. The bill, however, encountered fierce opposition, mostly from those in Congress who wanted the construction financed through tolls rather than a bond issue. Rural residents also objected because the system was designed to connect cities with populations over 50,000, and thus, so it seemed, bypass the rural parts of the nation.[36]

In its final form, the Federal Highway Act created 41,000 miles of superhighways called the National Defense and Interstate Highway System. The Highway Trust Fund was established to finance the project through taxes on gasoline, tires, and transport trucks. The program was extremely popular.[37] The only major complaints have been that the highways did not, at first, go through cities (that part of the project came later), and that the system increased the growth of the nation's suburbs at the expense of urban areas and small towns, leading to the severe decline of the nation's inner cities and rural areas.[38]

The 84th Congress also passed the Air Pollution Control Act. The act's political significance was negligible, but it was the beginning of a realization that the nation's air quality was deteriorating rapidly and that something needed to be done. The act declared that air quality was a danger to public health, but it did not go beyond the right of the individual states to control the problem. The role of the federal government was merely to conduct research on air quality and disseminate the information to the states. The 1955 bill did little to improve the nation's deteriorating air quality in the mid-1950s, but it became the foundation for legislation through the next decades that would slowly push the nation toward that goal.

Not surprisingly, little was done in Congress as the 1956 campaign approached. Johnson was beginning to feel the pinch from party liberals, led by Paul Butler, who complained that his moderation and his cooperation with the Eisenhower Republicans was damaging the Democrats' hopes for a victory in 1956. Eisenhower was feeling the same sort of pressure from his party's right. As the decade progressed, the pressure on the two party leaders would increase considerably.

‡

On February 29, despite all the health concerns, Eisenhower finally decided, again, that the nation needed him. Looking thin but fit, he appeared on television and made it clear that he wanted a second term. Republicans of all stripes got on board, realizing, of course, that the president's coattails would be generous. Knowland and others on the right pointed out that the president would need the votes of his party's right wing in his second term, and then they insisted the president dump Nixon and chose a Taft Republican as his running mate. Eisenhower did not respond.[39]

While Eisenhower pondered running, so did Stevenson. He was again the clear choice for the Democrats despite his horrible loss to Eisenhower in 1952. No other Democrats, in fact, truly chose to stand up and run against the president, although a few seemed to be willing to make the run in 1956 as a way of setting themselves up for a post-Eisenhower era election in 1960. At the same time, Stevenson had maintained control of the party machinery, he had the support of labor and the urban political machines, and he believed he had been drafted prematurely in 1952 and pushed to run against Eisenhower with almost no campaign strategy, planning, or money.[40]

After his 1952 defeat, Stevenson decided he would travel, make speeches, and try to pay off his party's half-million dollar deficit. Then he said goodbye to his supporters: "Now I must devote more time to my own concerns," he said. But *Time* noticed that "the presidential virus is not that easy to shake off." Then in July 1955, he told Truman that he might be interested in running in 1956, but he said he would like to do it without campaigning. Stevenson deplored the campaign trail and had come to believe that he could run an old-style front-porch campaign. He soon realized, however, that in the new postwar political world, voters wanted an active, visible candidate.[41]

In the summer of 1955, Stevenson told his friends he would run, that he would announce at the first of the next year, and he began convening a series of organizational meetings at his farm near Springfield, Illinois.[42] Among the ideas that came from these meetings was that Eisenhower was vulnerable on foreign affairs because of his severe cutbacks in military spending. Stevenson wrote to one of his most important advisors, Arthur Schlesinger, Jr., that this situation had "gravely weakened our military forces and particularly our air power."[43] This advisory group also tried to determine why the nation was so clearly Democratic (they controlled both houses of Congress) yet so enamored with the Republican Eisenhower. They concluded that the president was a man of such evident goodwill and trust that the people of the nation were relieved of the necessity of following day-to-day political developments. They described this as "apathy," finally determining that "[t]he popularity of Eisenhower is thus one side of the coin; the flight from politics is the other." Then in the final analysis, the strategists concluded the obvious: "There can be no question, in short, that the country likes both the Democratic Party and Eisenhower."[44]

Stevenson and his advisors also concluded that part of their problem was Johnson and his collaborative strategies. They determined, in a series of memos (most of which were written by Arthur Schlesinger), that Johnson's backroom dealings had taken the political process out of the line of sight of the American people." Our present congressional leadership seems so obsessed with its virtuosity at backroom manipulation that it has forgotten its obligation to the American public. . . . The result is that the Johnson strategy has promoted and fortified the political apathy which is Eisenhower's main strength." This memo concluded that "[u]nless we start opposing [the administration] soon, the danger is that, when we finally do so during the campaign, it will sound wholly ritualistic and irrelevant and impress no one."[45] For Stevenson and those around him, moderation (from either side of the political spectrum) was not helping their cause. Johnson, of course, saw it differently. To him, confronting a powerful and popular president was not realistic and would produce nothing. Compromise was the only way.

Any possibility of beating Eisenhower was a long shot, at best, and that kept several Democratic candidates out of the field and, instead, packing their war chests for 1960. All that changed, however, when Eisenhower suffered his heart attack in September 1955. Almost immediately, New York governor Averell Harriman announced that he would run, and then there were rumors that Tennessee senator Estes Kefauver might also enter the race. Stevenson complained that "Harriman rushed out almost within the week [of Eisenhower's heart attack] and said he was no longer supporting [me]. Kefauver was not far behind." Stevenson announced in mid-December, 1955, that he would run.[46]

Once Eisenhower announced his intentions, another question immediately arose: would he keep Nixon on the ticket? Although Nixon had moved away from his party's right wing and toward the political center and the relative safety of Eisenhower-style moderation, several moderates close to the president still saw Nixon as the representative of the Republican right, the wing of the party that Eisenhower and the moderates detested most. Those moderates close to Eisenhower who disliked Nixon and wanted him out included Sherman Adams, presidential assistant Harold Stassen, and Massachusetts governor Christian Herter. But the majority of those who opposed Nixon probably kept their own counsel. Nixon was, after all, the vice president and a major political power inside the party. The decision, of course, was up to Eisenhower, and he refused to decide. His indecision cut deeply at Nixon, who believed he had been loyal and (at the very least) done everything he had been asked. The president continually suggested that Nixon might be bettor off somewhere else, at one point suggesting that he take a cabinet post in the administration, even secretary of state or defense. In his diary, Eisenhower saw the "Nixon question" in football terms: "[My] concern is where is Nixon going to be 4 years from now? What does 8 years on the job do for him? In the long run, he is thought of as the understudy to the star of the team, rather than being a halfback in his own right."[47]

The situation must have been agonizing for Nixon. Perhaps his biggest problem was that he had nowhere else to go. In 1952, had he been dumped off the ticket, he could have simply retained his seat in the Senate. But in 1956 about all he could do was fight to stay in the administration or return to California and practice law. So, Nixon stayed the course and did all he could to hang on to his job.

One reason Eisenhower chose to run in 1956 was that he felt he had no real successor; or more exactly, as he wrote Hazlett, "I [have] failed to bring forward and establish a logical successor for myself."[48] At the same time, Eisenhower liked Nixon, or at least he appreciated him. Eisenhower's military background led him to value a subordinate who served loyally and to the best of his ability. And Nixon had certainly done that. But Eisenhower clearly understood that his health might keep him from completing his second term, and he feared that Nixon was simply not up to accepting power. So, with the president conflicted on the point, Nixon sat on the bubble. He had the president's respect and admiration, but not his support. A Nixon friend told Earl Mazo (Nixon's campaign biographer for the 1960 campaign) that Eisenhower's failure to endorse Nixon was "one of the greatest hurts of [Nixon's] whole career."[49]

On March 13, Eisenhower listed in his diary his likes and dislikes about Nixon. "I am happy to have him as an associate," he wrote, "and I am happy to have him in government." However, he added, "That still doesn't make him vice president. He has serious problems. . . . I am not going to say he is the only individual I would have for vice president." At the same time, he added, "There is nothing to be gained politically by ditching him. He is going to be a 'comer' four years from now. I want a bevy of young fellows to be available [then]. Nixon can't always be the understudy to the star."[50]

Eisenhower probably would rather have run without Nixon in 1956. He believed that another candidate might do more to help him continue his inroads into the South, and if he chose a more moderate running mate he might well pull big vote numbers from independents and Democrats and be better able to control the political center. Perhaps most importantly, however, Eisenhower feared that his health might fail and Nixon would become president, and he clearly did not think that Nixon had the ability to be president. That was most likely how Eisenhower saw the situation. He may also have realized that he had chosen Nixon in 1952, and he was stuck with him in 1956—whether he wanted him or not.

Through most of the spring, Eisenhower responded to questions by the press in what seemed an unequivocal manner. "I am very happy that Richard Nixon is my friend," he said in a press conference in late March. "I am very happy to have him as an associate in government. I would be happy to be on any political ticket in which I was a candidate with him." Then in his usual manner, he admonished the press corps for their continued badgering on the point, even though he had been dodging the issue for months. "Now, if those words aren't plain, then it is merely because people can't understand the plain unvarnished truth. I have nothing further to add."[51] That may have been "plain," but it was not an official announcement. Finally, on April 26, Nixon took the situation into his own hands. He called on the president at the Oval Office and announced that he would be "honored to continue as vice president under you." Nixon added that he had waited so long only because he did not want to appear to be forcing himself onto the ticket. Eisenhower responded that he wondered why Nixon had, in fact, taken so long. The decision was announced that day. The press treated the announcement as a matter of political course.[52]

‡

Eisenhower pushed hard for the southern white vote, but he also continued to court black voters, many of whom continued to support the Republican Party, the party of Lincoln. This led to an administration-sponsored civil rights bill, submitted near the end of the 1956 congressional session and just months before the 1956 election. The bill was clearly designed by the administration to continue the trend of winning back black voters in the coming election while not offending southern whites. It was also intended to divide the Democrats, between the party's liberal northern

wing (that traditionally supported civil rights) and its conservative southern wing (that did not). No one from either party believed that the bill
would pass. For Eisenhower, however, the objective was moderation, as
it always was. He directed his attorney general, Herbert Brownell, who
was authoring the bill, to avoid offending the South. Do not, he told
Brownell, act like "another [Charles] Sumner."[53]

By 1956, southern Democrats in Congress had come to the conclusion that the *Brown v. Board* decision of 1954, along with the Republican
Party's desire to continue the trend of winning back black voters, would
eventually lead to a civil rights bill. In the face of the 1956 presidential
election, the Democrats responded just as the Republicans had hoped:
they began fighting a rear guard action in anticipation of a bill, and then
they split over the issue. The southerners in Congress did all they could
to delay the bill as long as possible, or at least show their constituents that
they would not go down without a fight.[54]

The result was the Southern Manifesto, an encouragement of massive
resistance against the *Brown* decision. It was also intended as a clear threat
toward any civil rights bill submitted by the administration. "We pledge
ourselves to use all lawful means to bring about a reversal of this decision
which is contrary to the Constitution and to prevent the use of force in its
implementation."[55]

The Southern Manifesto had its origins sometime in the spring
of 1956, when the Senate's southern power brokers began a series of
regular meetings in Richard Russell's Senate office. Russell had always
been one of the most influential senators in Washington, and thus an
important leader for southern issues, but his defeat for the Democratic
Party's presidential nomination in 1952 had, by some accounts, forced
him inward, away from his party's center. "Dick Russell had been a
great leader," party strategist James Rowe recalled, "a great influence
for good, but after he ran for the presidency and got knocked off as
a southerner in 1952, I always thought that Dick became a much
narrower southerner and was parochial."[56]

Those meetings in Russell's office included the biggest names in southern politics at the time: James Eastland (D-MS), Allen Ellender (D-LA),

John Stennis (D-MS), Sam Ervin (D-NC), Harry F. Byrd (D-VA), Strom Thurmond (D-SC), and Walter George (D-GA). By most accounts, the original idea for the manifesto came from Thurmond, but was finally drafted by Russell to soften Thurmond's vitriolic temperament. Russell worked diligently to modify the final version in an attempt to draw as many southern legislators into the process as possible. Then, on March 12, 1956, the text of the Declaration of Constitutional Principles (better known as the Southern Manifesto) was released to the press.[57] The document was signed by 101 members of Congress. All were southerners; all but four were Democrats.

The Southern Manifesto, however, is best known for who refused to sign the document. Albert Gore and Estes Kefauver, both Democratic senators from Tennessee, would not sign. Rayburn did not sign, and neither did Lyndon Johnson. Gore and Kefauver had presidential aspirations; Rayburn, as House Speaker, felt he could not be viewed in the House as a regional leader. Johnson was all of these. He had aspirations to run for the presidency, and, as Senate majority leader, he could not be pigeon-holed as a southerner and keep his party united.

Johnson's image had been his bane since the beginning of his political career. Because of civil rights, it was nearly impossible for a southerner to become president. "There was no question whatsoever," George Reedy recalled, "that anybody that signed that manifesto could never become president. . . . It was solely and simply a cry of defiance from one region. It was really cutting off the South from the rest of the nation. Russell . . . was conscious of the fact that if he put Lyndon Johnson on the spot with that manifesto, that it would wreck all of Russell's major plans. Russell was very determined to elect Johnson president of the United States."[58] Johnson, in response, had fought his entire political life against the narrow southern image, trying almost desperately to fashion himself a westerner.

So Russell did not push Johnson to sign the manifesto, offering the excuse that the majority leader in the Senate should represent the entire party, and not just one region. Southern senators, it seemed, understood. "Just senator to senator," John Stennis recalled, "we wanted [Johnson] to sign it, but at the same time we recognized that he wasn't just a senator from Texas, he was a leader and had a different responsibility in that degree. It wasn't held against him . . . by the southerners, that he did not sign it."[59]

Johnson had other reasons for not signing the manifesto, reasons that explain Johnson's nature. He always believed that the time had come for the South to accept desegregation, that racial segregation would have to end for the South to achieve economic development and attract significant financial investment. One of Johnson's close advisors wrote that he felt race "obsessed the South and diverted it from attending to its economic and educational problems; that it produced among white Southerners an angry defensiveness and parochialism. . . ."[60] In addition, Johnson had worked to unify his party. He realized, of course, that he could not continue in that role as a sectional leader.[61]

‡

When Stevenson announced that he would make the run in 1956, he also announced that he would run in five primaries: Illinois, Minnesota, Pennsylvania, Florida, and California.[62] He had always resisted primary runs; he simply disliked slogging through a primary campaign. But the party regulars were demanding that their candidate pay his dues and prove that he could still draw voters. Only a series of successful primary runs could do that.

Stevenson was immediately trounced in the mid-March New Hampshire primary by Tennessee senator Estes Kefauver. Stevenson, however, had not campaigned there. That victory gave Kefauver the status of front-runner, and he immediately challenged Stevenson to engage the campaign in Minnesota, later that month. Minnesota allowed crossover voting, and a strong Republican stop-Stevenson vote there resulted in another embarrassing defeat for Stevenson and rewarded Kefauver with the state's thirty delegates.[63] Stevenson responded with a vigorous campaign that brought him victories in the District of Columbia, New Jersey, Illinois, Oregon, and Florida. In Florida, Stevenson and Kefauver squared off for a debate, the first ever on both national radio and television. In California, Stevenson scored a knockout punch with a two-to-one victory over Kefauver. And in July, Kefauver dropped out, throwing his support and delegates to Stevenson.[64]

While Johnson recovered from his heart attack, the thought of running for president was not far from his mind. Rayburn, however, told Johnson that he thought he was too ill to run and that he might instead consider running as a favorite son from Texas—and then lead the Texas delegation at the convention. For Rayburn, this had more to do with Texas state politics than anything else. If Johnson headed the Texas state delegation, it would push out Allen Shivers, the conservative Democratic governor who had, in 1952, dragged Texas into the Eisenhower camp. To Rayburn (who wanted Stevenson to get the nomination and for Texas to go Democratic in the election) that meant that Johnson would be rounding up delegates in Texas and then turning them over to Stevenson at the convention.[65]

Through the summer, however, Johnson still seemed to be considering a run for the nomination, but he refused to acknowledge his candidacy or enter any primaries. As the convention neared, journalists began to speculate that if Stevenson failed to win the nomination on the first ballot that the nomination might go to Johnson. That, in fact, seemed reasonable since many Democrats realized that Stevenson was probably a sure loser against Eisenhower and they had begun looking around for someone else to nominate.[66]

As the convention approached, Stevenson won most of the primaries, and Kefauver had withdrawn. In mid-August, however, just as the delegates were beginning to collect in Chicago, Truman stepped in from the wings, insisted that Stevenson was, in fact, a loser, and then threw his support to Harriman.[67] This seemed to open things up, making Stevenson a less likely first-ballot contender. But Stevenson said later that he actually welcomed Truman's interference—and thus his exit from Stevenson's own campaign. Stevenson had always believed that Truman's endorsement (and raucous campaign swings) in 1952 had actually hurt his campaign.[68] At the same time, Reedy continued to advise Johnson that he was still a contender, that Stevenson's primary victories did not guarantee him the nomination, and that the party nomination was still up for grabs.[69]

On August 12, the day before the convention began, Johnson finally summoned reporters and announced that he would run. His strategy was simple. He would be the compromise candidate, slipping through a Stevenson-Harriman deadlock and taking the nomination after several ballots. For three hectic days, Lyndon Johnson was a serious candidate.

Johnson had Richard Russell's support—probably in response to Johnson's support of Russell in 1952. But in keeping with the southern strategy of the time, Russell had refused to attend the convention, fearing that a southern walkout would force him to choose between loyalty to his state's delegates and his prized Senate seat. But he finally attended the convention for a few hours at Johnson's insistence. Even then he refused to be an important player in Johnson's candidacy—mostly because he believed that Johnson had no real chance of winning the nomination.[70] Johnson's biggest problem, however, was that Sam Rayburn would not support him. "That damn fool Lyndon thinks he's going to be nominated president," Rayburn told reporters.[71] Rayburn then sent James Rowe, a trusted Johnson advisor, to convince Johnson that this was not the time to make a run. In one of his many political memos, Rowe wrote to Johnson that labor organizers and the northern bosses would not support him and that his health would be used against him by the Republicans if he won the nomination. Then he added that Johnson would become the candidate of the South. "There is now a danger that [you] will become the Dick Russell of 1956."[72]

Harriman intended to use his candidacy to force Stevenson to the left, particularly on civil rights.[73] Johnson saw this as a direct threat to the unity of the party, just moments before a national election. He also saw that an argument over civil rights at the convention could split the party, even to the point of purging the South. He may also have believed that Harriman may have intended to use the civil rights issue to rid the party of the South (sending southerners into the Republican Party) for the purpose of making the Democratic Party more purely liberal. For this reason, Johnson may have decided to hang on to his doomed candidacy in hopes of accumulating enough southern delegates to force Stevenson into the center and keep him from surrendering to Harriman and the northern liberals.[74]

Johnson tried to salvage his situation by handing his Texas delegation over to Stevenson in exchange for concessions, mostly on civil rights, but Stevenson refused.[75] In the final analysis, Stevenson did not need support from either Harriman or Johnson; he was nominated on the first ballot before the alphabetical roll call reached Pennsylvania.

With Stevenson nominated again, the first order of business for the Democrats was to keep the South in line—mostly by giving southern leaders what they wanted on civil rights. Everyone knew, particularly Stevenson, that the party could not afford to lose the South, to let it dribble into the Republican Party as it had done in 1952. Just before the convention, Alabama senator and 1952 vice presidential candidate, John Sparkman, called a meeting of southern delegates "to work out our problems within the party rather than to walk out or bolt," as he explained the situation to his colleagues.[76] As the party began to devise its platform, even the party's most liberal figures and civil rights advocates seemed to be willing to trade civil rights advances for white southern support and potential electoral success. Hubert Humphrey, who had built a reputation as a strong supporter of civil rights, insisted that the 1956 platform be "acceptable to the South."[77] Even Eleanor Roosevelt called for reconciliation: "I think understanding and sympathy for the white people of the South," she said, "is as important as understanding and sympathy for the colored people." The result was a weak civil rights plank that excluded an endorsement of the *Brown v. Board* decision—and a generally satisfied South that would almost certainly remain in the Democratic column.[78]

The next order of business was to choose the candidate's running mate. Stevenson had planned for some time to open up that decision to the delegates and let them choose by acclamation. His intention, most likely, was to show that the Democrats were more open in their choices than the Republicans, who were about to nominate Nixon again even though many in their party did not want him. For most Democratic Party members, however, Stevenson's plan was a ridiculous move. Both Johnson and Rayburn saw it as a blatant lack of professionalism when the candidate (by carefully choosing a running mate) could make use of the process to unite the party. As George Reedy recalled, "[N]obody wants a fight over the vice presidency."[79]

Joseph Kennedy had pushed his son, John, to withdraw his name from vice presidential contention, insisting that a Stevenson-Kennedy ticket was a loser and ultimately a detriment to John's political future. In fact, the young Kennedy had stated several times that he was not a candidate for vice president. However, as the convention progressed, Kennedy decided to defy his father, and he offered himself as a candidate for the second spot on the ticket.[80] His staff had distributed a memo early in the campaign arguing that Kennedy's religion would actually aid the 1956 ticket rather than hurt it. Catholics were trickling out of the Democratic Party because the Republicans were seen as standing stronger against communism—which was perceived as atheistic and anti-Catholic. Kennedy, the memo argued, would bring Catholics back into the party. Stevenson, however, was never convinced that a Catholic candidate on the ticket would be anything but a detriment, and he continued to believe (as he had believed in 1952) that he needed a southerner on the ticket—or at least someone from a border state. Several New England governors continued to push Kennedy, but party bigwigs like Rayburn counseled Stevenson to look elsewhere. Stevenson finally decided to ask Kennedy to nominate him at the convention, but he probably never seriously considered him as a running mate.[81]

The vote on the floor of the convention to decide Stevenson's running mate went back and forth between Kennedy and Kefauver for most of an afternoon. Kennedy was hurt by his religion, but also for a lack of support from Eleanor Roosevelt and other liberals. Johnson at first wanted Albert Gore from Tennessee, then Hubert Humphrey, and finally he threw his support to Kennedy. It was Kefauver, however, who won. He had come to the convention with the second-largest number of delegates, and they threw their support to their candidate.[82] He was probably the candidate Stevenson disliked the most. "Kefauver is not Adlai's type," *Time* magazine explained. "[T]he Deep South dislikes him and so does his own Tennessee delegation; Congressional Democrats disown him."[83] Kennedy then went before the convention to ask the delegates for a unanimous vote for Kefauver. The events raised Kennedy's stock in the Democratic Party.

Eisenhower was not impressed. He wrote to Hazlett just before the election: "I believe that the Stevenson-Kefauver combination is . . . about the sorriest and weakest we have ever run for the two top offices in the land."[84]

The president decided that the best way to run his campaign would be through the media, avoiding all the rigorous barnstorming and campaigning—most of which he detested and considered below the dignity of the office.[85] His strategy was simple, as he explained to Nevada senator George Malone and his secretary took notes: "The President discussed his ideas of how he should conduct his campaign . . . mainly . . . reporting periodically to the American people the accomplishments of the Administration and its plans for the future."[86] And it seemed to work. As the campaign progressed, Henry Cabot Lodge wrote to the president: "[You] must be the first great television President just as Roosevelt was the first great radio President."[87]

The Democratic Party strategy was more specific. It would try to appeal to voters in the farm states by playing on the dissatisfaction with the Republican Party's farm policy. Then, by straddling the civil rights issue, they hoped to win back the southern states that had escaped from the fold and voted for Eisenhower in 1952. Finally, they expected to pick up one or two big urban states in the East. That could spell victory.[88] Johnson, however, thought it was a loser. He campaigned for Stevenson in Texas, and he even toured Texas with Kefauver. But Johnson focused his energies on maintaining Democratic control of Congress.[89]

By mid-September polls were showing what most observers had come to realize, that Eisenhower was a pretty sure winner.[90] A month later, *Time* observed that there were no real issues in the campaign. "There is no . . . preaching of crusades in either camp." And, Stevenson, the article added, has "little appeal."[91]

Stevenson did have a program and issues to discuss, but in the long run they actually damaged his campaign. At a time when the fear of international communism was perhaps at its height, he called for an end to nuclear testing and an end to the military draft—both convictions left him open to charges of being "soft" on communism. Then, in late October, just days before the election, Soviet Premier Marshal Bulganin wrote to Eisenhower suggesting that the United States and the Soviet Union end nuclear testing. In the letter was the phrase: "We are entirely in agreement with the view which has been taken by some respectable United States officials lately about the necessity and possibility of agreement on the banning of atomic tests. . . ." The letter was published in the U.S. press on October 21. It was immediately perceived that "some respectable United States officials" was a direct reference to Stevenson—linking Stevenson to the Soviet Union. Nixon hit back hard, insisting that Stevenson would "throw out the window" U.S. superiority in nuclear weapons.[92]

In the midst of the campaign, foreign policy took center stage and swayed all foreign policy dynamics to Eisenhower's favor. He was, after all, perceived as a great military leader, a great diplomat, and (perhaps most importantly) a leader with restraint, a man who would not drag the nation unnecessarily into war. In the summer of 1956, Egyptian leader Gamal Abdel Nasser announced that he would nationalize the British-run Suez Canal and accept Soviet aid to build a dam on the Nile River at Aswan after the United States and Great Britain withdrew funds to build the dam. Through the summer and fall, France and England considered a military strike to take back the canal. Israel, fearing a greatly enhanced Egyptian power on its southern border if Soviet aid began to flow into Egypt, was willing to join the attack. On October 29, without consulting Washington, Israeli tanks pushed into northeastern Egypt and rushed toward the canal. Two days later British and French planes began bombing Egypt, and on November 5, the day before the U.S. election, British and French paratroopers invaded Egypt. The Soviets immediately threatened to assist the Egyptians. Eisenhower refused to be dragged into a major conflict by his allies and would not support the invasion. Without U.S. support, Britain and France baulked at further advances. A cease-fire was quickly signed and forces on both sides pulled back.

Secretary of State John Foster Dulles was Eisenhower's closest advisor on foreign affairs issues.   (Eisenhower Presidential Library and Museum, Abilene, Kansas)

Just as the Suez crisis unfolded, the Soviets seemed to take advantage of the diversion by crushing a revolt in Hungary. On October 31, Imre Nagy announced that Hungary would withdraw from the Soviet-sponsored Warsaw Pact. In the first week of November, the Soviets sent 200,000 troops and 4,000 tanks into Budapest and crushed the insurgency. Some 40,000 Hungarian citizens, including Nagy, died in the two days of street fighting. Another 150,000 left the country. Although the Eisenhower administration was criticized for not assisting the people of Hungary against such raw aggression, the vast majority of Americans praised their president for not dragging the nation into World War III over the incident. Perhaps most importantly, the image of the Soviet Union was tarnished badly by their actions.

Eisenhower was confident that he would win the election, so he set his sights on attaining a Republican majority in Congress. He also hoped that he would establish more control over the wayward Republican right. He convinced John Sherman Cooper to resign as ambassador to India and return to run for the Senate from his home state of Kentucky, where a long-held Democratic Senate seat was vacant and up for grabs. He did and won. Eisenhower also convinced his Secretary of the Interior, Douglas McKay, to run against Oregon senator Wayne Morse. Morse had won his Senate seat as a Republican and then became an independent when Eisenhower was elected in 1952. He switched to the Democrat Party in 1955. Eisenhower wanted him beaten. McKay lost.

In late October, Eisenhower told his son, John, "This fellow's licked [meaning Stevenson] and what's more he knows it."[93] On November 2, just four days before the election, Eisenhower told Hazlett that he expected to win "by a comfortable majority. . . ."[94]

The margin was indeed comfortable. He took almost 58 percent of the popular votes, and 457 of the electoral votes to Stevenson's embarrassing seventy-three. Eisenhower's margin in the Electoral College was fifteen more than in 1952. He won by 9.5 million votes, three million more than in 1952. And he took forty-one states, two more than in 1952. In the South, Eisenhower won Kentucky and West Virginia, but he lost Missouri, a state he had won in 1952. All of Stevenson's victories were in the South, where he carried seven states, but again, not Johnson's Texas. *Time* reported that Eisenhower's victory was "the greatest personal vote of confidence since F.D.R. in 1936."[95]

Eisenhower ran far ahead of his party, with the result that the Democrats continued their control of Congress; they added one seat in the Senate and two in the House. "He was terribly disappointed," James Hagerty recalled the president's post-election thoughts. "It was a source of continual bewilderment to him. . . ."[96] It was the first time that a successful presidential candidate had not carried at least one house of Congress since Zachary Taylor in 1848.

In the 1956 election, black voters showed that they had become disaffected with the Democratic Party and their relationship with southern white supremacists. In April, *Newsweek* confirmed that black votes were up for grabs.[97] Then, in something of a political shift, Adam Clayton Powell, an African American congressman from Harlem and one of the primary leaders in the civil rights movement, announced that he was shifting his allegiance to Eisenhower.[98]

Thus, Eisenhower did well among black voters. In thirty-five northern congressional districts where African Americans made up more than 10 percent of the population, Eisenhower's vote totals rose to over 5 percent above his 1952 totals. Even in the South, votes for Eisenhower among African Americans rose more sharply than in the rest of the nation; and in the major southern cities, African Americans made a significant shift from Stevenson to Eisenhower.[99]

African Americans, like other voters in the nation, clearly liked Eisenhower. But since Eisenhower took office in 1953, the Republican administration had really done very little to warrant black support. Certainly, many black voters had decided to stay with the party of Lincoln; and many may have followed the lead of Powell and other black leaders who simply refused to share a political home with southern white supremacists. But the *Brown* decision must have also impacted black voters. The decision had been handed down during a Republican administration, by a court headed by a Republican Chief Justice who had been appointed by Eisenhower. And, although Eisenhower refused to endorse the decision, he also refused to repudiate it. For many black voters, that was enough for them to cast their votes for the president.[100]

The 1956 election brought an end to Stevenson's career, at least as a Democratic Party presidential nominee.[101] That, again, placed Johnson in the role as the party's dominant figure, even though he had failed to deliver Texas for the second time in two elections. In fact, Eisenhower won Texas in 1956 by a greater margin than in 1952. The election made Johnson majority leader again, but the position was immediately precarious. His margin of victory was only forty-nine to forty-seven, thus a shift of only one vote could have put Johnson and the Democrats out. In Texas, the junior senator, Price Daniel, had vacated his Senate seat to run for governor. A special election had to be called to replace Daniel, but that would not be scheduled until 1957.

In the meantime, the seat would be filled by an appointment made by the governor. That was Allen Shivers, a Democrat who had supported Eisenhower—and a Johnson political enemy. The situation gave Shivers the power to return Johnson and the Democrats to minority status. Eisenhower visited Shivers in Texas and applied pressure. But Shivers sided with the Democrats. In Ohio, voters had elected Frank Lausche, a conservative Democrat. There were rumors that he might caucus with the Republicans, but he cast his vote for Johnson and the Democrats retained their slim majority in the Senate.[102]

When parties lose elections they, at once, try to find out why, and that leads to inevitable finger pointing. And the fingers began to point toward Johnson and Rayburn, the two Texans who controlled the party's infrastructure in Congress, set legislative policy, and often collaborated with the Eisenhower administration. Johnson and Rayburn, in addition, had not been able to deliver their state in the last two presidential elections. The result was a liberal backlash within the party, mostly led by Paul Butler, now at the head of the Democratic Advisory Council. The members of the DAC were generally liberal and not in office—thus they were less likely to be punished by Johnson and the other party leadership. The plan they devised for the next session was to challenge Eisenhower on every front, and set an agenda for the next election, the 1960 campaign. DAC members included Stevenson, Harriman, Truman's secretary of state Dean Acheson, retired New York senator Herbert Lehman, Thomas Finletter, liberal economist John Kenneth Galbraith, and Butler. The idea, Galbraith later recalled, was to "take . . . some of the Texas image off the party."[103] Lehman complained, "In my judgment . . . the election of 1956 was lost before the campaign began. . . . The Democrats in Congress failed to *make* the issues during the eighteen months we were in control."[104]

Johnson and Rayburn engaged the conflict by refusing to accept seats on the DAC. There was an immediate split between Johnson (and his Senate supporters) and the DAC, and that split would continue through the next congressional session. The party was split between Johnson, Rayburn, and the moderates on one side and the liberals, led by a growing power on the left, led by the DAC and a group that Johnson would later call "the bomb throwers" in the Senate.

In the Republican Party, the right was about to surge, marginalizing Eisenhower and the moderates. The Middle Way was on its way out.

CHAPTER FIVE

Moderates Among Moderates: Eisenhower and Johnson at the Height of Their Powers

By the time Eisenhower stepped into his second term it was clear that he was winding down his presidency. As the candidates from both parties began to plan for the 1960 campaign four years later, Eisenhower was often derided as an inactive president, detached from all but the most important events, a president who spent too much time playing golf with his wealthy buddies at the Augusta National Golf Club. There were those who believed that he had been pushed into a second term by a political party that could not produce a viable successor.

In addition, because of the twenty-second amendment to the Constitution, Eisenhower had become the nation's first lame duck president, unable to run again. His vote-getting skills were no longer available, and thus no longer needed to keep several members of the GOP right in office. Consequently, many on the right began to grow increasingly rebellious toward Eisenhower's moderation; they no longer needed Ike.

Arizona Senator Barry Goldwater became the spokesman for the Republican right (and a critic of the Eisenhower administration) in the last years of the 1950s.   (Eisenhower Presidential Library and Museum, Abilene, Kansas)

Eisenhower, however, was not through. He worked with those who would work with him—no matter their party affiliation. And he excluded from the government's business those who would not. Perhaps most importantly, Eisenhower had concluded that he could pass significant legislation without the votes from his own party's right wing. The conservatives in his party, however, had also concluded that the era of Eisenhower moderation must end, and their power was beginning to grow.

Eisenhower continued to pride himself on his middle-of-the-road view of politics that included the rejection of the radical right within his own party, and the radical left among the Democrats, in an effort to hold the political center. It was, he believed, where the political posture of most Americans resided and from where he was called to serve the nation. Early

Arthur Larson, who wrote A Republican Looks at His Party, *was Eisenhower's closest advisor on the nature of "modern Republicanism." (Courtesy of Lex Larson)*

in his presidency he adopted the phrase "dynamic conservatism," and then, "the Middle Way," but neither really captured his imagination as a phrase that explained his political views.

In 1956, Arthur Larson published *A Republican Looks at His Party.* It caught Eisenhower's eye because of Larson's phrase "Modern Republicanism." According to Larson, "Modern Republicanism" worked because "despite old party labels, most Americans have gravitated toward a basic agreement on fundamental issues, toward the moderate approach to government. The Republicans, Independents, and Democrats who voted Ike into office are massed at," what he called, "an 'Authentic American Center.'" Republicans in the future, he argued, would have electoral success if they continued to maintain that course.[1]

There were, Larson wrote, five reasons for this realignment—as he saw it: 1) Without a depression or war emergency during 1950s, there was no longer a need for a strong central government. 2) Unemployment was low. Thus there was no need for emergency federal assistance. 3) Labor and management had developed basic equality, and thus they were no longer in conflict. 4) Great wealth was no longer held by individuals, but was instead in the hands of business and industry. 5) The nation had shifted from an agrarian to an industrial economy. This "Modern Republicanism," he predicted, would hold the center for a considerable time. The Democratic Party, he wrote, could not, mostly because the Democrats were burdened with a polarized party of ultraradicals and ultraconservatives.[2]

This new political idea, Larson said, did not fit neatly into the commonly described political categories at the time, such as "liberal," "New Deal," "prolabor," "probusiness," "left," or "right," because such categories had been "drawn from earlier decades [and] are now obsolete."[3] He described two political paradigms—in fact competitors to the ideology of "Modern Republicanism." He called them the "1896 ideology," and the "1936 ideology." The first, he wrote, was the ideological foundation of both political parties and emphasized states' rights, respect for the importance of private enterprise, hostility toward organized labor, and an indifference to the needs of individuals. The 1936 ideology was, in many ways, a reaction to the 1896 ideology. It emphasized the centralization of federal authority, an excessive hostility toward big business (and a related belief that business and industry could not work properly without government stimulation, intervention, and regulation), a penchant for organized labor (and the associated belief that it needed government assistance to overcome employers' bargaining advantages), and a sensitivity to the needs of the individual. Larson then went on to argue that whatever the merits of these two political and social philosophies at the times of their popularity, neither fit the needs of the nation in the 1950s.[4] Eisenhower liked Larson's analysis and the phrases he used to describe it.

Following the 1956 election, Eisenhower commented to the press on his landslide victory, along with his disappointment that the Democrats had maintained their majorities in Congress. "From my point of view," he said, "the United States has not yet been convinced that modern Republicanism is with us and is going to be the guiding philosophy of the Republican party." He continued by giving a detailed explanation of Modern Republicanism: "It is a type of political philosophy that recognizes clearly the responsibility of the Federal Government to take the lead in making certain that the productivity of our great economic machine is distributed so that no one will suffer disaster, [or] privation through no fault of their own."[5]

By this time, however, the press had picked up the phrase and had begun using it to describe the Eisenhower wing of the Republican Party rather than any political philosophy.

Those who were on board with Eisenhower's "Modern Republicanism" liked what they heard from the president. But, not surprisingly, those on the conservative right saw "Modern Republicanism" as a means for the president to write out of the party those who disagreed with him. Even Nixon—always willing to sway with the prevailing winds—was worried that talk of "Modern Republicanism" would alienate the faithful. He called it "either a boast," or "a threat that those within the party who did not share [the president's] views would gradually be replaced by those who did."[6] John Bricker, a Republican with conservative credentials, added that "[m]uch that sails under the banner of Republicanism today is certainly not Republicanism as we know it in Ohio."[7] And Illinois senator Everett Dirksen said on a popular news program, "I have always thought of myself as just a plain ordinary, garden-variety type of Republican. . . . I have never heard Modern Republicanism defined—a good definition—that you could sink your teeth into. . . . [U]ntil such time, I simply have to think of myself as a Republican, and I believe most of the party members will do likewise."[8]

Larson's political philosophy never caught on much beyond Eisenhower. Liberals saw it as an inadequate response to needed liberal programs, while conservatives argued that it was an attempt to incorporate a liberal philosophy into the Republican Party agenda, while marginalizing conservative ideas.[9]

‡

Almost immediately following Eisenhower's reelection, the Middle East threatened to flare up again. In the aftermath of the Suez Crisis, it appeared that the Soviets intended to make inroads into the Middle East, almost certainly in an attempt to gain control of the oil output from that region. It was a threat that Eisenhower could not abide—diplomatically or politically. On January 5, Eisenhower went before Congress to ask for the authority to provide economic and military aid to the nations of the Middle East because, he said, he feared "that power-hungry Communists [might] . . . estimate that the Middle East is inadequately defended, [and] be tempted to use open measures of armed attack." He added, "I am convinced that the best insurance against this dangerous contingency is to make clear" that the United States is prepared to act. He asked for $200 million per year for two years beyond foreign aid funds already appropriated. And, he said, he hoped troops would never need to be used.[10] There was precedent for such a request. In 1955, Congress had given the president open-ended authority to defend Formosa. That situation was different, however, because it was a response to China's open belligerence toward Formosa. The 1956 request was a response to an anticipated belligerence.

In the days before the speech, the president had summoned twenty-nine legislators to the White House for a briefing on his new Middle East policy—that would become known as the Eisenhower Doctrine. "If the Russians go into the Middle East and we don't stop them," Dulles warned, "we are gone." Johnson, present at the meeting, was not so sure.

He called the Eisenhower Doctrine a "far-reaching proposal," with "grave implications."[11]

The Eisenhower Doctrine was, however, something of a fait accompli. James Reston of the *New York Times* explained that the idea had been publicized so widely that congressional leaders would have no real choice except to support it. Had they rejected it, he added, it would have both damaged and embarrassed the administration. In addition, congressional rejection might well have triggered Soviet aggressions in the Middle East under a possible assumption by the Soviets that the American government was divided and conflicted over the issue.[12]

The Doctrine did put the Democrats in a precarious position. Johnson and Rayburn disliked handing over to the president what amounted to a predated declaration of war, with no knowledge of specific circumstances. In addition, a number of congressmen on both sides of the aisle were reluctant to make an alliance with the Arab states, a bloc of nations sworn to the destruction of Israel—an avowed American ally in the region and whose relationship with Washington impacted the sway of the Jewish vote in several key northeastern states. On the other hand, blocking such an initiative might make the Democrats appear "soft," unwilling to contain communist advances—an accusation that had dogged them politically since the end of the war.

Paul Butler and the Democratic Advisory Council pushed Johnson and the moderates to reject the president's doctrine outright. Instead, Johnson counseled congressional Democrats to force the administration to cut back on its economic requests and then to ease up on the resolution's language. Rayburn introduced a substitute resolution in the House that declared that the United States "regards as vital to her interests the preservation of the independence and integrity of the states of the Middle East and, if necessary, [will] use her armed forces to that end."[13] Dulles rejected Rayburn's proposal, and the president's Middle East Resolution passed the House. The battle then was engaged in the Senate.

Dulles and Johnson reached a compromise that the aid to the Arab states would come from regular foreign aid funds and not from a special fund allocated beyond the foreign aid budget. In addition, the president would give Congress at least fifteen day's notice before granting economic aid. The Senate resolution also stated that the United States would be "prepared" to send troops if the president deems it necessary. Republicans in the Senate objected, but the White House accepted the compromise. The Eisenhower Doctrine (which included the language changed by Johnson) passed the Senate in early March, 1957. It was signed by the president two months later.[14]

In the midst of all this, another event in the Middle East again threatened to split the bipartisanship of the previous four years. Israel refused to leave Gaza, a region controlled by Egypt that the Israelis had taken during the Suez Crisis. Eisenhower and Dulles favored sanctions against Israel, fearing that any opposition to sanctions would alienate the Arab states and invite Soviet interference. The Democrats in Congress, however, led again by Johnson, opposed the sanctions, arguing that no sanctions were imposed against Egypt for invading Israel at the beginning of the Suez Crisis; and there had been no sanctions against the Soviets for invading Hungary. So, why, they asked, should sanctions be imposed against Israel over this incident?[15] Eisenhower and Dulles backed away from their demands.

The significance of these two events is that they disturbed the bipartisan foreign policy. Bipartisanship had been founded on the Democratic Party's acceptance of an Eisenhower foreign policy. Foreign policy was undoubtedly the president's strength, his heritage, and the foundation of his popularity. On domestic policy, however, the Republicans and Democrats often disagreed, but even then the Democrats, led by Johnson, were willing to work with the administration and compromise on most issues. The Democratic Party's response to the Eisenhower Doctrine and the situation in Gaza was, for the first time, a clear break with the administration's foreign policy. Eisenhower had taken the currency from his November win to Congress and asked for two foreign policy initiatives that would have given him tremendous power. Johnson and the Democrats had rejected one proposal and forced the administration to severely modify another. William S. White wrote in the *New York Times*: "If bipartisanship is defined as faithful concurrence with the President in foreign policy . . . then bipartisanship lies in disarray in the Senate. . . . Not in many years has Senate leadership . . . directly and so massively challenged a President on a world issue. . . . Right or wrong, justifiably or not, the Administration's course in the Middle East has brought the hitherto cooperative Democrats close to general rebellion. . . ."[16]

Despite the differences with Eisenhower's Middle Eastern strategy, Johnson was still fielding assaults from party liberals who insisted he attack the administration for the expressed purpose of building a case for Democratic victories in the future. Many of these assaults on Johnson came from Butler and the Democratic Leadership Council. Johnson, however, continued to maintain control of the liberal faction in the Senate.[17] He always insisted that he had, in fact, opposed the president on a number of issues, and that Stevenson in the 1956 campaign had simply failed to exploit those differences. However, all doubts would be swept clean when the leader bumped heads with the president over the 1958 budget.

‡

By 1956, the economy was booming. This can mostly be credited to (and in part caused by) the baby boom and the baby boom patterns of the decade. Families began moving to the suburbs and buying cars to make the transition. They spent money, and as the economy expanded, their purchasing power increased dramatically. By most accounts, it was the beginning of what would become the new postwar consumer culture. But by the beginning of 1957, the economy had begun to sag and a worldwide recession was underway. That was followed by a further drop in prosperity by the summer. By the spring of 1958, the economy had hit bottom. It was, in fact, the worst economic downturn since the Great Depression.

By late 1957 the president's approval rating began to drop—to 57 percent, down from 79 percent in February 1957. And then by March 1958 his ratings hit an all-time low at 52 percent.[18] In late November 1957, the president suffered a stroke, usually considered mild. He recovered quickly and attended a NATO summit in Paris against his wife's requests and his doctors' orders. When he returned, he was described by a reporter for *Time* as appearing weak, which gave "an open invitation to his opponents to walk all over [him]." At the same press conference, the president said he would do nothing to help the economy "at this moment."[19]

Despite his talk of reducing deficits and balancing the federal budget, Eisenhower still had to appropriate funding for the military, foreign aid, and the growing need for various domestic programs. Consequently, the federal budget soared, nearly doubling the budgets from the Truman years—something of a baseline for conservative complaints about government spending deficits. When Eisenhower proposed a budget of $73.3 billion for fiscal year 1958 (up $2.8 billion from the year before), Secretary of the Treasury George Humphrey warned that the deficit could cause "a depression that might curl your hair." Eisenhower then seemed to throw down the gauntlet to the Democrats. "If Congress can cut the budget, it is their duty to do it." For most Democrats that meant: "See if *you* can do any better."[20]

Eisenhower believed he had done everything he could to keep his budget under control. It was, in fact, only 18 percent of the gross national product, the lowest since 1939; and the president saw that as responsible. But the members of the Old Guard conservatives in his party were not interested. They wanted the budget balanced. "The Republican Old Guard is back on its feet," *Time* reported. "Not since 1952 has it been so in evidence. Its battle flag is the curl your hair Eisenhower budget."[21] When William Knowland and New Hampshire Republican Stiles Bridges attacked the president, claiming that he had abandoned his party and actually embraced New Deal programs, Eisenhower shot back, insisting that their comments were nonsense and that such social programs had "now become accepted in our civilization as normal, that is . . . social security, unemployment insurance, health research by the Government, assistance where States and individuals are unable to do things for themselves."[22] Asked in a press conference if he had grown more liberal in office, Eisenhower replied that "[i]f anything, I think I have grown more conservative. . . . I believe that unless a modern political group does look these problems in the face and finds some reasonable solution . . . then in the long run they are sunk."[23] After five years, Eisenhower had done very little to mollify the Old Guard conservatives in his party; he had not pulled them into his coalition or convinced them of his way of thinking. The budget battle showed that clearer than any other issue. It also showed that the GOP conservatives no longer feared Eisenhower, or needed his vote-getting abilities.

Eisenhower had originally hoped that the Democrats would approve of his budget. It did, after all, give support to several traditional Democratic Party programs. But Johnson and the Democrats had also begun to see a partisan opportunity. Instead of asking for increases, or even supporting the president's proposals, they began cutting into Eisenhower's budget—by at least $4 billion, or about 5 percent.[24] This immediately undermined the GOP and its long-established role as the custodian of fiscal conservatism, and it allowed the Democrats to grasp the leadership on the budget issue.

With the fight engaged, the president, in mid-May, responded by taking his side of the argument to the nation. In a televised address on May 14, he insisted that "[n]o great reductions in [the budget] are possible unless Congress eliminates or curtails existing Federal programs, or unless all of us demand less service from our country." He continued to express a need to confront the communist threat abroad and, to that end, keep the American military at the top of his economic agenda. In defense, he added, further cuts would require sacrifices "of our sons, our families, our homes and our cities to our own shortsightedness."[25] The president's efforts, however, changed few minds. *Time* called the address "the closest thing to a political flop that Ike has ever had." In fact, only one television network station carried the speech live, and only about 11 percent of the public bothered to watch. *Time* added that it was "too little too late." The president's enemies, the magazine continued, have taken "possession of the field." In the same article, *Time* reported that Johnson, working "behind the scenes," has been "prying and jimmying for hours on end with the sharpest touch in politics." He "has been so successful in exploiting the G.O.P. troubles that he has almost hidden his own party's more basic division."[26]

Another aspect of the budget battle brought Johnson into conflict with Eisenhower's political philosophy of the Modern Republicanism. In 1956, Eisenhower had appointed Arthur Larson to head the United States Information Agency (USIA), the nation's chief international public relations and propaganda bureau.[27] In that role, Larson had decided to take his political agenda on the road to try to convince the nation's moderates that "Moderate Republicanism" was the way of the future. In April 1957, in a speech in Hawaii, Larson called the Democrats un-American. The next day, House Democrats cut the USIA 1958 budget from $144 to $105 million. Johnson was on the Senate Appropriations Committee, and he argued that the House cuts should have been deeper in the interest of balancing the federal budget. For four days, Larson sat for questioning before Johnson and the Senate Committee. Johnson slashed at Larson, accusing him of asking for more funding than his agency needed and insisting that Larson defend his requests. "We look to you as the distinguished author and spokesman for your party . . . to enlighten us." The committee finally cut Larson's budget to a bare $90 million, and Johnson pushed the appropriations cut through the Senate. The conference committee added an additional $6 million, but even then, the president called the entire affair "irresponsible." In October, Eisenhower removed Larson from the USIA.[28] Again, the lame duck president was challenged and the challengers won.

In the midst of the budget fight, an event of seemingly minor significance turned out to be a milestone in the growth and development of the GOP right. In April 1957, Barry Goldwater, a conservative senator from Arizona, stood to speak in the Senate against the Eisenhower budget. In an attempt to deflect what was to come, the president had asked Goldwater to the White House for lunch, "to discuss ways of helping him in his bid for re-election in 1958."[29] But Goldwater refused. He was scheduled to speak, and he would speak—although he apologized to the president for the statement he was about to make before he even took to the Senate floor. To an almost empty chamber, Goldwater made it clear that he was ready for a break. He began with an almost obligatory compliment to the president for his leadership in his first term. But now, he added, "I am not so sure." He accused the administration of being charmed by the "the siren of socialism" and that it had "aped New Deal antics." The president's budget, he said, "was a betrayal of the people's trust," and, he added, "it weakens my faith in the constant reassurances we have received from this administration that its aim was to cut spending, balance the budget, reduce the national debt, cut taxes—in short to live within our means. . . ." Too many Republicans, he added, have adopted the Democratic principle that all Americans should be "federally born, federally housed, federally clothed, federally educated, federally supported in their occupation, and die a federal death, thereafter to be buried in a federal box in a federal cemetery." He went on to attack the president's concept of Modern Republicanism, calling it a "splintered concept of Republican philosophy," and then he promised he would fight "against waste, extravagance, high taxes, unbalanced budgets, and deficit spending" as proposed by the Democrats, but that he would also battle "the same elements of fiscal irresponsibility in this Republican administration."[30] It was a stinging attack.

Goldwater's high-profile break with Eisenhower catapulted him to a leadership position among GOP conservatives in Congress. In 1958, Goldwater would win reelection—and Knowland would lose. Goldwater quickly became the successor to Robert Taft, the leading conservative political voice that the right had been looking for since Taft's death in 1953. Immediately after the 1958 elections, Goldwater was approached by a group of Midwest conservatives to discuss the possibility of organizing a Goldwater-for-President committee, with an eye on the 1960 campaign. Goldwater realized that Nixon, with Eisenhower's blessing, would be unbeatable for the Republican nomination that year, and he declined the offer.[31] But following Nixon's loss in 1960, Goldwater would take a second look.

Goldwater's 1957 speech set the tone for the Republican right for the remainder of the century. They would embrace fiscal restraint, a balanced budget, and low taxes, while opposing big government, statism, and all manners of socialism and social welfare. They would also reject Eisenhower's middle-of-the road Modern Republicanism and keep the Republican Party away from the centrism and conciliation that Eisenhower pursued with Johnson and the moderate Democrats. It was also an indication that the Republican right no longer needed Eisenhower and his long coattails. Goldwater's speech was a game changer. American politics would never quite be the same.

None of this made Eisenhower happy. Not only had he lost control of the budget issue, but his budget proposal had given the Old Guard conservatives new life and a new leader. In a pre-press conference briefing, he commented that he did not believe that "Senator Goldwater was entitled to make that kind of attack."[32] And then a few days later his postmaster general recorded the basic contents of a meeting with the president: "During the last few minutes the President indicated in no uncertain terms his anger over the Senate speech . . . given by Senator Goldwater of Arizona."[33]

‡

By the mid-1950s it was fairly apparent that civil rights legislation was on the horizon. The *Brown v. Board* decision of May 1954 showed for the first time that desegregation was in the nation's immediate future. Eisenhower was not enthused by the court's decision, stating only that he would uphold it as required by his office. By some accounts, Eisenhower's reticence emboldened white southerners, and southerners in Congress responded with the Southern Manifesto, an encouragement of massive resistance against the *Brown* decision. That document made it clear that southern leaders would continue their age-old fight against desegregation.

Eisenhower may have had little regard for the *Brown* decision, but he still hoped to maintain voter support from the African American community. Voting rights seemed a less divisive issue than desegregation. To that end, Eisenhower, in his State of the Union message in January 1956, asked for a bipartisan committee to determine why African Americans in the South were being denied the right to vote.[34] That appeared to be the origins of what would become the Civil Rights Act of 1957, but Attorney General Brownell had actually written the bill a month before and presented it to the cabinet. It received mixed reviews there, but Eisenhower allowed

Brownell to send the bill to the House on April 9.[35] The bill had four distinct parts:

1. It allowed for the creation of a bipartisan civil rights commission, designed to recommend additional civil rights legislation.

2. It proposed the creation of a civil rights division in the Justice Department.

3. It would give the federal government the authority to use civil procedures to protect civil rights. It also gave the attorney general the power to seek injunctions against the obstruction of civil rights, and it increased penalties when such obstructions resulted in a loss of life. Thus, this section of the bill gave the attorney general the authority to enforce court orders to desegregate public schools and to enter into such cases as the 1955 Emmett Till murder case.

4. It allowed the attorney general and the federal courts to guarantee the right to vote to anyone who had been denied that right by state laws and practices This section of the bill also provided for trials by federal judges in cases involving civil rights contempt charges.[36]

In its original form, the bill had no real chance to pass. It slipped through the House without much fanfare, but it was killed quickly in the Senate where the Judiciary Committee, chaired by Mississippi Democrat James Eastland, kept the bill from reaching the floor. The Eisenhower administration blamed the Democrats for killing the bill; the Democrats responded that Eisenhower had submitted the bill in an election year only to win black votes. Just after the Senate rejected the bill, in August, Russell lamented: "I merely say that when such nefarious schemes as these are presented in the future . . . there will be members of the Senate who will resort to every weapon at their command to prevent such proposals being imposed on the people of the U.S."[37]

The civil rights bill was then submitted in the next congressional session in 1957 (85th Congress, 1st session). By then, the year-long Montgomery bus boycott (that ended in December 1956) had been a rousing success, and in February a victorious Martin Luther King, Jr., appeared on the cover of *Time*. All of that seemed to say that a bill would pass—or at least a bill would have a more serious consideration than in 1956. The primary question was what type of bill would it be? "It seemed likely," wrote *Time*, "that Lyndon Johnson and his conservative colleagues would settle for some compromise form of civil-rights legislation in this session."[38]

Eisenhower had done well among black voters in the 1956 election, which convinced the Democrats that if they did not pass a civil rights bill before the 1958 midterm elections they might lose the African American vote entirely. It was a difficult dilemma for both parties. The bill might help Republicans get more black votes, but they might lose the white South (an area where they had made strong gains) in the process. For Democrats, such a bill might well split their party—as the party had split in 1948 over civil rights, but it might also allow the Democrats to win back those African American voters who had been defecting to the Republicans since 1952. Democratic liberals assumed that Eisenhower was pushing the bill to split the Democrats. Others thought that the administration's objective was to tie up other domestic legislation, particularly Social Security reform and foreign aid. A few liberals, particularly Illinois Democrat Paul Douglas and New York Democrat Herbert Lehman (along with several leaders of liberal organizations like the NAACP and the ADA) wanted to turn the tables on the Republicans by forcing the issue and getting Republicans on record for opposing the bill.

Thus, the bill again slipped through the Democratic-controlled House with little fanfare, passing by a vote of two to one in mid-June. But the big battles would be in the Senate.

In the meantime, the president had begun shifting away from a bill that was designed to enforce desegregation, to one that would be more focused on the right of southern blacks to vote. In fact, Eisenhower had always been skeptical of Part 3, the portion of the bill that allowed the executive branch, through the attorney general, to enforce court orders to desegregate public schools. The president believed that a focus on voting rights would allow the bill to pass, avoid many of the political pitfalls over the bill, and give southern blacks the means to demand further rights. He also hoped that a bill that focused on voting rights would allow the

Republicans to continue the trend of winning over more and more African American voters.

On the day the bill passed the House it was sent on to the Senate, and then to Eastland's Judiciary Committee where, most thought, it would die. But in a rare bit of bipartisanship, liberal Paul Douglas and conservative Republican Bill Knowland joined to circumvent Eastland's Judiciary Committee by having the bill placed directly onto the calendar, allowing it to be called up at anytime by a majority vote. That procedural motion passed 45 to 39. What would become the Civil Rights Act of 1957 had jumped its biggest hurdle.[39]

Johnson had to shore up his Texas constituency by voting against the motion that allowed the bill to go directly to the floor, but he had also made certain that the motion passed without his vote. He had worked to convince western liberals to support the civil rights bill. In exchange, southern senators agreed to vote to drop their opposition to the bill and then to vote to appropriate the Hell's Canyon Dam on the Snake River in Idaho. This water-power project was dear to the hearts of several western senators, and they were willing to make the deal to get the project.[40]

Behind the scenes, Democratic Party leaders had reached the conclusion that a bill would in some form finally pass, and that they—rather than the administration—should take control of the outcome. Lyndon Johnson, of course, took the lead. His objective was a compromise bill, one that would satisfy those who wanted a civil rights bill, but without offending southern segregationists. Johnson, *Time* reported, wanted to enact a bill "that most of the South could swallow, that Dick Russell would not filibuster against, and that Bill Knowland and Northern Democrats could hold up as a symbol of civil rights progress."[41] Johnson also believed that if he could achieve that objective, he would be in a good position to win his party's nomination for president in 1960.

Not everyone agreed. Johnson's chief political advisor, James Rowe, wrote, "Your friends and your enemies . . . are saying that you are trapped between your southern background and your desire to be a national leader. . . . If you vote against [this] civil rights bill you can forget your presidential ambitions in 1960." In the same memo, however, Rowe added: "It would be most important that [you] get all the credit for getting a compromise bill through, with emphasis in the South on compromise, and emphasis in the North on getting a bill."[42] That became Johnson's objective.

With that, Johnson and Russell met to pound out a compromise—one that Russell could live with, and one that both men believed would satisfy the liberals in their party. They decided that Part 3 (which gave the federal government the power to take an active roll in desegregating southern schools) had to be eliminated. And they wanted to make certain that anyone cited for contempt of court in any civil rights case would receive a jury trial. The point was clear: all-white juries in the South would not convict white defendants of civil rights violations. The compromise they proposed was designed to weaken the bill severely.[43]

In early July, Russell attacked Part 3 and Part 4 (which sanctioned contempt of court trials by federal judges without juries) of the bill. He called Part 3 "cunningly contrived" and then added that he "would be less than frank if I did not say that I doubt very much whether the full implications of this bill have ever been explained to President Eisenhower." It was significant that Russell attacked only a section of the bill and not the entire bill. That was immediately perceived as a willingness to accept a civil rights bill of some sort—as long as the two offending provisions were removed or moderated.[44]

At a news conference the next day, the president said that Russell was right, that he, in fact, did not understand the bill. "I was reading part of the bill this morning," he told reporters, "and . . . there were certain phrases I didn't completely understand." He added that he would speak to Brownell (who wrote the bill) "and see exactly what they do mean." Then he added that he would be happy if the bill only protected voting rights.[45] Critics used this to begin rewriting the bill. The Senate was headed toward a compromise.

There were some valiant attempts to save Part 3, but it was clear that for the bill to pass, Part 3 would have to be eliminated. Part 3, George Reedy later said, "evoked all the old specters of reconstruction acts." Johnson convinced Republican senator George Aiken of Vermont and liberal Democrat and civil rights supporter Clinton Anderson, senator from New Mexico, to cosponsor an amendment eliminating Part 3. Anderson wrote in his memoir: "It seemed to me that a weakened bill was better than no bill at all, if especially the voting guarantees remained intact."[46] Herbert Brownell recalled that Johnson then went to Eisenhower and convinced him to drop his demands for Part 3.[47]

At the same time, Russell was convinced that because of the growing success of the civil rights movement, a filibuster would no longer work as a strategy for killing civil rights bills. He told a group of southerners who met in his office in early July that the South was not as solid as it once was, that there were, at best, only eighteen staunch southerners who could be depended on to work a filibuster; and worse, conservative Republicans were no longer willing allies. The members of the southern caucus agreed to follow Russell's lead. Russell and Johnson agreed. The best way to handle the civil rights bill was to cripple it: cut Part 3 and to add a jury trial provision to the bill.[48]

On July 24, Part 3 was eliminated by a vote of 52 to 38, with eighteen Republicans (including Knowland) voting to cut the section. The crucial western liberals went along, and several other senators agreed to vote to eliminate the section because they thought it might keep the bill from final passage. Eisenhower conceded that he had never been very enthusiastic about Part 3 and would not insist on its restoration.[49] With that, attention shifted to the jury trial provision of the bill.

It was written into the bill that criminal contempt cases would be tried without juries. A criminal contempt case punishes an individual for challenging the authority of the court. Generally, criminal contempt cases are decided by the court alone—without a jury. Russell and other southern leaders insisted that these cases be tried by juries, while northern liberals argued that all-white southern juries would not convict white defendants charged with criminal contempt in a civil rights case.[50]

Johnson effected a compromise that was little more than allowing jury trials in criminal contempt cases (which was what southerners had wanted) but not in civil cases. The administration opposed Johnson's compromise, sending Nixon to argue before the press that the inclusion of the jury trial amendment was "a vote against the right to vote," and "one of the saddest days in the history of the Senate."[51] Johnson wrote to Adlai Stevenson that the issue was now politicized: "We are faced right now with an effort to kill the Bill on the pretext that it does not go far enough. I believe the real reason is that those who are using this pretext prefer the [political] issue to a solution, and there will be bad days ahead for our country if they succeed."[52] In the final analysis, the bill stated that a judge in a voting rights case could decide whether or not to call a jury. However, if the case was tried without a jury, the maximum penalty could not be greater than a fine of $300 and a short jail sentence.[53]

The next day, after a fourteen-hour session, the Senate passed the amended bill, 72 to 18. Eisenhower said he was "damned unhappy about the vote last night," and the "Senate Democratic leadership skillfully gutted the first civil rights bill to approach congressional approval in eighty-two years." It was, he added, "a hard slap in the face of a nation generally trying to live up to its own constitutional guarantees."[54] By the end of August, the two houses of Congress had reconciled their differences, and the bill came back to the Senate for a final vote. South Carolina senator Strom Thurmond, however, decided that he would make the point that he opposed the bill and began a filibuster that lasted twenty-four hours and eighteen minutes. This personal statement was an embarrassment for most southerners in the Senate who had worked hard to achieve the compromise, and they considered the bill a victory. The House passed the bill on August 27; the Senate two days later.[55]

Eisenhower's legislative leaders encouraged him to sign the bill. Even Knowland insisted that it was the best the Senate could do under the circumstances and that the administration might take the opportunity to build from it.[56] Martin Luther King, Jr., the new leader of the civil rights movement, and Roy Wilkins of the NAACP encouraged the president to sign the bill. Wilkins made the analogy: "If you are digging a ditch with a teaspoon and a man comes along and offers you a spade, there is something wrong with your head if you don't take it because he didn't offer you a bulldozer."[57] Prominent African American Ralph Bunche said, "It would be better to have no bill than one as emasculated as that which has come out of the Senate." In a telegram to the president, Jackie Robinson wrote, "I am opposed to civil rights bill in its present form [and I] disagree that half a loaf is better than none." "[h]e added his support, however. I "Have waited this long for a bill with meaning, [I] can wait a little longer." A. Phillip Randolph insisted that it was "worse than no bill at all." And Eleanor Roosevelt wrote that Congress was "trying to fool the people."[58]

Johnson said later—a point that became the most common explanation for the Civil Rights bill of 1957—"I got all I could on civil rights in 1957. Next year I'll get a little more. The difference between me and some of my northern friends is that I believed you can't force these things on the South overnight. You advance a little and consolidate; then you advance again. I think in the long run my way may prove to be faster than theirs."[59]

By the time the president finally signed the bill, on September 9, events in Little Rock had changed the entire nature of the civil rights debate in the United States.

‡

The events surrounding the desegregation of Central High School in Little Rock, Arkansas, were one of the first big news stories in television history. It was also the first time that northern whites would see televised scenes of hate-filled white mobs rampaging to preserve the system of southern segregation. Never again would the argument be adequate that blacks and whites in the South both wanted a segregated system. The events at Little Rock would also precipitate the most severe test of the Constitution since the Civil War.

On July 17, 1956, about a year before the Civil Rights Act of 1957 was passed, the president, in a press conference, said, "I can't imagine any set of circumstances that would ever induce me to send Federal troops . . . into an area to enforce the orders of a Federal court, because I believe that common sense will never require it."[60] This may have been a signal to southern segregationists that the president would not intervene to enforce the *Brown* decision and desegregate southern schools, and it may have been one of several triggers that set off events that exploded at Central High School in Little Rock in September 1957.[61]

The Little Rock school board had been one of the first in the South to announce that it would comply with the *Brown* decision and desegregate its school system. In late May 1955, it released a plan for gradual desegregation. The plan was modest: one school, Central High School, was scheduled to desegregate at the beginning of the fall semester 1957, and the remainder of the school system would be desegregated over the next seven years. The Federal District Court approved the plan in the last days of August, and everything was set to go forward at the beginning of the school year in September. To begin the process, the board chose nine African American students (six girls and three boys) out of some seventy-five who applied. The students were chosen mostly for their good grades and their willingness to be a part of the program.

Little Rock was generally perceived as one of the cities of the celebrated New South. It was a progressive community, looking toward the future of business and prosperity rather than to its past of racism and provincialism. The mayor was a moderate on race issues, and the local newspaper supported the desegregation efforts. The governor, Orval Faubus, could hardly be called a liberal, but he seemed above race baiting. Faubus, however, was facing a difficult run for reelection from a popular segregationist candidate, and he had concluded that he would lose the election if he stood by and allowed Central High School to be desegregated.

On August 29, county Judge Murray O. Reed, a Faubus appointee, issued an injunction blocking the desegregation of Central High School. The next day, Federal District Judge Ronald N. Davies nullified Reed's injunction and ordered the school board to admit the nine black students. Then, on September 2, the day before school opened, Faubus called out the Arkansas National Guard to surround the school. He then went on local television to announce that it would "not be possible to restore or to maintain order if forcible integration is carried out tomorrow." No city officials in Little Rock had anticipated any trouble. When it became clear that Faubus had directed the National Guard to stop the desegregation process at Central High, it became apparent to the Justice Department in Washington that Faubus's actions were, in fact, an attempt to nullify the Constitution and disregard a federal court order.[62]

Eisenhower had just begun a vacation at Newport in Rhode Island, but he kept close watch on the events unfolding in Arkansas. At a news conference on September 3, he professed ignorance of the situation. He was, however, well aware of the events in Little Rock and had even directed General Maxwell Taylor, the army chief of staff, to order the 101st Airborne Division at Fort Campbell, Kentucky, to begin contingency planning in anticipation of a possible deployment. He had also given Brownell the authority to issue a public warning to Faubus.[63]

On September 4, the Arkansas National Guard, under Faubus's direction, barred the nine African American students from entering Central High School. The action was supported by some four hundred whites who had shown up at the school to harass the students and block their entrance into the school.[64] The next day, Faubus sent a telegram to the president asking him to understand his efforts to stop integration in his capital city. Eisenhower responded immediately that he would defend the Constitution "by every legal means at my command."[65]

On September 8, Little Rock mayor Woodrow Wilson Mann complicated the situation further by sending a panicky telegram to Eisenhower insisting that the situation was about to explode and asking for federal assistance.[66] Eisenhower wanted to avoid using military force to desegregate a southern school, but Mann's request changed the dynamic. As president of the United States, he had an obligation to protect American citizens. For that reason it may have been Mann's request that forced the president to act.

All of this had placed Faubus in a very bad situation. He was about to be flicked aside by the federal government. To work his way out, he began negotiating with Brooks Hays, an Arkansas congressman. Hays was convinced that Faubus would stand down if he could find a way out of the situation without embarrassment, without his hand being forced by Washington. Sherman Adams and others at the White House believed that the situation could be resolved if Eisenhower simply explained to Faubus the consequences of his actions. Adams, then, arranged for the president and Faubus to meet.[67]

Against advice from Brownell (who questioned Faubus's intentions) the president and the governor met on September 4 at the Newport Naval Base. The meeting lasted only fifteen minutes. Faubus described the progress that Arkansas had made in civil rights and then asked for ten days, without federal interference, to resolve the issue peaceably. He even asked for a contingent of federal marshals to assist. Eisenhower proposed, instead, that Faubus leave the National Guard troops in place, but change their orders to maintaining the peace while allowing the nine African American students to enter the school. The president made it clear that in any conflict between federal and state authorities, "there could be only one outcome—that is the state would lose." And, he added, he "did not want to see any governor humiliated."[68] It was clearly an ultimatum, and Faubus seemed to understand the consequences. According to Brownell, "Everyone was relieved over the apparent agreement."[69] Faubus returned to Little Rock, where he was expected to change the guardsmen's orders and allow desegregation of the school.

Faubus, however, did nothing. On September 20, a federal judge in Little Rock ordered the governor to cease with his interference of the integration process. Faubus responded by appearing on local television and announcing that he was withdrawing the troops. He then left for a governors' conference in Georgia. It seemed like an end to the stalemate, but as the troops left, white rabble-rousers from all over the South moved in to fill the gap. Quickly, the Little Rock police force was outnumbered, overwhelmed, and outgunned. Mayor Mann again wired the president that the situation was worsening quickly. Lives were in danger, he wrote, and troops were needed to deal with the escalating events.[70]

All this placed the president in a difficult position. Faubus had defied a federal court order and then lied directly to the president of the United States. The president had little choice but to act. Since the beginning of his administration, Eisenhower had dealt with a number of crises simply by waiting for a cooling of passions. Here things were not cooling down. In addition (despite the insistence of his attorney general to the contrary) he was not certain he had the authority as president to do anything. To Sherman Adams he said, "[T]he whole U.S. thinks the President has the right to walk in and say 'dispense—we are going to have negroes in the high school and so on.' That is not so."[71]

Eisenhower had allowed the situation to get out of control. His attempts at negotiation, moderation, and deemphasizing the escalating events had all failed to resolve the problem. The result was a full-scale constitutional incident that endangered American lives. On September 24 he ordered General Taylor, and 1,000 paratroopers from 101st Airborne Division to rush to Little Rock. The soldiers, trained in riot control, showed up on Little Rock's Main Street in full combat gear. To make certain that Faubus's power was totally destroyed and to avoid any confrontations or questions of authority, the president also nationalized the Arkansas National Guard.[72]

The incident ended. The threat of violence ended, and the school was desegregated. Eisenhower, however, was left with a great deal of political residue. Southern politicos were appalled. Olin Johnston, a Democratic senator from South Carolina, even called for the federal troops to be arrested and for Faubus to force a constitutional showdown with the president. South Carolina's governor, James Byrnes, insisted that "the United States Government has declared war on Arkansas." Senator James Eastland of Mississippi accused the president of attempting to destroy the social order of the South. And Richard Russell complained that while "totalitarian rule" might be able to "put Negro children in white schools in Little Rock," it would "have a calamitous effect on race relations and on the cause of national unity."[73]

By most accounts, Eisenhower backpedaled on the issue to preserve his standing with southerners—in the South and in Congress—in order to continue his political strategy of winning back the white South for the Republican Party. But a primary aspect of his reticence in dealing with the Little Rock incident was that he did not believe that the federal government had the authority to force a state to desegregate its schools. He also did not believe in the merits of the *Brown* decision or the authority it gave the executive branch.[74] Consequently, his immediate responses were measured. When he returned to Washington, he told the press that he had been forced to send in troops because of his "inescapable" responsibility to enforce the law. He went on to blame "disorderly mobs" led by "dema-gogic extremists." Then he added that the nation's attitudes toward its minorities could hurt its image abroad, explaining that communists were "gloating over this incident."[75] He added that he would act to preserve order, but that he would not act—specifically—to desegregate the nation's public schools.

By mid-October, the situation in Little Rock had calmed. The president withdrew most of the troops and returned the Arkansas National guards-men to state control. On October 25, the nine black students entered the school without military protection. The guardsmen remained in Little Rock throughout the school year. Then, in September 1958, Faubus, still running for governor, closed Central High School in Little Rock, and then threatened to close the entire Arkansas public school system rather than allow desegregation.

The violence at Little Rock went a long way toward undermining the southern argument that race relations in the South were generally consensual and peaceful. Southern congressmen and senators could no longer argue that they were working to preserve a southern social system that everyone wanted. The result was that the southern stance became little more than bigotry and racism—a stance that no longer held any intrinsic moral value. The Little Rock incident was the beginning of a pullback by southern legislators from their historic opposition to civil rights legislation.

‡

The issue of space followed almost directly on the heels of the events in Little Rock. The Soviet satellite *Sputnik* was launched into space at 7:30 p.m. on October 4, 1957, and the space race took the spotlight away from civil rights. The Democrats were, in fact, able to exchange an issue that divided them badly for one that not only united them, but appeared to expose the administration as inept and weak in the face of Soviet advances. "The integration issue is not going to go away," George Reedy wrote Johnson. "The only possibility is to find another issue which is even more potent. . . . Sputnik fulfills that requirement."[76]

The launch of *Sputnik* had a major impact on the nation's politics mostly because it allowed the Democrats to take control of national defense policy from Eisenhower and the Republicans. Eisenhower's leadership in defense had gone unchallenged for over five years. He had, after all, orchestrated the European victory in World War II and managed the Soviets firmly, while at the same time diminishing the threat of a nuclear holocaust. For most Americans, he was both strong and safe. *Sputnik* changed that. The event called into question the military and technological superiority of the United States. Perhaps more importantly, it placed into focus Eisenhower's complacency, his willingness to play down events—even to the point of hoping that bad things (given enough time) would eventually go away. Then, as events progressed it became clear that Eisenhower had failed to come to grips with the basic fear, along with the profound anxiety, and even the sense of impending doom, that had overwhelmed the American people as a result of the *Sputnik* launch.

Eisenhower's nonchalance was predictable. He understood all that was happening, along with most of the consequences. High-altitude U-2 over flights of the Soviet Union had shown ICBM (Intercontinental Ballistic Missile) bases at Tyuratum in Kazakhstan as early as mid-1956; and within a year, U.S. scientists knew that the Soviets were on the verge of launching a satellite. Two years earlier, the United States had announced that it would launch a satellite during the International Geophysical Year (IGY) that was to begin in mid-1957 and end in December 1958. But instead of handing the project over to the military (which had shown the most promise of sending a satellite into space) Eisenhower decided instead to focus on Project Vanguard, a purely scientific endeavor, in an attempt to show the world that the American space program was entirely peaceful. From a purely technological standpoint, this proved to be a mistake.

When the Soviets launched *Sputnik*, Eisenhower played down the event. He refused to recognize anything except the presence of "a small ball in the air," and he insisted that there was no contest with the Soviets over space exploration. What the president failed to realize was that the

Soviets had achieved more than just a scientific victory. Cold War fears were growing in the mid-1950s. And for the first time, the American people saw themselves as vulnerable to a Soviet nuclear attack from space, and that led to near panic.[77]

The Republicans followed the president's own deemphasized response, insisting that *Sputnik* was of no real significance and that soon enough the United States would get on the scoreboard with its own space program. The president said that the event "does not raise my apprehensions one iota."[78] James Hagerty, the president's press secretary, insisted that the United States had never considered competing in any sort of space race with the Soviets, and that the U.S. program "is proceeding satisfactorily in accordance with its scientific objectives."[79] Secretary of Defense Charles Wilson called the Soviet launch "a neat scientific trick" and agreed with Hagerty that there was no "race" for space.[80] White House Chief of Staff Sherman Adams wrote in his memoirs that he had responded to the president's call for "deemphasis" by insisting that the administration was not "intent on attaining a high score in any outer-space basketball game."[81] Senator Alexander Wiley, a Republican from Wisconsin, called *Sputnik* "a great propaganda stunt" and "nothing for us to worry about."[82]

The Democrats responded by calling the Soviet launch a direct threat of a nuclear attack on the United States. Presidential hopeful Senator Stuart Symington of Missouri claimed that the incident involved nothing less than "national survival." Florida senator George Smathers said "the Russians [are] taking a lead in science that threaten[s] the survival of the free world."[83] Senator Mike Mansfield, the Democratic Party whip from Wisconsin, said, "For too many years the United States has been all too prone to underestimate the capabilities of the Soviet Union, and now the chickens have come home to roost."[84] From these argument grew the "missile gap" issue that dominated the presidential campaign of 1960. No missile gap existed, and Eisenhower knew it because of the secret U-2 spy plane flyovers of the Soviet Union. He decided that the U-2 program should remain a government secret, and he chose to keep the information from the American people.

In response, Eisenhower was forced to accept defense expenditures high enough to get the U.S. space program off the ground, while giving the American people the peace of mind that their nation, and their science, was not second best. Part of this was the constant pressure to show the world (particularly the newly emerging developing world) that the United States was more technologically advanced than the Soviets. Thus for the Soviets, the Soviet *Sputnik* launch was an important scientific victory, but it also served as a tremendous propaganda victory. It seemed to show that Soviet technology was unchallenged, and that the Soviet Union—not the United States—held the keys to the future of the world. This was, perhaps, more damning to the Cold War efforts of the United States than any military capability.

By late October, the president's approval ratings began to drop.[85] Then, just as the nation began to accept Eisenhower's explanation that the Soviet launch was little more than an insignificant stunt, the Russians launched a dog into space on November 4. *Time* magazine could not resist calling the satellite "Mutnik" and then naming the dog "Little Curley."[86] The president had been able to slough off *Sputnik I* as a Soviet trick, but this *Sputnik II* was clear evidence of an obvious Soviet technological advance.

With the Democrats on the attack, Eisenhower finally responded that he would take steps to shore up the technological deficit. He named a special assistant for science and technology and promised that a single manager at the Pentagon would administer the space program. He said he would also push for a national effort to train more and better engineers—in answer to those who believed that the events had been caused by a complacent national education system.[87]

Eisenhower and Johnson met within days of the Soviet launch. The president's greatest fear was that Missouri senator Stuart Symington would turn the entire *Sputnik* affair into a partisan political issue, something Eisenhower wanted to avoid at all costs. Symington had called for a complete investigation of the Senate Armed Services Committee, followed by a special session of Congress.[88] And he was laying blame for the entire incident onto the administration's fiscal policies of restraint and even insisting that Eisenhower had grown detached from his office and his responsibilities. Eisenhower warned Johnson that if Symington's rhetoric was not softened that he would blame the situation on the Truman administration for cutting nearly all funds for missile research.[89] Johnson's objective, then, turned to containing Symington, keeping him under control so he would not turn the hearings into a partisan battle. "Contain Symington," Reedy told Johnson, "so [you] will become the expert on space and the missile gap."[90]

Symington's call for an investigation of the Armed Services Committee went to Richard Russell, who turned the matter over to Johnson. Johnson announced on November 5 that the Preparedness Subcommittee of the Senate Armed Services Committee would conduct an inquiry into the U.S. missile and satellite programs. The committee would be made up of seven senators. Of those seven, four were Democrats: John Stennis of Mississippi, Symington, Kefauver, and Johnson; and three were Republicans: Stiles Bridges, of New Hampshire, Leverett Saltenstall of Florida, and Ralph Flanders of Vermont. Johnson was most worried about Symington, who clearly intended to turn the inquiry into a stepping stone for his own presidential bid in 1960. As Truman's Secretary of the Air Force, Symington also wanted to undercut any Republican charges that the Truman administration was in any way responsible for the U.S. lag in missile development. Johnson and Russell hoped to keep the partisan bickering to a minimum, fearing that an investigation dominated by Symington might open the Democrats to charges of playing politics with national security. In his press release announcing the organization of the committee and its purposes, Johnson promised that it would be nonpartisan and that the committee would not attempt to fix any blame.[91]

Eisenhower had no intention of allowing Johnson and his committee to produce all the answers. Within two weeks of the *Sputnik* launch, the president ordered a review of the nation's missile program—going back into the Truman administration. It was soon discovered that budget cuts during Truman's second term in 1949 had led to the elimination of the early Atlas ICBM program, and that it was Symington who had approved the cuts. The entire report was completed by the end of 1957, and a copy was delivered to the Republican members of Congress. The report blamed

Truman for the cutbacks that eventually led to America's losses and the Soviet's gains. It then pointed out how the Eisenhower administration had spent billions on missile development.[92]

Johnson knew that the Democrats were not without blame in cutting funds to missile development, allowing the Soviets to make their surprising advancements. Johnson's response was to control the committee by controlling who testified, with a focus mostly on witnesses who were prominent scientists and public figures. His hope was to avoid partisan attacks against Truman's record. When the hearings concluded at the end of January, Symington insisted on producing a report sharply critical of the administration, the president, and its past policies. Johnson refused. Instead, he settled for a carefully worded report that called for an increase in defense spending that would allow for further missile development. Eisenhower agreed. In the end, Johnson achieved his goals: The hearings damaged the Republicans by making it look as though Eisenhower was oblivious to the Soviet missile threat, which generally benefited the Democrats. At the same time, he avoided any serious clash with Eisenhower.[93]

On February 6, 1958, the Senate created a committee designed to devise legislation for a permanent space agency. Later that month, Johnson was named chairman. On April 2, legislation drafted by the administration with the aid of Johnson and his committee was submitted to Congress establishing NASA (National Aeronautics and Space Administration). After some wrangling over who would devise space policy, Johnson set up a nine-member Space Council (including the president, the secretaries of State and Defense, the NASA director, and the head of the Atomic Energy Committee). The council was to oversee nearly all aspects of NASA.[94] The bill was signed on July 29, 1958. NASA was to be civilian controlled, giving it a peaceful focus.[95]

On February 1, 1958, the United States successfully placed *Explorer I* into orbit, and the nation seemed to breathe a sigh of relief. On March 5 *Explorer II* was launched, but a booster failed to ignite, and the satellite did not reach orbit. A *Vanguard* rocket, launched on March 17, sent into orbit America's second satellite, known affectionately as the "grapefruit" for its diminutive size. By that time, the Soviets had launched *Sputnik III,* a massive one-and-a-half-ton satellite, shot into orbit by a rocket with over one and a half million pounds of thrust.[96]

By December, the United States carried out Project Score, the launching of an entire Atlas missile into earth's orbit, along with a small communications satellite. It was hardly a major step in the advances of space science, but it let the nation (and the world) know that the United States was engaged in the space race and that it intended to win. On Christmas day, the satellite broadcast to the world a Christmas greeting from President Eisenhower. "Now the whole picture has changed," *Newsweek* commented. "[T]he 'missile gap' has closed."[97]

‡

James Hagerty called it "the saddest thing I think that happened during the Eisenhower Administration."[98] In June 1958, the House Committee on Legislative Oversight released documents that accused Bernard Goldfine, a wealthy New England textile manufacturer, of providing gifts to Sherman Adams, Eisenhower's chief of staff, in return for influence with the Federal Trade Commission and the Securities and Exchange Commission. The press then reported that Goldfine had paid for a "sheaf of hotel bills, an oriental rug and other gifts. . . ." Somehow, the $69 vicuna coat that Adams received from Goldfine seemed to impact Americans harder than anything else. Vicuna was considered a luxury that most Americans could not afford in 1958. And considering Nixon's reference in his 1952 Checkers speech to his wife Pat's "Republican cloth coat," the gift seemed more important to the American people than anything else that had changed hands.[99] As the scandal widened, it became more and more difficult for the president to stand behind his trusted aide.

Eventually, Adams admitted to receiving the gifts with an almost amoral attitude toward the entire event. He insisted that the gifts were simply part of a reciprocal, personal relationship, and he denied using his influence to Goldfine's benefit. Adams did, however, make inquiries on Goldfine's behalf to the FTC and the SEC, and, apparently, he turned

Illinois Senator Everett Dirksen became one of the leaders of the Republican right in the last years of the 1950s. (Eisenhower Presidential Library and Museum, Abilene, Kansas)

over information to Goldfine that was confidential. "But I did not stop to consider," Adams wrote in his memoir, "that in making a personal [telephone] call . . . in which he was involved I might be giving the officials in the federal agency the erroneous impression that I had a personal interest in their ruling or decision on the case."[100]

There were two important political concerns in Adams's indiscretions. First, Eisenhower had claimed during his first campaign that his administration would be "as clean as a hound's tooth." That promise was in direct response to the corruption that had emerged near the end of the Truman administration. A lack of corruption, *Time* observed "was the base of the President's tremendous moral authority in the nation and the world. . . . In violating it," *Time* continued, "Sherman Adams had committed a grave impropriety."[101] The second problem was that it was an election year, and beleaguered Republicans mostly from the party's right wing, wanted Adams, a moderate, gone from the White House before they began their campaigning.

In a press conference, the president conceded that Adams may have shown some bad judgment, but, he added, "I need him."[102] But as the scandal grew in the press it was apparent that Adams would have to go. Eisenhower sent Nixon to do the dirty work of convincing Adams to resign for the good of the administration. But Adams refused to step aside. The president then sent Meade Alcorn, the chairman of the Republican Party, to explain to Adams that his presence in the administration in an election year was damaging the party's prospects. Adams finally agreed to resign on September 22. He then went on television to explain his side of the story.[103]

‡

Just as the budget fight ended and the events in Little Rock calmed, the situation in the Middle East flared up again, and then the nation dipped into another economic downturn—that developed into a full-blown recession by 1958. Fueled by a drop in production of durable goods and a declining demand for commodities and other raw materials, the expanding recession pushed unemployment to just above 7 percent, the highest rate since before the war. America's industry was hurt badly, with steel and auto production being damaged the worst, operating at about 50 percent of capacity. Auto sales were off by over 30 percent, owing in part to rising interest rates. Not surprisingly, the city of Detroit received the blunt of the crisis, with unemployment rates there soaring to over 20 percent. All that caused corporate profits across the board to fall by 25 percent, and that, in turn, led to a sharp decline in investment capital.[104]

Like most recessions, the impact was spotty. The industries hit worst included durable goods, lumber, metals, mining, and textiles. Agriculture and general retail sales were impacted less. Job losses were heaviest in the Northeast industrial states, the steel- and automobile-producing regions of the Midwest, and the mining and lumber districts of the West. The South felt little impact, with the notable exception of the textile regions of the Piedmont and the mining regions of Tennessee, Kentucky, and West Virginia. Perhaps the most debilitating aspect of the recession was that Americans believed it was more than just a temporary downturn, that it was the beginning of another Great Depression and that high unemployment and tight money might drag on for years. In March 1958, 40 percent of Americans who were polled responded that the economy was the nation's biggest problem, while only 17 percent were worried about international relations and the need for a lasting peace.[105]

At first, Eisenhower had no response, encouraging widespread doubts about his leadership at a time when the American people were looking to the president for answers. He even refused to recognize the recession until the late fall 1957; and then in early 1958, he said simply that he would do nothing to solve the problem. In his diary he wrote, "We are basically conservative. . . . We believe in private enterprise rather than a 'government' campaign to provide the main strength of recovery forces. We want to avoid a succession of budgetary deficits because of the inflationary effect."[106] He hoped the crisis would pass.

Johnson saw the recession as an opportunity to shore up his relationship with the liberals and the Democratic Advisory Council, build a record for his party for the coming elections (1958 and 1960), and even place himself in a position to run for his party's presidential nomination in 1960. All of this would, of course, come at the expense of Eisenhower and the Republicans, who seemed willing to do little more than allow the recession to run its course.

The Democratic response was partisan. Just months before, Johnson and the Democrats had presented themselves as budget cutters, working with the GOP right to pare down Eisenhower's big spending. Now, in the face of a potentially debilitating recession, their answer was to spend their way out of economic disaster. Johnson was reading the nation well. He sold the American people on the need to cut spending from the 1958 budget, and then he turned around and contradicted himself by trying to persuade the nation of the necessity of increasing spending to rescue a sagging economy. He had managed to convince the American people that it was the Democrats, and not the Republicans, who held the keys to economic prosperity in the mid-1950s.

Johnson introduced his plan at a dinner honoring President Truman. He argued the need to double the rate of spending on the federal highway program; increase funding for public housing, military housing, and hospital construction; and increase unemployment compensation. He also proposed a bill to improve the nation's rivers and harbors, a bill to build flood control projects, and a farm bill that would freeze farm supports.[107] This was hardly a strong liberal program. The various bills were introduced individually by various congressmen with no coherent plan to target sectors of the economy for recovery. It was, in fact, more for political advantage than economic development. The Democrats, for instance, worked hard to aid farmers, a group generally not hurt by the recession, but whose votes were expected to impact the upcoming elections. River and harbor works projects allowed powerful congressmen to pack in the pork for projects in their districts and states. And southern legislators, fearing federal control of education, halted aid for school construction, a measure that might have brought tangible growth to a number of areas hit hard by the recession.

Johnson, however, worked hard to pull those bills together into a coherent recovery program. As was always the case with Johnson, his main objective was still political. As one journalist observed, he wants to "make it look as though the Democrats are doing everything, the Republicans nothing."[108] Johnson was also faced with the problem he had always faced. Controversial bills and programs had a tendency to split the Democrats into factions—factional divides that were often much worse than the Republican moderate–Old Guard split. As his party's leader in Congress, he had to keep the party together if he was going to succeed in controlling the legislative agenda. And if he intended to run for president in 1960, he needed to head a united party. For Johnson, controversy was the enemy. That was most apparent in his handling of the 1957 Civil Rights Bill. His strategy was much the same here.

The Democratic initiative, as weak as it was, forced Eisenhower to react. He vetoed several of the bills, calling them a "waste of public funds," and insisted that they would cause inflation if he allowed them to become law. As Johnson had hoped, each incident made the president appear insensitive to the needs of the American people.[109] At the first of the year, Eisenhower announced his own plan to stimulate the economy, a plan to upgrade the nation's post offices over the next several years. *Time* called that a "gimmick-ridden four year-old plan . . . that was a puny anti-recession weapon."[110] To shore up his side of the argument, Eisenhower went to the nation with a televised speech that *Time* said "came through [as] an echo of the hollow prediction popularly attributed to Herbert Hoover in the early 1930s: 'Prosperity is just around the corner.'"[111]

Eisenhower finally sent an anti-recession package to Knowland that included a recommendation for a boost in defense department spending and an increase in spending for military construction projects. He also sent a message to the Federal Reserve suggesting a cut the discount rate. But these were barely noticed in the press. The American people seemed to be waiting for the other shoe to drop, a tax cut that would pump billions into the economy and end the recession.

Nixon predicted a tax cut "[in] a few weeks," he said. But Eisenhower made it clear that he believed a tax cut was dangerous because it might lead to inflation.[112]

In June, Eisenhower simply threw up his hands and declared the recession over. A few liberals insisted that it was not, that unemployment was still high, and that such a declaration allowed the president to avoid dealing further with the problem—and bring an end to any possibility of a tax cut.[113] Paul Butler accused Eisenhower of depriving the nation of the public programs necessary for prosperity. Truman blamed the administration for high prices, high unemployment, and high taxes. And Johnson accused Eisenhower of maligning a Democratic program that was designed to help the people and bring an end to the recession.[114]

The recession became the primary issue of the approaching 1958 campaign, along with *Sputnik* and Sherman Adams's resignation. All three of these issues had brought into question Eisenhower's leadership. In addition, big business had chosen the 1958 campaign to launch a series of statewide "right-to-work" laws, outlawing compulsory union membership. Organized labor, mostly outside the big political fights since the late 1940s but still a powerful political entity, reared up and prepared for an all-out political battle against Republican candidates who supported "right-to-work" laws. In foreign affairs, there was another crisis in the Formosa Straits. There, renewed shelling by the Beijing government of the little islands of Quemoy and Matsu reminded voters that Eisenhower still had no solution for what was being called "the China problem."[115]

In addition, the recession had dragged American industries down to less than 70 percent of their total capacities, and unemployment had jumped to above 7 percent. The *Sputnik* launches seemed to confirm what Democrats had been saying for some time, that Eisenhower had let the nation get behind the Soviets. By mid-July, political pundits were predicting that the Democrats would pick up a significant number of seats in the coming election, particularly in the House.[116] There was talk of a landslide and even a realignment of the national party system. For many Democrats, vivid recollections of the majority congresses in the 1930s and 1940s wound them up.

Republicans tried to counterattack in the face of certain defeat. In a White House conference in early October, GOP leaders produced a document insisting that a Democratic victory would "lead the nation down the left lane which leads inseparably to socialism." In Baltimore, Eisenhower called Democrats "political free spenders," "radicals," "extremists," and "gloomdogglers."[117] The attacks seemed to work. As the election got close, the press agreed that the Republicans were beginning to gain back ground. At the same time, the economy had begun to bounce back. "Prosperity is rising," *Time* reported. "[U]nemployment is dropping, and the Republicans have gained points because they have refused to push the panic button on emergency tax cuts and all-out Government spending. . . ." They have stood "firm on the doctrine that a sound economy would lead to a solid return to prosperity."[118]

Rayburn responded to Eisenhower's attacks, saying that the president had gone "pretty far in accusing us of being radicals and left-wingers." But, he added, "in the past about 85 percent of the time Eisenhower's programs

were just an extension of Democratic principles."[119] But for Rayburn and the Democratic leadership, the prospect of an election landslide did not necessarily bring thoughts of a new New Deal. Rayburn, particularly, understood the difficulty of trying to keep a large majority in line. "I'd just as soon not have that many Democrats," he told a colleague. "Believe me, they'll be hard to handle. It won't be easy."[120]

It was a landslide. In the Senate, the Democrats went from a narrow two-seat majority to an overwhelming majority of thirty seats. In the House, the Democratic majority jumped from a solid 234–201 to a crushing 282–154. At the state level, the Democrats gained five governorships for a national total of thirty-five.[121] Bill Knowland ran for governor of his home state of California, and the California governor, Goodwin Knight, ran for Knowland's Senate seat. Both lost. Nine Republican incumbents lost their seats in the Senate, including John Bricker. The only bright spot for the Republicans was Nelson Rockefeller's election as the governor of New York.[122] If there was a decisive factor for the Democrats, it was the recession. The economic downturn had been the most severe in thirty-eight out of the forty-nine House districts in which the Democrats defeated Republican incumbents.[123]

Of those Republicans who did win, most were moderates like Rockefeller, Pennsylvania's Hugh Scott, and Oregon's Mark Hatfield. The real losers were those on the far right, including Bricker, Nevada's George Malone, Indiana's Harold Handley, Knowland, and Chapman Rivercomb from West Virginia.

Eisenhower did little in the campaign; he made only three trips and spoke in only six states. He appeared on television in a "people ask the president" format. But the process appeared contrived and uninteresting. In response to those who criticized the president for his lack of campaigning, White House aides insisted that the president's modest efforts might well have saved the Republicans from losing another twenty seats in the House.[124] It was clear, however, that the president had not responded adequately to a number of issues that affected the nation. If it were true in past elections that the voters had liked Ike but not the Republicans, it seemed true after 1958 that they liked neither.

By the end of 1958 it was apparent that the Eisenhower administration was on a very slow descent. Crises had not been managed well, and it had become apparent to the American voter that the president's management style of allowing events to resolve themselves was not adequate. The volatile and difficult situations had included the incidents at Little Rock, the *Sputnik* challenge, the budget and the recession, and the Sherman Adams scandal. Eisenhower had allowed each of these situations to run their course with little interference or even involvement. The recession and the Adams scandal did, for the most part, resolve themselves without the president's interference. But the nation's race relations grew worse without presidential input; and without any assertions from the White House to the contrary, the American people began to fear for their safety in light of apparent Soviet technological and scientific advances. Eisenhower, in 1953, had brought to the nation a sense of safety and moderation, but by 1958 the American people were beginning to grow tired of (what was slowly becoming) an inactive presidency.

In addition, the president's lame duck status and his waning popularity among voters had allowed the opposition (among Johnson and the Democrats and among his own party members) to rise up and make a series of successful attacks on the administration. At the same time, the right wing within the Republican Party was beginning its ascendency. The right had not fared well in the 1958 elections, but many of those losses served to allow a younger generation (mostly from the West) to replace the old-line conservatives from the Midwest. As the Republican Party became more conservative, and as Eisenhower became less effective as a party leader, the Republican Party began its slow realignment that purged the moderate Northeast and brought together the more conservative coalition of the West, the South, and the old Midwest conservatives.

CHAPTER SIX

Bipartisanship in Decline—and the Election of 1960

The day after the 1958 midterm elections, in which Democrats won in a landslide, Eisenhower was mad. "Pretty bad, wasn't it?" he said to his press secretary. Then he added, "I'm going on the attack . . . [and] relate every bit of legislation from now on to the pocketbook of the individual American. I'm going to put a price tag on everything." He believed that the Democrats had done well in the elections because of their populist campaign strategy of forcing him to veto their expensive social programs. That had made the Republicans appear insensitive to the needs of the American people.[1] Eisenhower must also have realized that the new Congress, with its large Democratic majorities, would no longer need to work with Republican moderates to pass legislation.

At the same time, the new Congress was not necessarily prepared to jump on Lyndon Johnson's bandwagon in the Senate—or onto Rayburn's in the House. Immediately, factions developed within the party, and as Rayburn predicted, a small majority was much easier to organize and control than a party with a large majority. In addition, liberals generally disliked Johnson's leadership; they had (for six years) considered the Democratic leader much too conservative in the face of Republican control of the White House. He had, in fact, killed or weakened a number of liberal bills since he became leader, all in the interest of bipartisanship and compromise. Five of the fifteen new Democrats who came to the Senate following the 1958 elections were avowed liberals, Young Turks who immediately allied themselves with the old liberals like Douglas and Kefauver. Together this new liberal coalition began pushing back against Johnson's leadership—and his strategy of working with the president against Republican conservatives.

Liberals inside Johnson's circle of advisors tried to get him to see the new order and to change his strategy to meet it. James Rowe wrote to Johnson just after the election: "You know there has been this undercurrent of emotion against your leadership in the past six years. . . . [I]t is much stronger today," he added, "than it has ever been in the past."[2] In fact, the liberals within the Democratic Party (not unlike the conservatives in the Republican Party) were beginning to assert themselves, weakening Johnson's power and eroding the political center. Johnson, however, was slow to change. When Joe Clark (a newly elected liberal Democrat from Pennsylvania) combined his forces with a group of other liberals to insist that Johnson appoint more liberals to the Senate Policy Planning Committee, thus giving liberals a greater voice in the Senate leadership, Johnson refused.[3] On February 23, all this came to a head when William Proxmire, a party liberal who had replaced Joe McCarthy as the junior senator from Wisconsin, complained on the Senate floor that Johnson's "one-man" rule should be replaced by regular party caucuses. Two weeks later he said, again on the floor of the Senate, that Johnson had been making party policy "on an ad-lib, off-the-cuff basis." He agreed that Johnson's methods were "a brilliantly instinctive performance by a man who has been called an authentic political genius." But he went on to criticize Johnson for his lack of response to other Democratic senators, party factions, and to the party's basic platform. Then he added, "Unless we stop this trend, more and more crucial matters will be decided over the telephone, in the cloakroom or almost any private place where dissent can be silenced without public knowledge." There were other critics. Oregon's Wayne Morse said Johnson was a "Charlie McCarthy in a political ventriloquist act." The reference was that Johnson was the dummy and Eisenhower was the ventriloquist, the real talent pulling the strings and doing all the talking. And Michigan Democrat Pat McNamara accused Johnson of directly and intentionally blocking all liberal legislation.[4] The Democratic Party's political center was beginning to collapse.

Johnson finally responded, not by attacking the liberals, but by attacking Eisenhower and the Republicans. At an AFL-CIO rally, he accused them of blocking "prudent proposals to expand the economy of our country."[5] He followed by introducing a program designed to meet liberal demands—one that would directly oppose the administration's agenda. The idea seemed to energize party leaders, but when the president complained about the cost of such a program, Johnson backed off.

By mid-March 1959, Lyndon Johnson still looked like the party leader on the Senate floor, but he was quickly losing his grip on his party's legislative machinery to the surging liberals. He had been a genius at keeping Senate Democrats together when the majority was small and every vote counted. Now, in 1959, with a Democratic majority of over two-thirds in the Senate, and with a liberal faction within the party on the ascendency, any attempt by Johnson to keep the party together was nearly impossible.

At the same time, Eisenhower was also weakened badly—both in Congress and in his own party. Several Republican Party leaders, particularly on the right, had come to see him as inattentive to their needs, and they blamed the November defeats on his willingness to work too closely with Johnson and the Democrats. The 1958 elections marked an end to Eisenhower's time as a popular vote-getter, with long coattails that could keep Republicans (of all types) in office. The GOP right had opposed his moderation since 1953. Now they emerged in open revolt against the administration.

Eisenhower and the Eisenhower presidency were in the process of changing. Sherman Adams had been the focus of Eisenhower's liberal conscience. Now that he was gone, and not really replaced, conservatives close to the president began to assert themselves. Chief among this group was Treasury Secretary Robert Anderson. In addition, Eisenhower was, himself, becoming more and more conservative. Under Anderson's influence, the president had begun to see budget balancing as an economic necessity, even a sacred cause that he would fight for, even as Republican strength waned in the face of Democratic (and progressively more liberal) economic programs.

The Republican Party was also changing. It was becoming more conservative, with competent conservatives replacing incompetent ones. In the Senate, Everett Dirksen had replaced the always-difficult Bill Knowland as the party leader. Dirksen often voted with the Old Guard, but he consistently supported the president on economic issues and had gone down the line with Eisenhower in the budget battle. *Time* magazine called him "a much smoother operator than the bumbling" Knowland.[6] And in the House, Charles Halleck of Indiana had replaced Joseph Martin as the Republican leader. Halleck's leadership was stronger and more attentive to an overall Republican program and strategy. In addition, the Republicans were in the minority. Not unlike the Democrats in the early years of the decade, there was a sense that they had to unite their forces, circle their wagons, if they were to put up any effective display of opposition. Even though congressional conservatives baulked at Eisenhower's moderation, they were willing to work with the president on most issues. By June, *Time* saw the party unity: "This year, with [Charles] Halleck [in the House], and with Illinois's Everett Dirksen replacing Knowland in the Senate, the Republicans in the White House and on Capitol Hill work as an effective team." The president had even come to admire Halleck, calling him a "political genius."[7]

It was the battle over the next budget, however, that brought the two interparty conflicts to a head. The president insisted that his 1960 budget be balanced. This would be his last budget, or at least the last budget he would administer in its entirety, and he wanted to leave office with a balanced bank account. He also wanted to cut taxes before he left office. He had, in fact, promised tax cuts in his January 1959 State of the Union message and then later in other speeches, always making it clear that he considered inflation to be the real enemy of prosperity and that it could be controlled only through fiscal responsibility.[8]

While the 1960 budget was being debated, the 1959 budget was getting out of hand, with deficits running over $12 billion, including defense spending that was finally $1.4 billion above the original estimate. Most of the Pentagon overruns could be traced to increased missile production, an unexpected military crisis in Lebanon, and anticipated conflicts with China over the contested islands of Quemoy and Matsu. It was farm subsidies, however, that had caused the greatest overrun, adding nearly $2 billion to the budget.[9]

Balancing the budget would be difficult, at least because the Democratic majority in Congress was much more interested in social programs than achieving a balanced budget. In fact, liberal Democrats in the House cheered approvingly as the first bills were passed that shot beyond the administration's budget requests. Charles Halleck warned, "the budget busters are on the move." In addition, there were demands from the military for a more effective (and expensive) space program; and there were increasing demands from farmers for higher subsidies.[10]

Eisenhower sent to Congress a request for a balanced budget of $77 billion. During the next few months, he vetoed one Democratic-sponsored bill after another, including two bills each for increased spending for housing and agriculture. In his veto messages he argued, simply, that the nation could not afford such expenses. Congressional Democrats often cut the costs of these bills hoping to gain enough support to override the president's veto, but they were not successful. Johnson complained that Eisenhower's actions were "government by threat of veto."[11] By the time Congress adjourned their first session in the fall, they had hardly increased spending at all. In fact, there was a budget surplus of $1.3 billion.[12]

Eisenhower's balanced budget also did not sit well with all Republicans. Nixon, for one, believed that a balanced budget would damage the GOP by placing too little emphasis on social programs, or what he called "dynamic programs."[13] Nixon, of course, intended to run for president in 1960, and he did not want to run on a program of fiscal retrenchment, a program that would be unpopular with many voters. There were others who believed much the same, including Eisenhower's Labor Secretary James Mitchell, Attorney General William Rogers, and a very vocal Senator George Aiken from Vermont. But it was Treasury Secretary Robert Anderson and Budget Director Maurice Stans who had the president's ear, and they pushed for a balanced budget.

‡

Through 1957 and 1958, Johnson continued to insist that he did not want to run for president in 1960, but, not surprisingly, few believed him. "[I am] not a candidate," he told a group of Democrats in Albuquerque. "[I] would not be a candidate and would not permit anyone to make me a candidate."[14] But Johnson continued to make noises about running. In late 1958, he decided he needed some foreign policy experience. Eisenhower had, after all, orchestrated the nation's foreign policy (mostly with approval from his own party and moderate Democrats) since he came to office in 1953. Thus, Johnson (and the other Democrats) had been kept out of the foreign policy loop. With the election approaching, Johnson realized that (if he decided to run) he would be vulnerable without some foreign policy background. In mid-November he spoke at the United Nations on America's role in space.[15] Then later that month he traveled to Mexico to speak with that country's president-elect, Adolfo Lopez Mateos, about international trade.[16]

Johnson began moving toward a candidacy in other ways. A few weeks after his trip to Mexico, he joined the Western Regional Conference of Democrats, again attempting to throw off his "southern-ness" and embracing a western character that most believed was a reasonable route to the presidency. The press realized the significance. *Time* reported, "Political geographers, noting that the road to the White House is impassable from the South but wide open from the West, suspect that Johnson might have more than one reason for his western shift in thinking." The magazine added that Johnson had stopped meeting with the southern caucus "a couple of years ago."[17]

American presidential candidates have often appeared shy about running for office—at least in this period in history. If for no other reason, they did not want to seem overly ambitious. The ultimate honor was to be drafted, to be asked to come to the aid of your party (or better, the nation). Both Eisenhower and Stevenson, in 1952 and again in 1956, sat back, denied their desire to run, and appeared to wait for the convention to come to them. But Johnson's reluctance was real; he was, actually, conflicted about running in 1960. George Reedy blamed Johnson's indecisions on his inner demons. Johnson "*was* flirting with the idea of a presidential race [in 1960] but only half flirting," Reedy wrote in his memoir. "It was a period in which he put on one of the greatest Jekyll-Hyde shows in history. He would authorize the establishment of a campaign headquarters and then refuse to allow it to do anything. He would authorize his staff to draw up campaign proposals and then forbid any action. . . ."[18]

Johnson may have decided to run for president simply because he believed he had done all he could in the Senate. His power as leader was being usurped by the liberal Young Turks, and he was on the verge of being marginalized. "I am quite convinced of this point," Reedy recalled. "[B]ecause strange things began to happen during the last two years of his Senate leadership. He lost votes that he should not have lost, he made enemies that he should not have made."[19] His genius of building political coalitions out of a thin majority of senators was no longer valuable in a Senate controlled by a large Democratic majority, and a party on the verge of being dominated by liberals.

Also, Johnson could not abide failure. It was a thread that ran through his entire life. In January 1959, Stewart Alsop, writing in the *Saturday Evening Post* just as the 1960 campaign got underway, insisted that Johnson's "hatred of failure" would not allow him "to become an active candidate and thus risk the humiliation" of losing.[20]

Even as the 1964 election approached, with a landslide victory at his fingertips, he told Reedy and several others that he would not run, and he was so emphatic that he convinced people around him that he was serious about the decision.[21]

Johnson decided that he would run for the presidency by continuing to be the most effective majority leader in American history. Most likely he hoped that the American people would see that, see his value as a national leader who could reach out, compromise, and hold a balance in the Senate. He would be a James Madison or a Henry Clay. But by 1960, presidential campaigns were changing. The campaign that year would be more about image than issues, more about candidate appeal and the power of the media than about legislative leadership. Johnson's strategy of presenting himself to voters as the grand legislator would not go far enough. He was also a moderate among moderates, in a political would in which moderation was being usurped by the growth of extremist wings of both parties. His time was passing.

‡

When Eisenhower came to office in 1953, he declared in his first State of the Union address that the Taft-Hartley Act "has shown the need for some corrective action, and we should promptly proceed to amend the act."[22] Taft-Hartley was enacted as the Labor Management Act of 1947 and was designed to weaken the New Deal–era Wagner Act of 1935, which gave workers the right to join unions and to strike. In June 1947, the Republican-controlled 80th Congress passed Taft-Hartley, immediately described by organized labor as the "Slave Labor Act." It allowed the president to appoint a board of inquiry to investigate disputes, seek injunctions, and call for "cooling off" periods. It also outlawed the closed shop and secondary boycotts.[23] Even Robert Taft, the chief architect of Taft-Hartley, had come to believe in his last years that the law needed amending, that it was, in fact, too restrictive on labor. Eisenhower saw himself standing somewhere between the nation's pro-labor and the pro-business forces, an example of his Middle Way.

In 1953, Eisenhower named Martin Durkin as his secretary of labor, a Democrat who had headed the AFL's Plumber's Union. It seemed like a bipartisan gesture, an attempt to reach out to the other side, but the decision caused problems. The president set up a committee to recommend changes to Taft-Hartley. The result was nineteen recommendations. The report was leaked to the press; Eisenhower insisted that the report was not yet ready for public consumption and that there would be additional changes. Durkin saw this as undercutting his position, and he resigned under protest.[24]

Eisenhower continued on his Middle Way on the Taft-Hartley issue, explaining in his diary how he felt about the bill: "I am personally opposed to the principle of the closed shop and would not find it possible to approve a federal bill containing such a provision. At the same time," he added, "I believe . . . unions to be an absolutely essential factor of modern industrial life in order that men who work may be assured of fair wages, proper working conditions, and other benefits that flow to them as a body."[25]

In 1954, Eisenhower proposed fourteen amendments to Taft-Hartley, but he excluded the amendment that would have prohibited states from passing "right-to-work" laws. The bill was killed in the Senate by a coalition of conservative Republicans and southern Democrats. In his State of the Union addresses in 1955 and again in 1956, the president asked that Congress amend Taft-Hartley, but Congress took no action, and the president generally dropped the issue.[26]

Labor legislation, with minor exceptions, lay dormant until revelations emerged that several unions, particularly Jimmy Hoffa's Teamsters, were mismanaging their pension funds. In 1957, the Senate's Select Committee on Improper Activities in the Labor and Management Field, headed by Arkansas Senator John McClellan, held a series of hearings that revealed widespread corruption and organized crime influence inside several unions. The McClellan Committee's chief counsel, Robert Kennedy, targeted Hoffa and the Teamsters, leading to their expulsion from the AFL-CIO.[27]

The next year, John Kennedy, in an attempt to boost his presidential prospects, introduced a bill to impede the power of organized crime inside unions. The bill, introduced with Republican senator Irving Ives, was pushed through the Senate by Johnson. It was generally a mild reform bill that did little to curtail the power of the unions. But it did give Kennedy a major legislative success, something he lacked as he headed toward the 1960 campaign. The Kennedy-Ives bill, however, died in the House where a coalition of pro-business and pro-union representatives considered the bill either too harsh or too mild. Northern Democrats charged that conservative Republicans killed the bill because they wanted strong anti-labor legislation, while Eisenhower insisted that liberal Democrats killed it because they wanted a weaker bill.[28]

The question of corruption in the unions, however, remained in the air. In March 1959 Kennedy and North Carolina Democrat Sam Ervin introduced another anti-corruption bill. Republicans were willing to allow it to pass, but insisted it still did little to curtail union power. Eisenhower also wanted a stronger bill, and on August 6, 1959, he went on television and insisted that Congress enact a labor law to eliminate the racketeering and corruption exposed by the McClellan Committee. He associated corruption with organized crime inside the unions, calling the problem a "national disgrace," and said it was time to pass a law that would "protect the American people from the gangsters, racketeers, and other corrupt elements who have invaded the labor management field." He also called for an end to such "coercive" practices as secondary boycotts and blackmail picketing.[29]

By 1959, Eisenhower had become more conservative on economic issues, and that clearly included his outlook on organized labor. In the early years of his administration, he wanted to maintain a balance on labor-management issues—truly a Middle Way between the two sides that would give ground to labor's demands and needs, even to the point of naming a union official to his cabinet. But by 1959, his tone had changed considerably; he had grown increasingly hostile to the nation's unions and their legislative demands. That shift was undoubtedly caused by the corruption uncovered by the McClellan Committee, but a number of moderating influences no longer impacted the president. Taft's death and Sherman Adams's resignation quieted the most moderate voices around him, and that void allowed for the increased influence of the conservatives in his administration. In addition, party conservatives in Congress like Barry Goldwater were gaining influence, and they were not sympathetic to the needs of organized labor.

Senator Lyndon Johnson celebrates his fifty-second birthday with his good friend, Illinois Senator Everett Dirksen.   (Lyndon Baines Johnson Presidential Library, Austin, Texas)

Just as liberals in the Democratic Party were pushing Johnson to set a more liberal agenda for the coming presidential campaign, conservative Republicans were pushing Eisenhower to adopt a more conservative stance. Perhaps more importantly, the results of the 1958 elections had removed the need for Democratic moderates like Johnson to work with the president to reach their legislative objectives; no longer was it important for moderate Republicans to work with moderate Democrats to find common ground, to compromise, and to work out their differences to get legislation passed. For the first time since 1953, the Democrats did not need Eisenhower; and thus Eisenhower felt no need to work with the Democrats. At the same time, GOP conservatives no longer needed Eisenhower's coattails to hold their seats in Congress. The result was a more conservative Republican Party led by a growing conservative leadership in Congress; and a Democratic Party that was in the process of rejecting Johnson's leadership and becoming increasingly more liberal. The Middle Way was eroding rapidly. Issues surrounding organized labor made that increasingly clear.

A second labor bill was introduced in 1959, one much preferred by the president over the Kennedy-Ives bill. The bill was introduced by Georgia Democrat Phil Landrum and Michigan Republican Robert Griffin. The Landrum-Griffin bill included much of the anti-racketeering, anti-corruption language from the Kennedy-Ervin bill, but it also contained anti-labor provisions favored by Eisenhower. Added were sections prohibiting blackmail picketing and secondary boycotts.[30]

Along with Kennedy-Ervin and Landrum-Griffin was a third labor bill sponsored by senators Don Shelly and James Roosevelt, both California Democrats. Conservatives, however, believed that the Shelly-Roosevelt bill was inadequate in dealing with corruption in the unions. After some heated discussion in the House, Landrum-Griffin passed, and then in the Senate. The president signed the bill on September 14.[31]

‡

By mid-July 1960 the Democrats had jumped ahead of the Republicans in a national poll as the party best able to deal with the world situation.[32] This was an amazing turn of events, considering Eisenhower's past popularity and reputation as a military strategist, and the Republican Party's place as the harbinger of national security. Most Americans saw Eisenhower as a combination of both comfortable in domestic policy and firm in dealing with world affairs. Under Eisenhower's protection, so it seemed, the people of the nation need not worry about the world's problems.

At the same time, the Democrats, since the war, had been forced to fend off nearly constant accusations of being too "soft" in the world of diplomacy, of allowing the nation's enemies too much advantage in a weak attempt to negotiate and find common ground. As the 1960 election approached, however, the Democrats had managed to eclipse the Republicans as the party most able to deal with the nation's enemies. Mostly, this sentiment resulted from Eisenhower's mishandling of the

Sputnik launch in 1957 and then the Cuban Revolution, an event that occurred just as Eisenhower was leaving office in the months before the 1960, presidential election. In both cases, Eisenhower told the American people that there was really nothing to worry about—which turned out to be something less than a complete explanation of events. The result was that the American people began, really for the first time, to question Eisenhower and his ability to deal with international affairs.

In January 1959, Cuban revolutionary Fidel Castro entered Havana after defeating the armies of Cuba's corrupt and reactionary dictator Fulgencio Batista. Batista saw the end coming and fled to Dominican Republic; in mid-February, Castro was sworn in as Cuba's prime minister. He immediately initiated a land-reform policy that expropriated private property, although he continued to deny accusations that he was a communist. In April, he visited New York in a celebrated whirlwind tour. He apparently intended to meet with Eisenhower in Washington, but the president chose, instead, to play golf. Castro considered the president's choice a snub, but he finally met with the vice president at the White House. Following the three-hour meeting, Nixon said that he thought Castro did not really understand communism and was probably not a communist.[33]

Eisenhower responded with a customary holding action in hopes that a third choice in Cuba might appear, a figure or group that would cast itself somewhere between the corrupt and rightist Batista, and Castro—who had maintained an anti-American sentiment that included talk of a redistribution of wealth in Cuba. Meanwhile, Castro began to drift into the Soviet sphere. In February 1960, the Soviets signed an agreement with Cuba to buy Cuban sugar. In exchange, Cuba was to receive Soviet oil. When American oil refineries in Cuba refused to refine the Soviet oil, Castro nationalized the refineries. Eisenhower responded by cutting U.S. purchase of Cuban sugar. Soviet premier Nikita Khrushchev announced that Moscow would purchase all sugar produced in Cuba. By late summer, 1960, Khrushchev had announced that he would defend Cuba from an American invasion with rockets, if necessary.

Eisenhower liked the idea of dealing with anti-communist dictators through clandestine CIA-sponsored missions. It was inexpensive, more often than not decisive, and generally under the political radar. In 1953, a CIA-led operation removed Mohammed Mossedegh from power in Iran. In 1954 another CIA-led mission overthrew Jacabo Arbenz in Guatemala with little more than a few CIA-flown, vintage P-47s. Not surprisingly, Eisenhower looked to those easy successes as a formula for dealing with Castro. But those around him insisted that removing Castro by force without a viable, American-sponsored replacement might bring to power someone even worse than Castro. So, Eisenhower waited.[34]

In January 1960, Eisenhower visited several Latin American nations in an attempt to counter Castro's growing popularity and convince those nations that the United States was a good friend and a good neighbor. He was generally unsuccessful. In March 1960, in the midst of the presidential campaign, the president approved a CIA-directed program that included an attempted assassination of Castro. The plan also called for the organization and training of an anti-Castro paramilitary force for the eventual invasion of Cuba. When Eisenhower left office at the beginning of 1961 that program remained in place, but not executed. As the 1960 election approached a growing number of American voters came to believe that Eisenhower had mishandled the situation in Cuba, and they began to look to the Democrats to deal with that situation. Eisenhower is also often criticized for handing over to the next president an unresolved situation in Cuba.[35]

‡

One of Eisenhower's greatest defeats in the 86th Congress was the Senate's rejection of Lewis Strauss for Commerce Secretary. Strauss had headed the Atomic Energy Commission for five years, and Eisenhower expected an easy confirmation for such a seasoned public servant. But Strauss was arrogant, combative, and aggressively conservative in the face of an increasingly liberal Senate. Strauss was also responsible for labeling J. Robert Oppenheimer, the leader of the Manhattan Project, as a national security

risk, leading to the revocation of Oppenheimer's security clearance and generally ending his career. Liberals saw this as a ridiculous overreaction to a few of Oppenheimer's prewar associations and even an extension of McCarthyism. Strauss was also an outspoken opponent of public power, and he had resisted congressional oversight into the development of atomic energy.[36] Despite the obvious conflict, few expected Strauss's nomination to be rejected.

Johnson disliked Strauss, although he assumed he would be approved; Johnson had even counseled Strauss that his approval was nearly inevitable. In the final vote, however, Johnson voted against Strauss's nomination and saw to it that the other Senate Democrats did the same. For Johnson, it was a good choice. By doing so, he lined up with his party's liberals, and because of Strauss's ultraconservatism, Johnson really offended no one in his own party. Had Johnson supported the nomination, the liberal outcry against him would have certainly increased and probably ended his chance's of being nominated for president in 1960.[37]

Strauss's nomination was rejected in mid-June. It angered Eisenhower, who blamed Johnson for Strauss's defeat. The president, however, had done nothing to see that Strauss was approved. He called it the "most shameful day in Senate history."[38]

The coming presidential campaign put the brakes on most legislation coming out of the 86th Congress. Neither party wanted to give the other an advantage by allowing it to pass significant legislation in an election year. Besides Landrum-Griffin, the only other important legislation to pass Congress in 1959 and 1960 was Hawaiian statehood. Other legislation included a $750 million pay raise for federal employees, which was passed—over the president's veto. Congress also passed the president's defense budget mostly intact, but the next year, 1960, congressional Democrats added another $600 million to the budget to combat the so-called "missile gap." Real or imagined, the "missile gap" would become an important issue in the 1960 campaign.

The 1960 Civil Rights Act has been mostly overlooked as just another bill that angered southerners and split the Democrats, while doing little to ameliorate the problems of racial inequality and voter rights in the

South. It is, however, a good example of Johnson's waning abilities in the Senate to keep civil rights legislation off the table in his increasingly failed attempts to keep the Democrats united. The bill allowed for federal inspections of voter registration polls and rolls and assigned penalties to anyone obstructing a citizens' right to vote. The bill's greatest claim to fame was that southern Democrats managed to sustain the longest filibuster in the history of the Senate in an attempt to kill the bill, forty-three hours between February 29 and March 3, 1960. The bill passed and was signed by the president on May 6, 1960. Despite the passage of both the 1957 and 1960 civil rights acts, voting among African Americans in the South in the 1960 presidential election increased by only about 3 percent, leading to the erroneous argument that African Americans in the South did not want the right to vote.

Congress met in August following the party conventions; each party stymied the initiatives of the other to make certain that no one got a political advantage. The Democratic candidate, John Kennedy, tried to push a minimum wage bill through the Senate, but it was killed by conservatives in the House. Medical care for the aged was killed in the Senate, and a school construction bill died in the House. Congress adjourned on September 1, and the campaign began in earnest.[39]

‡

Massachusetts Senator John Kennedy had been, more or less, unofficially running for the Democratic nomination since the 1956 vice presidential convention floor fight. His political organization in 1960 was unparalleled, and, of course, his pockets were deep. But it would take more than just good political organization and Joe Kennedy's money to make him president. He had to convince party leaders that he could attract voters. To that end, Kennedy decided the key to his nomination was in the primaries, and just after announcing his candidacy in early January 1960, he said that any candidate who did not run in the primaries did not deserve the Democratic Party's nomination. It was obvious that he was pointing directly at Johnson. For Kennedy, running in a series of primaries and showing his face to the voting public (who generally did not know him) was a major advantage over a candidate like Johnson, who chose to remain in Washington in hopes that his successes in running the Senate would be enough to garner voter appeal.

As the campaign progressed, a stop-Kennedy movement emerged, mostly designed to further Johnson's candidacy, but it was poorly organized, and Johnson did almost nothing to advance the effort. He had not yet made the transition to the new politics of television; he campaigned as politicians had campaigned for decades, presenting himself as a statesman and waiting for the campaign and the nomination to come to him. In fact, the nomination of Kennedy rather than Johnson in 1960 can be seen as an example of the new style of campaigning prevailing over the old, the future replacing the past. A strong record in Washington was no longer enough.

Eisenhower was expected to choose a successor—endorse a candidate to carry on his moderate policies. But for Eisenhower in 1960, that impulse was not particularly strong; he felt no real need to name a successor or even to place his stamp on Nixon. As he told Swede Hazlett as the 1956 campaign got underway: "I have failed to bring forward and establish a logical successor for myself."[40]

Eisenhower liked Nixon well enough. The vice president had done his job, served the administration well, and to Eisenhower those were good traits. But he also saw the office of the president as a particularly difficult job, one that took specific skills and a certain temperament. He really never believed that Nixon had acquired those qualities. In 1952, Eisenhower considered dumping Nixon over the slush fund scandal, and then again in 1956 he entertained thoughts of naming another running mate. In 1960, the situation had really not changed much. Nixon would, of course, make the run, and if Eisenhower gave his enthusiastic endorsement, he would win the nomination. But Eisenhower simply did not have enough confidence in Nixon to give over a full-scale presidential endorsement.

All this placed Nixon, again, in a difficult situation. Eisenhower's approval numbers had fallen, but he was still a major player in the Republican Party and in national politics. Without that "arm around the candidate" endorsement from Eisenhower, Nixon could easily lose the election; with an enthusiastic presidential endorsement, he would certainly win. With an endorsement from the president that was less than enthusiastic, the election could go either way. And Nixon had other problems. As vice president, he represented the Eisenhower administration; it was part of his job to support and defend the administration's policies. But he was also a candidate who was running for office on his own merits. He had to show that he had his own ideas and that he was independent, or the Democrats would rip him apart for being little more than an extension of Eisenhower.[41]

Eisenhower seemed to understand all this. He stayed clear of much of the campaign, his brother Milton said in an interview, "at least in part to allow Nixon to show himself as a leader on his own. . . ."[42] Eisenhower may have understood that, but every time Nixon made a campaign statement that varied from the Eisenhower script, the president made it clear that he thought Nixon was ungrateful and trying to dismantle his policies.

Part of the problem came from Eisenhower's belief that the next president, whoever he was, would almost surely destroy his vision. It had been Eisenhower's primary goal to leave the nation at peace and prosperous. Prosperity meant a balanced budget that would, in turn, build business confidence. To do that, he needed to keep spending low, and that meant keeping military spending as low as possible without compromising national security. The candidates in the campaign wanted to appear strong on defense, and they argued hard for more military spending. In addition, the Republicans wanted a big tax cut, and the Democrats were clearly willing to take the budget as far out of balance as necessary to serve their social agenda and push the economy upward.

As the campaigns began to take shape, both candidates identified Eisenhower's two terms in office as the stationary years, the age of no growth and no progress—while the Soviets had made big gains in several areas. The call from both parties was to move forward again, to get the nation moving again. For Eisenhower, all of this was an abomination that threatened to undo all he had done. At the same time, he also felt that neither candidate had what it took to be the next president of the United States.

At a press conference during the earliest days of the 1960 campaign, Eisenhower was asked if he would endorse Nixon. He refused, stating "that there are a number of Republicans, eminent men, big men, that could fulfill the requirements of the position. . . ." He added that Nixon understood how he felt on this point. Then he inserted a comment that made it clear that if it had to be Nixon, he would go along. "I am not dissatisfied with the individual that looks like he will get it."[43] Again, Eisenhower refused to use his influence to effect change. He had an opportunity to lead his party and the nation into the next decade, but he responded by allowing events to take their course without his input.

While Eisenhower evaded the issue, Nixon did all he could to win the president's endorsement, including adopting a new political personality. The "New Nixon" was an Eisenhower Republican and a middle roader, although he rejected such titles, knowing full well what they meant to his party's right wing.[44] And it generally worked; he managed to embrace the party's center without alienating the right too badly— at least until the convention. Following a speech in Florida, the press noticed the difference. His tone was "leaning over backward toward moderation. . . . It was hard to believe that this was the Nixon who used to be known for his 'instinct for the jugular,' whose no-holds barred campaigns since 1946 [have] earned him the hatred of Democrats from Harry Truman and Sam Rayburn right on down." Nixon went out of his way to praise his Democratic rivals. He even called Truman a strong president and said he had "real respect" for John Kennedy.[45]

Nixon's stock had risen considerably in the summer of 1959 when he confronted Soviet Premier Nikita Khrushchev in the kitchen of a model American home display at Sokolniki Park in Moscow. Nixon attended the opening as the representative of the Eisenhower administration. In an impromptu "debate" over which economic system produced better products, Nixon held his own with the Russian Bear as the two men pointed and jabbed fingers at each other just outside the display. The Kitchen Debate was covered in the U.S. press, with photos of Nixon and Khrushchev clearly arguing. The event helped clear away the doubts that many voters had of Nixon's ability to stand up to the Soviets.[46] The "Kitchen Debate" brought Nixon strong poll numbers, shored up his relationship with the right, and showed voters that he was a leader.

Eisenhower's obvious ambivalence toward Nixon (and the campaign itself) brought Nelson Rockefeller into the campaign. In the 1958 elections, with Republicans falling like dominoes from one end of the country to the other, Rockefeller defeated Averell Harriman to become governor of New York. Rockefeller was a moderate Republican, with close ties to labor and civil rights issues. He supported most social-progressive programs, particularly federal construction of low-income housing. He also believed in a strong national defense. Almost immediately, he began running for president by making exploratory trips here and there to gauge his popularity outside the Northeast. He never entered any primaries, and he never officially announced that he would run for the nomination. By December 1959, it was clear that his candidacy was a dead issue, and he withdrew from the campaign that he had never entered.[47] But the lack of interest in his run showed that Eisenhower-style moderation (at least in the Republican Party) was on its way out the door.

By June, Eisenhower was still keeping any opinions he had about the campaign or the candidates to himself. To Rockefeller that meant that the president was looking for someone else, perhaps someone like himself, someone more moderate than Nixon. Rockefeller put in a call to the president to ask if he should make a run—obviously pining for an endorsement. Eisenhower told Rockefeller plainly that Nixon had the nomination sewn up and that if he really wanted to run for president, he should consider a run at the next opportunity, probably in 1964.[48]

As the power of the Republican right increased, the Goldwater phenomenon that would become a clap of thunder four years later was just getting underway. A small Goldwater-for-president boomlet began to gain momentum in the spring and early summer of 1960 when a few Goldwater supporters convinced the Arizona senator that Nixon was not a true Republican. In March 1960, Goldwater spoke to a crowd of supporters in South Carolina and, to his own surprise, roused them to pledge their thirteen delegates to him at the 1960 Republican convention.[49]

Adlai Stevenson had lost badly to Eisenhower in 1952 and again in 1956. Despite those trouncings, he refused, in 1960, to stand down and withdraw from the campaign. By most accounts that meant that he would run—under the right circumstances, of course, and that meant a convention draft. With Stevenson on the sidelines, refusing to commit, Johnson was Kennedy's only significant rival for the nomination. But Johnson refused to engage Kennedy in the primary battles. So, Kennedy decided to battle the man who would fight, and that was Hubert Humphrey. Humphrey wanted to run in the Wisconsin and West Virginia primaries. He believed he could win in Wisconsin because voters there were concerned with many of the same issues as voters next door in his home state of Minnesota. In West Virginia, Humphrey hoped to excite an electorate with a strong New Deal heritage, few Catholics, and a large labor vote. Humphrey was a Protestant, was strongly associated with New Deal and Fair Deal programs, and he had strong national support from organized labor. Kennedy accepted the challenges and beat Humphrey in both states.

For Kennedy, the primary campaigns (which were covered extensively in the national press) allowed him to become more and more familiar to the American people. In Wisconsin, he pounded the pavement, canvassed small towns from one end of the state to the other, and worked the neighborhoods and cafes, often in the harshest climatic conditions. In West Virginia he confronted his religion, insisting that his Catholicism would not stand in the way of his ability to govern; and he showed himself to be sympathetic to the needs of the working classes, organized labor, and the poor. His victories in Wisconsin and West Virginia removed Humphrey from the campaign, neutralized the Catholic issue, and gave Kennedy a commanding momentum that took him into the party convention with almost unbeatable strength.

At the Democratic convention in Los Angeles, it was Kennedy and Johnson who controlled the most delegates, but a stop-Kennedy movement began to coalesce around Stevenson, who still refused to campaign for the nomination or withdraw his name from contention. Stevenson's strategy was to grab the vast majority of undecided delegates following the first ballot and take the nomination on the second or third ballot.[50]

Johnson arrived having just pushed through the Senate the 1960 Civil Rights Act. The *New York Times* praised it, stating that it would lead to Johnson's nomination.[51] But Johnson still had no real chance of winning the nomination. Despite all his attempts to remove himself from his southern background, he was still stuck with the old southern conservative image in the minds of most northern politicians and northern voters. It was an image that was not popular in 1960. As Kennedy told his advisors just as Johnson announced that he would run, "Do you think that [Chicago mayor] Dick Daley or [Pennsylvania congressman] Bill Green and [New York congressman] Charles Buckley or [Michigan governor] Mennen Williams would ever accept Johnson? They know he would never get them any votes in the North in a fight against Nixon."[52] Following a last-minute push by Stevenson supporters to stop the Kennedy steamroller, Kennedy went over the top fairly easily on the first ballot.

At first glance, the convention had all the ingredients for a dramatic, old-time Democratic Party brawl. But it was quickly apparent that the Kennedy machine was unstoppable from the beginning. It was also clear that Stevenson's time had passed and that Johnson had arrived with too little too late. *Time* reported on the reality of it all: "Despite Lyndon Johnson's belated drive, despite the boisterous demonstrations for Adlai Stevenson, the efficient, machinelike Kennedy team had the nomination won before the first gavel."[53]

Kennedy's choice of Johnson as his running mate shocked northern liberal Democrats like Arthur Schlesinger, Jr., Arthur Goldberg, and Walter Reuther. Schlesinger told the press that he felt physically sick when he heard Kennedy's choice.[54] But it was the right decision. Kennedy was perceived as a liberal and a leader of the growing liberal wing of the Democratic Party. He had almost no appeal in the South, and he believed that he would need the South to win. Although Johnson had worked hard all his political life to avoid the southern conservative labels, southerners persisted in calling him one of their own, and (at least in Texas) they were willing to give him their votes. In addition, the Kennedy-Johnson ticket was almost an archetype of what a political ticket should be. Although Johnson was only a few years older than Kennedy, he looked much older and represented to America the past generation of politicians, while Kennedy represented youth, vigor, and the future. Kennedy was from the Northeast and was strong in the industrial states, popular with labor, ethnic groups, and of course, Catholics. Kennedy was also popular with liberals in his party (although at first he had some difficulty in winning many of them to his side), and he was strongly anti-communist. That combination had great appeal to many voters in 1960, who saw a need for domestic programs but had, through the decade of the 1950s, feared the Democrats' "soft" approach to what they perceived as the communist threat. Johnson's appeal just about covered the rest of the country. He was considered a conservative. He was popular in the South, the West, and large parts of the Midwest. He was popular with farmers in the West and the South—and he could carry Texas. Kennedy attracted northeastern liberals, and intellectuals. Johnson knew how to appeal to the grassroots, the average American, the farmer in the field, the southern landowner. Whatever Johnson was, Kennedy was not; whatever Kennedy was, Johnson was not. Despite the consternations of northern liberals, it was truly the perfect ticket.

‡

The Republicans assembled in Chicago to nominate Nixon, the heir apparent. Nixon's only real problem was Nelson Rockefeller. Rockefeller had already dropped out of the campaign, but as the governor of New York he was still powerful enough to force a liberalization of the Republican Party platform. Nixon, however, realized that a floor fight over Rockefeller's demands might alienate Barry Goldwater and the growing power of the Republican right.

Nixon at first tried to appease Rockefeller by awarding him the second spot on the ticket. Rockefeller, however, insisted that he was not interested and submitted his own party platform and threatened to turn any fight into a floor fight. Nixon rushed off to Rockefeller's Fifth Avenue apartment in New York to make a deal. The result was a party platform that was clearly stamped with Rockefeller's moderation. Conservatives called it "The Surrender of Fifth Avenue;" Goldwater called it the "Munich of the Republican Party." Nixon had propped up his left, but had managed to alienate his right. The event set the stage for the Republican Party for the next twenty years. Nixon would never again be trusted by his party's right wing, and the "Rockefeller wing" of the party, the moderates, would be their nemesis.[55]

Nixon received the nomination against no real contenders. At Eisenhower's insistence, he chose Henry Cabot Lodge as his running mate. Lodge was an internationalist, a northeastern moderate who had lost his Massachusetts Senate seat to Kennedy in 1952, at least in part because he had headed a "draft-Eisenhower" committee instead of attending to his own campaign. He was chosen mostly because of his foreign policy background that was intended to offset Nixon's strengths as a domestic politician. Lodge had served as Eisenhower's ambassador to the United Nations and had been seen on television often accompanied by the world's most prominent leaders.[56]

During the campaign, Kennedy seemed to make the most headway by insisting that the nation needed to get moving again under new and stronger leadership. He insisted that the United States was losing prestige abroad and that the economy was lagging at home. He also called for a stepped up defense effort to keep the United States from falling further behind the Soviets.[57]

Nixon defended the Eisenhower administration's record, but in keeping with his need to portray himself as a candidate in his own right, he said several times that it was "something to build on." Eisenhower never really endorsed Nixon, and he only entered the race on Nixon's behalf at the eleventh hour. Nixon later speculated that had the president campaigned in Illinois and Missouri, states that Nixon lost to Kennedy by razor-thin margins, that he might have won those states and the election.[58] Nixon spent most of the campaign attacking Kennedy as immature—lacking the strength to stand up to Khrushchev and the Soviets. He also called for continued fiscal responsibility and claimed that the Democratic Party platform might add as much as $18 billion to the national budget.[59]

The 1960 campaign was unique for a number of reasons, but mostly because of the televised debates. Both candidates expected the debates to aid their campaigns. Nixon saw himself as a great debater and a master of the television speech. He had arrived at that conclusion mostly because of his 1952 Checkers speech that had brought him back into Eisenhower's good graces. In fact, he believed he was so good at debating that he might sucker-punch Kennedy right out of the campaign by exposing him as inexperienced in handling and understanding of world affairs. Kennedy hoped to use the debates to show his face to an electorate who really knew little about him and to exhibit his maturity and capability—to show voters that he could be president. Kennedy's strategy worked. Nixon's did not.

The two met for four debates, one hour each. They were questioned by panels of newsmen and permitted to rebut each other's answers. Some seventy-five million Americans watched the first debate. Nixon was advised that the number of watchers would increase from the first to the last debate, but in fact, it was the first debate that drew the most attention, and the number of TV watchers declined as the debates continued.

For a series of reasons, Nixon looked awful during the crucial first debate. The lighting was so strong that it washed out his complexion; his shirt did not fit well, and the color of his suit was too light to contrast with the background. He also chose to wear heavy face makeup to hide his heavy beard, and that began to streak under the hot lights as the debate progressed. Kennedy, in turn, had spent the week before in California. He was tanned, and he looked, as producer Don Hewitt recalled, "like a young Adonis."[60]

The debates were generally a tie, in the sense that no one won or lost more "debate points" than the other. But Kennedy was able to show voters that his religion did not make him un-American, that he had mature leadership qualities, and that he was a viable candidate. His numbers rose immediately, particularly among undecided voters. It was personal image that was the deciding factor among voters, not issues. U.S. presidential campaigns would never again be the same.[61]

The largest number of voters in American history cast their votes on November 8, 1960. Kennedy took a solid majority in the Electoral College (303 to 219), but the popular vote was thin, 34.2 million to 34.1 million. Kennedy's geographical coalition included the Northeast (including New York, Pennsylvania, and New Jersey), much of the South (including Johnson's Texas), and the central industrial states (including Michigan, Illinois, and Minnesota). He lost most of the farm states and the entire West. Nixon ran strongly in the West and Midwest, winning key states like California, Indiana, and Ohio. He also carried several border states. Republicans complained bitterly about voter fraud, particularly in Illinois and Texas, but they were never able to produce any significant evidence that fraud had occurred.[62]

In Congress, the Republicans gained two seats in the Senate, but the Democrats maintained their majority at sixty-four to thirty-six. In the House, Republicans gained twenty seats, giving the Democrats a majority there of 263 to 174.

The 1960 presidential election marked the end of one era and the beginning of another. Never again would American voters cast their votes without the input of television or without taking into account a candidate's character, his image, or even his physical appearance. For many Americans the year 1960 was the departing point for a new future, a new America that the new president said would "get moving again." That implied, of course, that the Eisenhower administration and the 1950s somehow represented the past, a time that had ended. It was all very optimistic: A brave new world was on the horizon. And for at least thirty years, Eisenhower was seen as the symbol of the nation's past.

The last two years of the decade had shown the decline of bipartisanship in Washington. The 1958 midterm elections had brought a strong (and growing) liberal element into Congress, an element that opposed Johnson's moderation and an element that Johnson could not control. Although Kennedy was not a model liberal, he represented a new liberalism—that opposed all that Lyndon Johnson stood for. Also by then, a newly empowered right wing began to emerge in the Republican Party, led by new faces like Goldwater and Dirksen, making Eisenhower's job of holding his party's middle all the more difficult. By the end of Eisenhower's second term, much of the Middle Way was gone, replaced by the extreme wings of the two parties.

CHAPTER SEVEN

Conclusion:
The End of a Decade and
the Beginning of the
Future of American Politics

Samuel Lubell, in his *Revolt of the Moderates,* called Eisenhower's 1952 victory a "crucial turn" in American political history.[1] Two years earlier, Lou Harris wrote in his *Is There a Republican Majority?* "that the basic Democratic majority has been broken. But, perhaps more important, the Republicans have put together a permanent majority of their own. That forecasts a state of flux in American politics for some time to come." There is, he added, "the possibility of a permanent political revolution stemming out of the 1952 election of Dwight Eisenhower."[2] Both Harris and Lubell were correct. The 1952 election was a significant departure from the past. The remainder of the decade would be a new era in American political history and set the stage for the tumultuous sixties.

The first departure from the past is the simplest to explain. Harry Truman was the last of the New Dealers; his Fair Deal programs grew out of Roosevelt's depression-era policies. Truman's plans and programs, however, had more to do with politics, of getting elected, than any need to solve the nation's economic problems. In fact, the economic problems the nation faced in those years immediately following the war (overabundance and a fear of inflation) were the exact opposite of the problems that Roosevelt faced in the 1930s. Nevertheless, Truman's policies were, for most observers, a direct extension of the New Deal. His successor as Democratic Party standard bearer in the next decade was Illinois governor Adlai Stevenson. Stevenson was no Truman, and he certainly was no Roosevelt. Many of his followers, however, hoped he would become the direct political successor to both. He was urbane, witty, even charming— many of the characteristics often attributed to Roosevelt. But he had no desire to carry on the New Deal–Fair Deal legacy of the Democratic Party. In fact, by comparing statements and deeds over time, Eisenhower may well have been to the left (at least on some social issues) of Stevenson.

Stevenson came to realize that Truman (with a dismal approval rating at about 30 percent) might, in fact, damage his campaign against Eisenhower in 1952. That may have been a mistake; Truman had considerable appeal to the common man, something that Stevenson truly lacked. At the same time, Truman wanted a successor, someone who could follow him in office, carry on the New Deal–Fair Deal tradition, and keep the Republicans out of Washington. Stevenson accepted the nomination, but he rejected all of Truman's advances, and he even spurned Truman's assistance on the campaign trail. He also wanted to rid himself of the albatross of corruption in the Truman administration, or "that mess in Washington," as events there were often called. The result was a significant break in the history of the Democratic Party between the politics of the past and the politics of the future. Out went much of the old New Deal–Fair Deal Democratic traditions, and in came a new political tradition that seemed a better fit for the times. Stevenson's new tack represented a more moderate, more business-friendly philosophy that pulled away from the paternalism and economic management of the previous decades. He was also inclined to support civil rights for African Americans at the expense of southern white votes. Truman had made a few gestures in that direction at times;

and Stevenson might be called a "gradualist" on civil rights who often feared the political repercussions of a civil rights stance. But through-out his two campaigns, he was generally a supporter of the 1954 *Brown* decision and civil rights for African Americans.

Lyndon Johnson's moderation through the 1950s added to all this. He was the Democratic Party leader through the decade, even more so that Stevenson or even the Democratic National Committee chairman Paul Butler. Johnson's moderation in the Senate set the stage for most party policy during the decade, as did Sam Rayburn's equally moderate leader-ship in the House of Representatives. Their moderation had as much to do with their relationship with Eisenhower and Eisenhower's popularity with voters as with their own convictions. The result was a moderate Democratic Party through the 1950s, with a much more moderate stance in Congress than the old Democratic Party that had controlled Washington during the Great Depression. Toward the end of the decade, liberalism began to gain strength in the Democratic Party, and it pushed out Johnson's style of moderation and conciliation. By 1960, the liberal leaders in the party saw their futures in John Kennedy—a direct rejection of Johnson and the politics of the 1950s.

At the same time, Eisenhower's own policies in the 1950s caused a directional shift in the Republican Party that was also significant. Like Stevenson, Rayburn, and Johnson, Eisenhower was a moderate. He was so moderate, in fact, that he often bandied about the word "liberal" to describe some of his own policies. Through his first administration this moderation brought very little pushback from the powerful right wing in his party. The president was extremely popular, and his coattails were generous and predictable. To confront Ike might mean losing an election. So, through much of the decade, the right pandered to the general. But that soon changed. Following the 1956 general election (and certainly by the 1958 congressional elections) Eisenhower had lost much of his relevancy among the members of the GOP right. He was no longer the popular president whose elections kept Republicans (of all stripes) in office. The Twenty-second Amendment to the Constitution made it clear that Eisenhower could only serve two terms. Following the 1956 election, he became a lame duck, with no election to look forward to, and no promise of long coattails to keep his party members in line. By 1958, with Eisenhower effectively on the sidelines, the GOP right rose to control the party. Nixon's loss in 1960 made the right wingers even stronger, with a sharp eye toward the next presidential election in 1964.

By the end of the 1950s, the future of American politics was coming into focus. Both parties were undergoing major transformations. In addition to the rise of the Republican right in opposition to Eisenhower's moderation, a new Republican Party geographic coalition was forming. The conservative South was joining with midwestern conservatives and generally rejecting the historically more moderate northeastern wing of the party—surrendering that region to the Democrats. By 1964, with Barry Goldwater's run, that coalition would add large parts of the American West. The Republicans suffered an ignominious defeat that year, but by the next election cycle in 1968 the southern-midwestern-far-western Republican coalition would be in place. Add to that the age-old traditional Republicans (a group almost always overlooked in the calculations of coalitions) and the increasing strength of the nation's growing suburbs, and a new Republican coalition was born. It was strong, strongly conservative, and it would stay in place for the remainder of the century. When Lou Harris asked in 1954 *Is There a Republican Majority?* the answer he gave was yes.

This new coalition was much more conservative, and it would field conservative candidates clear into the next millennium. Prior to 1960 or so, Republican presidential candidates had been moderates, like New York governor Tom Dewey. Eisenhower (always supported by Dewey and his circle) and a short time later, Nelson Rockefeller, also fell into that group. Alf Landon and Wendell Willkie, both of whom lost presidential campaigns to Franklin Roosevelt, were also Republican moderates. By the mid-1960s, however, that wing of the party had been purged. With the northeastern moderates out, the new coalition turned its focus toward the issues of anti-communism, lowering taxes, and reducing the size of the federal government. By 1980, when Ronald Reagan ran and won with that coalition, the Republican Party had achieved its transformation from Eisenhower moderation to Reagan conservatism. It was, by then, a more conservative (and a much stronger) party.

It was Eisenhower who first saw the future of the Republican Party in the South. Since Reconstruction, race and race issues had defined southern politics. African Americans voted (when they were allowed to vote) Republican, the Party of Lincoln; and whites were generally Democrats. By the end of World War II, much of that had begun to change. The Democrats slowly took on the mantle of the party of civil rights, the party that would be the future for African American voters. If there was any question about the Democratic Party's growing support for civil rights, there was the 1948 Democratic convention. The party members refused to give their support to the white southern delegations when they insisted on their usual state's right clause in the party's platform. After a raucous floor fight, Hubert Humphrey (then the mayor of Minneapolis and running for a Senate seat from Minnesota) called for the party to "get out of the shadow of states' rights and to walk forthrightly into the bright sunshine of human rights." With that, the entire Mississippi delegation and part of the Alabama delegation walked out of the Philadelphia convention and formed the States' Rights Party, better known in history as the Dixiecrats. They nominated their own candidates for president (South Carolina's Strom Thurmond) and vice president (James Eastland from Mississippi).

The final impact of the Dixiecrats on the 1948 election was minimal. But the nature of the campaign sent African American voters to the polls to cast their votes for Truman, the Democrat. The shift had begun. White southerners (always conservative) saw their future in the Republican Party; and the Democratic Party became the party of civil rights, or at least the party that made the most promises to African Americans. In 1952, Eisenhower saw this—in fact before most anyone. He saw that the Solid South was breakable, that there were southern white votes to be had there. Against the advice of his campaign staff, Eisenhower campaigned in the South. His inroads into the white South in 1952 made no difference in his final victory over Stevenson, but both the 1948 and the 1952 elections set a strong foundation for the future. The process would be slow, but white southerners would find a home with the Republicans, and the nation's African Americans would eventually abandon the Party of Lincoln and become Democrats. That process eventually served to make the Republican Party more conservative and the Democratic Party more liberal. The Eisenhower and Johnson Middle Way was deteriorating.

In 1952, Eisenhower took Texas, Oklahoma, Missouri, Tennessee, Virginia, Maryland, Delaware, Kentucky, and Florida. Four years later, in 1956, he held on to most of those states, losing only Missouri, but adding Louisiana. Democrats always assumed that it had been Eisenhower's personal appeal that had brought white southern voters to his side in 1952 and again in 1956. But Nixon's numbers in the 1960 campaign showed that the white South was actually in transition from the solid state of the post-Reconstruction-era Democratic Party into the Republican Party— and that the transition was continuing, even picking up steam as the 1950s ended and the next decade began. Not only did Nixon, in 1960, increase voter strength throughout the South, he outran Eisenhower's 1956 numbers in four of the South's most southern states: Alabama, Georgia, Mississippi, and South Carolina. Although he ultimately lost all of those states to Kennedy, he won Virginia, Kentucky, Florida, Oklahoma, and Tennessee. In a national losing effort, Nixon maintained Eisenhower's 1956 strength in three of those states: Virginia, Florida, and Tennessee. Nationally, Nixon showed best in the rural regions of the nation, but in the South his support came from what was being touted as the New South, southern cities like Atlanta, Birmingham, Dallas, and Houston— and the large and growing white suburbs that had begun to spring up on the outskirts of those cities.

By the end of the 1950s, much of this was in place. In 1968, Nixon lost much of the South to George Wallace, then running as a third-party candidate. But in 1972, Nixon swept the South. Georgia governor Jimmy Carter returned the South to the Democrats briefly in 1976. But from 1980 until 1992, the South remained firmly in Republican hands. Arkansas Democrat Bill Clinton made some significant inroads back into the South in 1992 and again in 1996, but much of the South, even then, remained Republican in two losing causes.

As the 1950s came to a close, the new Democratic coalition was fairly solid and increasingly liberal. It had taken control of the industrial Northeast (generally abandoned by the Republicans) and kept control of most of the nation's industrial regions. The Democrats also won the votes of the nation's African Americans. That shift could be seen in national voting numbers, and not only in the South. Gallup reported that seven out of ten African Americans nationwide voted for Kennedy in 1960. In 1956, 64 percent of New York City's African American population had voted for Stevenson. But in 1960, that number jumped to 74 percent. For Kennedy, the numbers went from 63 to 78 percent among Chicago's African American voters. In Pittsburgh, the increase was from 68 to 78 percent; 48 to 74 percent in Baltimore, 36 to 64 percent in Atlanta, and 19 to 65 throughout the rural South.[3]

The black vote was instrumental in establishing Democratic majorities in many of the nation's large northern urban areas, particularly New York, Chicago, Detroit, Pittsburgh, Cleveland, and several others. These urban black votes were often instrumental in awarding the Democrats the electoral totals of states that were much more conservative. Perhaps Michigan and Illinois are the best examples. Although both states had generally conservative white populations, they often tilted to the Democrats because of the huge African American votes in those states' big cities. Some of this shift was apparent in the polls as early as 1948. In that election, Truman made several gestures toward African American voters and won the electoral votes of Illinois, California, and Ohio. Of course, it was not only black voters who pushed those states into the Democratic column; the labor vote, for instance, was equally important in Truman's victories in several industrial states. In addition, Truman missed winning the electoral votes of Pennsylvania, Indiana, and Michigan by less than 1 percent of the popular vote in those states. By the end of the 1950s—and then into the next decade, the Democrats maintained firm control of the black vote (both nationally and in the South). In addition, by 1960, the Democrats were pretty solid in most of the nation's industrial states like Pennsylvania, Michigan, and Illinois. Again, this electoral strength was at least in part a result of the urban black vote (in conjunction with other Democratic voters, particularly the labor vote).

During and after the 1950s, the Democrats continued to rely on portions of the old New Deal coalition that had formed in the mid-1930s.

They had managed to pull into their party structure African Americans and other groups like urban immigrants, voters in the lower income brackets, various minority groups, and organized labor in the industrial states and cities. However, through the next decades, the demographics of these groups changed considerably. The immigrants became second-generation Americans; people in the lower income brackets moved up into the middle class; the ranks of organized labor decreased significantly; and whites in the cities began moving into the more conservative suburbs. The result was that many of these groups abandoned their Democratic Party–inspired liberalism for a more conservative view of the world. The result was that the size of the Democratic Party began to shrink in both popularity and numbers. By the 1980s, that process was generally complete and the Democrats found it difficult to maintain majorities at almost all levels of government. Pundits complained that the Democrats were resting on their laurels of the New Deal–Fair Deal programs and that blaming the Republicans for the 1930s economic depression and the narrowness of McCarthyism no longer appealed to voters. The Democrats, they argued, needed new ideas and new leadership. All of these changes began in the 1950s. By 1980, the political realignment was generally in place.

By the end of the 1950s, the Republicans had become more conservative, made up of a much more conservative coalition, and led by leaders (like Goldwater and Dirksen) who were more conservative than their predecessors. The events of the decade also made the Democrats more liberal, made up of a much more liberal coalition of African Americans, labor, and the urban populations. The Middle Way that was envisioned by Eisenhower and his moderation, and accepted by Johnson, was generally gone. Its death was brought on by the demands of extremism in both parties.

Another change in American politics in the 1950s was that a greater significance was being placed on the personal images of the political candidates, with the result that American politics would never be the same again. Political writers still want to explain how the 1960 campaign (when the attractive Kennedy beat the unattractive Nixon) was at the origins of a new age in political advertizing, the first presidential campaign in which image trumped substance. But as with most aspects of the 1960s, that trend began in the 1950s. Eisenhower was well aware of his own image. He had what the press often called an infectious smile. He even had an appealing nickname. Add to that his hero status, his past accomplishments, his clean image, and even his place as something of an all-American symbol, and he became one of the most appealing candidates of the twentieth century. His opposition had yet to realize the significance of image. Bob Taft may have, in fact, understood it, but he was never able to overcome his stiff image, and he failed to portray himself as the man of the people that he believed would bring him the Republican nomination. As early as the 1948 campaign, Taft had even gone so far as to hire a media consultant, something mostly unheard of in those years. The consulting firm he hired was headed by General Oscar Solbert (who had been chief of the nation's psychological warfare strategy during the war). The plan was to pump up Taft's image from a stale legislator to a bright, vibrant, electable political candidate with a forward-looking agenda. The result was the predictable campaign literature filled with the beaming smiles and the slap-on-the-back personal life of a very human figure: "Bob Taft is by no means an austere or aloof person."[4]

Eisenhower's Democratic adversary in both elections, Adlai Stevenson, refused to consider image control as an important part of his campaigns—much to his detriment. There were seventeen million television sets in the United States in 1952, and that medium was about to jump onto the American political scene. But Stevenson did not watch television, and he never really understood it or its potential impact on politics. It was Lyndon Johnson, however, who even more so represented the anti-image personality in the 1950s. Johnson was not an attractive man; he did not have an infectious smile, and in fact, if he represented anything it was the American South—an image that he tried to brush off through most of his career by proclaiming himself a westerner and not a southerner. His greatest talent was, of course, his ability to maneuver the Senate, to build coalitions and get legislation passed. Somehow, he believed that ability would make him an appealing figure to American voters; and several times throughout his career he seemed to want to do little more than point to

his accomplishments and present the American people with his résumé
of congressional victories. Most Americans, however (if they knew of
Johnson at all), saw him as a political wheeler-dealer, a southerner whose
primary ability was to weaken legislation. As vice-presidential candidate
in 1960, and then as vice president in the Kennedy administration, the
Kennedys (family, friends, and advisors) referred to him as "Colonel
Cornpone." Even as president, Johnson was unable to shake that terrible
image. Only in the 1964 presidential campaign did he take the advice
of others (from people around him like Bill Moyers) that a campaign to
destroy your opponent's image might be as successful as building your
own. In the 1950s, however, Lyndon Johnson knew little or nothing of
the significance of image in American politics.

Eisenhower's advertising campaign was run by the advertising guru,
Rosser Reeves. It was Reeves who concluded, in 1952, that the best way
to sell a political candidate was through what he called "spots." "This new
way of campaigning," Reeves wrote in a memorandum designed to sell
his idea, "is a new use of what advertising men know as 'spots.' A spot
is a 15-second or 1-minute announcement on radio—or a 20-second or
1-minute announcement on television."[5] These campaign spots in the
Eisenhower campaign were little more than short question-and-answer
episodes between Eisenhower and fictitious Americans asking the candidate about various issues, usually on the economy, the war in Korea, or
taxes. Eisenhower also ran a series of primitive cartoon ads on television
created by Roy O. Disney, Walt's older brother. Stevenson ran a few of
his own spots, but their impact was of little significance compared with
Eisenhower's barrage of TV and radio ads. By 1956, Stevenson seemed to
understand the significance of advertisement spots. In his first 1956 TV
ad, he stated the obvious: "Thanks to television, I can talk to millions of
people."[6] To many Americans, who by then were used to political ads and
seeing candidates on their television sets, Stevenson's statement must have
seemed quaint, perhaps even out of touch with the new progress. At the
same time, Eisenhower ramped up his advertising operation (mostly in
an effort to use media ads in place of personal campaigning) and buried
Stevenson in both the polls and in the quality and quantity of on-air

advertising. In the next campaign, Kennedy came to realize that he would have to engage in heavy advertising in order to beat Nixon.[7]

American politics at the end of the 1950s was considerably different than it had been at the beginning of the decade. The New Deal–Fair Deal era was at an end, even though large numbers of Democratic loyalists continued to long for those years of Franklin Roosevelt, New Deal liberalism, and a tradition in the party of economic planning and problem solving. The Republican Party had realigned, recalculated its conservatism, and reached a genuine parity with the Democrats.

This shift had made the Republican Party much more conservative, much less willing to work with the moderates in their own party or with the Democrats. The Democrats, now pushed forward by party liberals, were much less inclined to work with the moderates in their own party or with the Republicans. At least from a political standpoint, the stage was set for the 1960s.

Notes

Introduction

1. There is some evidence that Eisenhower, Johnson, and Sam Rayburn met (clandestinely) more than once to hash out various issues. The evidence, however, is sparse. See D. Hardeman and Donald Bacon, *Rayburn: A Biography* (Lanham, Maryland, 1987), 392.

Chapter One

1. Dwight Eisenhower, *Mandate for Change: 1953–1956* (Garden City, New York, 1963), 4–5. The correspondent was Virgil Pinckney. See William B. Pickett, *Eisenhower Decides to Run: Presidential Politics and Cold War Strategies* (Chicago, 2000), 8.

2. Dwight Eisenhower to Arthur Eisenhower (Oct. 20, 1943), Family File, EP, DDEL, Abilene, Kansas. Also in Louis Galambos and Alfred D. Chandler, Jr., eds., *The Papers of Dwight D. Eisenhower* (Baltimore, 1983), #1352, vol. 3, pg. 1518–19.

3. Stephen Ambrose, *Eisenhower: Soldier, General of the Army, President-Elect: 1890–1952* (New York, 1983), 269.

4. Dwight Eisenhower, *Crusade in Europe* (Garden City, New Jersey, 1948), 444. In 1958, Truman denied that he ever made this statement, but at that time the Truman- Eisenhower relationship was at a low point. Omar Bradley recalled Truman's statement. See Omar Bradley, *A Soldier's Story* (New York, 1951), 444. See also Steve Neal, *Harry and Ike*: *The*

Partnership that Remade the Postwar World (New York, 2001), 44; and Harry C. Blutcher, *My Three Years with Eisenhower: The Personal Diary of Captain Harry C. Blutcher, USNR* (New York, 1946), 434; Pickett, *Eisenhower Decides to Run*, 7.

5. John Gunther, *Eisenhower: The Man and the Symbol* (New York, 1952), 133. William Tecumseh Sherman had said: "If drafted, I will not run. If nominated, I will not accept. If elected, I will not serve."

6. Robert H. Zieger, *American Workers, American Unions, 1920–1985* (Baltimore, 1986), 104; Gary Donaldson, *Dewey Defeats Truman* (Lexington, Kentucky, 1999), 71.

7. Donaldson, *Dewey Defeats Truman*, 71.

8. Ibid., 5–19.

9. Ibid., 48.

10. Ibid., 29–48.

11. Gallup Poll cited in *Reader's Digest* (Dec. 1947). See also *Time* (Dec. 2, 1946). Pickett, *Eisenhower Decides to Run,* 146–60.

12. *Time* (Dec. 2, 1946); *Life* (Dec. 2, 1946).

13. Eisenhower to Thomas J. Watson (Aug. 21, 1947), Galambos and Chandler, eds., *Papers of Dwight Eisenhower*, #1700, vol. 9, pg. 1890. Also in Eisenhower Manuscripts, DDEL. Pickett, *Eisenhower Decides to Run,* 123.

14. Gunther, *Eisenhower*, 133.

15. Eisenhower to Walter Bedell Smith (Sept. 18, 1947), Eisenhower Manuscripts, DDEL. Also in Galambos and Chandler, eds., *Papers of Dwight Eisenhower*, #1742, vol. 4, pg. 1933.

16. Eisenhower to Earl Marvin Price (Oct. 31, 1947), in ibid., #1837, vol. 4, pg. 2027.

17. Dwight Eisenhower to Milton Eisenhower (Oct. 16, 1947), in ibid., #1800, vol. 4, pg. 1987.

18. Leonard Finder to Eisenhower (Jan. 12, 1948), in ibid., #1994, vol. 4, pg. 2191–93. See also Galambos and Chandler, notes in ibid., pg. 2192–94; and Pickett, *Eisenhower Decides to Run,* 34–42.

19. *NYT* (Jan.13, 1949). For the difficulty Eisenhower had composing the letter, see James Forrestal, *Forrestal Diaries* (New York, 1951), 365–66; and Eisenhower to Lynn Townsend White (Jan. 29, 1948), Galambos

and Chandler, ed., *Papers of Eisenhower,* #2016, vol. 4, pg. 2211. See also Peter Lyon, *Eisenhower: Portrait of a Hero* (Boston, 1974), 379–80; and Pickett, *Eisenhower Decides to Run,* 39–40.

20. The Finder letter is available in several places. The most accessible may be Eisenhower to Leonard Finder (Jan. 27, 1948), Galambos and Chandler, eds., *Papers of Eisenhower,* #2005, vol. 4, pg. 2202. A copy is also in the *New York Times* (Jan. 24, 1948). A good analysis of the Finder letter is in Pickett, *Eisenhower Decides to Run,* 34–42.

21. Gunther, *Eisenhower,* 137. Eisenhower told Bedell Smith, "I have experienced a great sense of personal freedom that I was rapidly losing." Eisenhower to Walter Bedell Smith (Jan. 28, 1948), Galambos and Chandler, eds., *Papers of Eisenhower,* #2009, vol. 9, pg. 2205. Also in Eisenhower Manuscripts, DDEP.

22. Donaldson, *Truman Defeats Dewey,* 136–44.

23. Polls that made this observation were fairly common. See Gallup poll in *Newsweek* (Oct. 6, 1947); *Public Opinion Quarterly* (Summer 1948); Roper poll in *Fortune* (June 1948).

24. Reinhold Niebuhr to James Loeb (June 23, 1948), Americans for Democratic Action Administrative files, ADA Papers, Wisconsin State Historical Society, Madison, Wisconsin.

25. "Statement on Political Policy," (April 11, 1948), in ibid.

26. Eisenhower to Walter Bedell Smith (April 12, 1948), Galambos and Chandler, eds., *Papers of Eisenhower,* #34, vol. 10, pg. 41. Also in Eisenhower Manuscripts, DDEL.

27. *Time* (April 19, 1948).

28. *NYT* (July 4 and 5, 1948).

29. Eisenhower to Robert Harron (July 5, 1948), Galambos and Chandler, eds., *Papers of Eisenhower,* #106, vol. 10, pg. 124. Also in Eisenhower Manuscripts, DDEL.

30. *Newsweek* (July 7, 1948).

31. Eisenhower to James Roosevelt (July 8, 1948), Galambos and Chandler, eds., *Papers of Eisenhower,* #110, vol. 10, pg. 129; *NYT* (July 3, 6, 1948). See also *Time* (July 12, 1948).

32. For a more in-depth analysis from this viewpoint, see Donaldson, *Truman Defeats Dewey,* 204–20.

33. Stevenson's largest margin of victory came from Cook County, Illinois. Douglas won easily as well, but by a narrower margin. See Jeff Broadwater, *Adlai Stevenson: The Odyssey of a Cold War Liberal* (New York, 1994), 83; Porter McKeever, *Adlai Stevenson: His Life and Legacy* (New York, 1989), 126–27.

34. Humphrey had been the mayor of Minneapolis and won a Minnesota Senate seat that year; Johnson defeated Coke Stevenson for a Texas Senate seat by a suspect eighty-seven votes. Kennedy won his House seat in 1946. He defeated Henry Cabot Lodge for a Massachusetts Senate seat in 1952.

35. After defeating Chicago alderman Paul Douglas in the Democratic primary, McKeough lost to Brooks in the November general election.

36. John Bartlow Martin, *Adlai Stevenson of Illinois* (Garden City, New York, 1976), 222. See also George W. Ball, *The Past Has Another Pattern: Memoirs* (New York, 1982), 152.

37. Martin, *Adlai Stevenson of Illinois*, 222.

38. Walter Johnson, ed., *The Papers of Adlai E. Stevenson, Washington to Springfield, 1941–1948* (Boston, 1973), 2: 393. The letter was to Edward G. Miller, Truman's assistant secretary of state. See also Martin, *Adlai Stevenson of Illinois*, 266–67; and Broadwater, *Adlai Stevenson*, 72. Even Richard Daly lost in 1946—for the only time in his political career, running for sheriff of Cook County, Illinois.

39. Johnson, ed., *Papers of Adlai Stevenson*, 3: 103.

40. Martin, *Adlai Stevenson of Illinois*, 405–7.

41. Ibid., 450.

42. Johnson, ed., *Papers of Adlai Stevenson*, 3: 411.

43. Ibid., 3: 416.

44. John Bartlow Martin wrote: "Despite his powerful appeal to intellectuals, he was not really himself an intellectual." Martin, *Adlai Stevenson of Illinois*, 473.

45. Ibid., 169; Ball, *The Past Has Another Pattern*, 136.

46. John Kenneth Galbraith, *A Life in Our Times* (New York, 1982), 289.

47. In fact, Stevenson may have been right. With some success, Republicans, through the 1950s, attacked as radicals all Democrats running for public office who had joined the ADA. Stevenson also refused to join the American Civil Liberties Union for the same reason.

48. Quoted in Steven Gillon, *Politics and Vision: The ADA and American Liberalism, 1947–1985* (New York, 1987), 48.

49. Johnson, ed., *Papers of Adlai Stevenson*, 3: 225.

50. Martin, *Adlai Stevenson of Illinois*, 511.

51. Johnson, ed., *Papers of Adlai Stevenson*, 3: 224–25.

52. See speeches reflecting this in Johnson, ed., *Papers of Adlai Stevenson*, 2: 135–46, 167, and 296–314. Stevenson's attitude toward the Soviets during the early days of the UN can be found in reflections by Henry Wallace. See John Morton Blum, ed., *The Price of Vision: The Diary of Henry A. Wallace, 1942–1946* (New York, 1973), 439–40.

53. See statements and speeches in Johnson, ed., *Papers of Adlai Stevenson*, 2: 369–82. See also Martin, *Adlai Stevenson of Illinois*, 255–56.

54. Martin, *Adlai Stevenson of Illinois*, 418.

55. Ibid., 485–88.

56. Ibid., 488. *Chicago Tribune* (March 15, 1952).

Chapter Two

1. Samuel Lubell, *Revolt of the Moderates* (New York, 1956), 2–3, 265.

2. Eisenhower manuscripts (Oct. 28, 1950), diaries, DDEL. For Eisenhower's movements toward a decision to run in 1952, see Pickett, *Eisenhower Decides to Run*, 76, 77–79.

3. Eisenhower manuscripts (Oct. 28, 1950), diaries, DDEL.

4. Eisenhower, *Mandate for Change*, 14.

5. Diary entry (Jan. 1, 1951), Galambos and Chandler, eds., *Papers of Eisenhower*, #1, vol., 12, pg. 5. See also, Eisenhower manuscripts (Jan. 2, 1951), dairies, DDEL. *NYT* (Jan. 2, 1951).

6. Pickett, *Eisenhower Decides to Run*, 107–14.

7. Lucius Clay to DDE (May 18, 1951) and DDE to Clay (May 30, 1951), both in Eisenhower manuscripts, DDEL; Eisenhower to Clay (May 30, 1951), Galambos and Chandler, eds., *Papers of Eisenhower*, #196, vol. 12, pg. 306–7.

8. Jean Edward Smith, *Lucius D. Clay: An American Life* (New York, 1990), 578–79, 584.

9. William Bragg Ewald, Jr., *Eisenhower the President: Crucial Days, 1951–1960* (Englewood Cliffs, NJ, 1981), 38–41. The significance of the Duff letter is explored in detail in Pickett, *Eisenhower Decides to Run,* 118–120. A copy of the letter itself can be found in *New York Times Magazine* (Nov. 14, 1993), 56–57. See also, Cliff Roberts, OH DDEL.

10. Smith, *Lucius Clay,* 585, 587.

11. Ibid., 590; Sherman Adams, *Firsthand Report: The Story of the Eisenhower Administration* (New York, 1961), 25–6.

12. Eisenhower to Lucius Clay (Feb. 12, 1952), Glambos and Chandler, eds., *Papers of Eisenhower,* #667, vol. 13, pg 974.

13. Smith, *Lucius Clay*, 591.

14. *U.S. News and World Report* (Mar. 21, 1952); James T. Patterson, *Mr. Republican: A Biography of Robert A. Taft* (Boston, 1972), 523.

15. *NYT* (Mar. 5, 1952). Patterson, *Mr. Republican,* 523.

16. *NYT* (Mar. 13, 1952).

17. Ibid., (Mar. 12, 16, 1952).

18. *Time* (Mar. 24, 1952). See also, Patterson, *Mr. Republican*, 535.

19. "1952 G.O.P. Presidential Primaries," (n.d.), Political Files, Taft Papers, LC.

20. Chester Pach and Elmo Richardson, *The Presidency of Dwight D. Eisenhower* (Lawrence, Kansas, 1991), 21; Patterson, *Mr. Republican,* 519. All of these accusations have been controversial, questioned by historians, and difficult to prove. In her second book, Kay Summersby accounts an affair with Eisenhower. Kay Summersby Morgan, *Past Forgetting: My Love Affair with Dwight David Eisenhower* (New York, 1976). Despite Summersby's memoir, that affair is still often disputed. According to Harry Truman, Eisenhower, during the war, asked permission to divorce his wife and marry Summersby. The request was denied. See Merle Miller, *Plain Speaking* (New York, 1974), 339–40. And Robert H. Ferrell and Francis H. Heller "Plain Faking?" *American Heritage Magazine* (May/June, 1995), 14–16. By most accounts, Mamie Eisenhower drank, but not heavily. See Ewald, *Eisenhower the President,* 11.

21. *Time* (April 12, 1952); Pickett, *Eisenhower Decides to Run,* 192; Robert H. Ferrell, *Harry S. Truman: A Life* (Columbia, Mo., 1994), 376–77.

22. *Time* (Mar. 24, 1952); *NYT* (Mar. 13, April 12, 1952); Harry S. Truman, *Memoirs: Years of Trial and Hope* (New York, 1956), 555; *Washington Post* (Mar. 30, 1952).

23. *Time* (Mar. 24, 1952).

24. Ibid., (Mar. 24, 1952).

25. Truman, *Memoirs: Years of Trial and Hope*, 552–53; Ferrell, *Harry Truman*, 75–77.

26. Truman was never shy about his opinions of Kefauver. See Robert H. Ferrell, ed., *Off the Record: The Private Papers of Harry S. Truman* (New York, 1980), 260–61, 268–69, 280.

27. Truman, *Memoirs*, 2: 555; Martin, *Adlai Stevenson of Illinois*, 523.

28. Martin, *Adlai Stevenson of Illinois*, 555.

29. Johnson, ed., *Papers of Adlai E. Stevenson*, 3: 533–34.

30. *NYT* (Mar. 30, 1952). *Washington Post* (Mar. 30, 1952); Ferrell, *Harry Truman*, 376.

31. *NYT* (Jan. 28, 29, 1952).

32. Ibid. (Feb. 29, 1952). See also, Russell's official announcement (Feb. 28, 1952), Series VI, Political Files, box 193, Richard Russell Papers, University of Georgia, Athens, Georgia.

33. Truman, *Memoirs*, 2: 561. Truman writes here that he suggested Sparkman. See also Martin, *Adlai Stevenson of Illinois*, 597–600, 606–7; Patterson, *Mr. Republican*, 552–55.

34. *NYT* (July 12, 1952); Patterson, *Mr. Republican*, 547–66.

35. Adams, *Firsthand Report*, 45–48. Adams disliked Nixon and may have counseled Eisenhower to remove him from the ticket.

36. Ibid., 46; Herbert Brownell, *Advising Ike: The Memoirs of Attorney General Herbert Brownell* (Lawrence, Kansas, 1993),124; Smith, *Lucius Clay*, 605–6.

37. Richard Nixon, *Six Crises* (New York, 1962),113–17; *U.S. News and World Report* (Oct. 3, 1952); *NYT* (Sept. 28, 1952). Stephen Ambrose, *Nixon: The Education of a Politician*, vol. 1, *1913–1962* (New York, 1987), 276–93.

Chapter Three

1. William Leuctenburg, *Troubled Feast: American Society since 1945* (New York, 1983), 88. That statement provoked Adlai Stevenson to reply: "I assume what it means is that you will strongly recommend the building of a great many schools to accommodate the needs of our children, but not provide the money." See also, *Time* (Feb. 8, 1954).

2. *NYT* (Sept. 6, 1949).

3. *Time* (Feb. 9, 1959). The meeting was of the GOP National Committee in Des Moines, Iowa. At the meeting, the president sat between conservative senator Everett Dirksen and liberal senator George Aiken. See also Eisenhower to General B. G. Chynoweth (July 13, 1954), Diary Series, Papers as President, Ann Whitman File, EP, DDEL. Also in Galambos and Chandler, *Papers of Eisenhower* (July 13, 1954) #977, vol. 15, pg. 1185.

4. Ambrose, *Eisenhower: The President*, 152.

5. Robert Ferrell, ed., *The Diary of James Hagerty: Eisenhower in Mid-course, 1954–1955* (Bloomington, Indiana, 1983) (Dec. 7, 1954, entry), 129.

6. William Manchester, *The Glory and the Dream: A Narrative History of America, 1932–1972* (Boston, 1973), 2: 812.

7. Eisenhower diary (May 1, 1953), Diary Series, Papers as President, Ann Whitman File, EP, DDEL. See also Galambos and Chandler, eds., *Papers of Eisenhower* (May 1, 1953), # 168, vol. 14, pg. 195–97. In the official report of the Legislative Leadership Committee, it was recorded that "Sen. Taft then stated [that] he could not possibly express the deepness of his disappointment at the program the Administration presented today." Arthur Minnich, Legislative Leadership Committee (May 9, 1952), Proceedings, White House Office Files, EP, DDEL. See also, Patterson, *Mr. Republican*, 599–600.

8. Taft to Herman Walker (Aug. 18, 1952), Subject Files, Correspondence with Senators, 1952, Taft Papers, LC. Taft also saw Eisenhower as a dupe of what he called "the New York financial interests and a large number of businessmen." See "Taft memo on the 1952 campaign," (n.d.), Box 1349, ibid.

9. Eisenhower, *Mandate for Change*, 219. Eisenhower had other good things to say about Taft after he died. See Eisenhower Diary (Jan. 18, 1954), Diary Series, Papers as President, Ann Whitman File, EP, DDEL. See also, Galambos and Chandler, eds., *Papers of Eisenhower* (Jan. 18, 1954), #669, vol. 15, pg. 826. Patterson, *Mr. Republican*, 599-611.

10. *National Review* (June 27, 1956).

11. The advisor was William Robinson. Eisenhower to Robinson (Mar. 12, 1954), Diary Series, Papers as President, Ann Whitman File, EP, DDEL. See also Galambos and Chandler, eds., *Papers of Eisenhower* (Mar. 12, 1954), # 773, vol. 15, pg. 949–51.

12. Eisenhower Diary (Jan. 18, 1954), Diary Series, Papers as President, Ann Whitman File, EP, DDEL. This quote can also be found in Robert H. Ferrell, *The Eisenhower Diaries* (New York, 1981) (Jan. 18, 1954, entry), 270. And Galambos and Chandler, eds., *Papers of Eisenhower* (Jan. 18, 1954), # 669, vol. 15, pg. 827.

13. *Time* (June 22, 1953).

14. Ibid. (March 9, 1953).

15. George Reedy, OH, #8, JLOHC.

16. Merle Miller, *Lyndon: An Oral Biography* (New York, 1980), 197–98; Hubert Humphrey, *Education of a Public Man: My Life in Politics* (Minneapolis, 1991), 163; Gilbert C. Fite, *Richard B. Russell: Senator from Georgia* (Chapel Hill, North Carolina, 1991), 302. See also Robert A. Caro, *The Years of Lyndon Johnson: Master of the Senate* (New York, 2002), 109–110, 475–76.

17. Hubert Humphrey, OH, #2, JLOHC.

18. Ibid., #1. Joseph Rauh, president of the Americans for Democratic Action (ADA), opposed Johnson's election as Democratic Party leader. See Alfred Steinberg, *Sam Johnson's Boy: A Close-up of the President from Texas* (New York, 1968), 393.

19. *NYT* (Jan. 6, 1953).

20. *Time* (June 22, 1953).

21. Reedy, OH, #1.

22. Cal Jilson, *American Government: Political Change and Institutional Development* (4th ed., New York, 2008), 230.

23. Miller, *Johnson*, 202; Reedy, OH, #1; Humphrey, OH, #2; Robert Dallek, *Lone Star Rising: Lyndon Johnson and His Times, 1908–1960* (New York, 1991), 430; Doris Kearns Goodwin, *Lyndon Johnson and the American Dream* (New York, 1976), 115.

24. Reedy, OH, #1; Goodwin, *Lyndon Johnson*, 115.

25. George Reedy, *Lyndon B. Johnson: A Memoir* (New York, 1982), 85.

26. Steinberg, *Sam Johnson's Boy*, 393–95.

27. Reedy to Johnson (Nov. 16, 1952), Senate Office Files, LBJP, LBJL; Reedy to Johnson (Nov. 6, 1952), ibid.

28. *Congress and the Nation, 1945–1964, A Review of Government and Politics in the Postwar Years* (Washington, DC, 1965), 110–11. The bill was introduced on January 7, 1953. Duane Tananbaum, *The Bricker Amendment Controversy: A Test of Eisenhower's Political Leadership* (Ithaca, NY: 1988), 23, 32–39.

29. *Congress and the Nation*, 111. Organizations that supported the amendment included the American Bar Association, the U.S. Chamber of Commerce, the Veterans of Foreign Wars, the American Legion, and the Daughters of the American Revolution. Tananbaum, *Bricker Amendment*, 35.

30. *PPP, Eisenhower,* 1953, 13–14.

31. Dwight Eisenhower to Edgar Eisenhower (Mar. 27, 1953), Name Series, Ann Whitman File, EP, DDEL. Edgar was an attorney practicing in Tacoma, Washington. He is usually considered more conservative than his younger brother Dwight. See also, Brownell, *Advising Ike*, 266. Galambos and Chandler, eds., *Papers of Eisenhower* (Mar. 27, 1953), #109, vol. 14, pg. 126–27. Also cited in Tananbaum, *Bricker Amendment*, 72.

32. Ferrell, *Eisenhower Diaries* (April 1, 1953, entry), 233. Also in Galambos and Chandler, eds., *Papers of Eisenhower* (April 1, 1953), #118, vol. 14, pg. 136. Other lawyers who advised the administration on the case included Assistant Attorney General J. Lee Rankin, Lucius Clay, Paul Freund, Erwin Griswold, Edward Corwin, John W. Davis, and John J. McCloy. All opposed the amendment. Brownell, *Advising Ike,* 267. Smith, *Lucius Clay*, 616–17.

33. *Congress and the Nation*, 111; Brownell, *Advising Ike,* 264.

34. *Time* (Jan. 18, 1954).

35. Tananbaum, *Bricker Amendment*, 78–79. Herbert Brownell disagreed, writing in his memoir, "Eisenhower's behind-the-scenes efforts and his attempts to stay above the political fray to avoid a head-on confrontation with the Senate led him to prevail." Brownell, *Advising Ike,* 270. The press conferences can be found at *PPP, 1953,* 109–10, and 132. In June 1953, Brownell and Dulles discussed this issue in a telephone conversation. See U.S. Department of State, *Foreign Relations of the United States*, I, 1952–1954 (U.S. Government Printing Office, 1984), 1812–13. Both men agreed that had the president been more forceful in his opposition to the amendment that enough Republicans would have withdrawn their support

to kill the resolution and end the controversy. See also, Ferrell, *Eisenhower Diaries* (April 1, 1953, entry), 233. And Galambos and Chandler, eds., *Papers of Eisenhower* (April 1, 1953), #118, vol. 14, pg. 136–37.

36. Ferrell, *Eisenhower Diaries* (April 1, 1953, entry), 233; Brownell, *Advising Ike,* 267–68; *Time* (Jan. 18, 1954). See also Galambos and Chandler, eds., *Papers of Eisenhower* (April 1, 1953), #118, vol. 14, pg. 1367.

37. *NYT* (July 2, 1953).

38. *Time* (Feb. 2, 1954); Smith, *Lucius Clay,* 617; *PPP, Eisenhower,* 1954, 273.

39. By some accounts, Johnson facilitated the George amendment. See Dallek, *Lone Star Rising,* 436; Miller, *Lyndon,* 203–04; Tananbaum, *Bricker Amendment,* chapters 8 and 9; and Humphrey, OH, #2. See also Caro, *Master of the Senate,* 527–41.

40. *NYT* (Feb. 27, 1956); Brownell, *Advising Ike,* 270; *Congress and the Nation,* 111–13. Johnson voted for the George amendment. Dallek argues that Johnson knew the amendment would be defeated and he needed to shore up his conservative base at home. Dallek, *Lone Star Rising,* 436; Caro, *Master of the Senate,* 527–41

41. *Congress and the Nation,* 119.

42. Reedy, OH, #1; Reedy made a similar statement in Miller, *Lyndon,* 203.

43. *Time* (Jan. 25, 1954). Polls showed McCarthy at 50 percent favorable and 29 percent unfavorable.

44. William S. White of the *New York Times* insisted that Johnson "do something about this damned fellow." Miller, *Lyndon,* 210. The same quote is in William S. White, OH, #3, JLOHC. Joseph Rauh, Drew Pearson, and Paul Douglas all approached Johnson to lead an attack against McCarthy.

45. White, OH, #3; Miller, *Lyndon,* 210; *NYT* (Feb. 14, 1954).

46. Miller, *Lyndon,* 214. Johnson told Humphrey, "One of these days he's going to violate the rules of this body, he's going to violate the code of the Senate, and that's when he'll get in trouble. . . ." Humphrey, OH, #1.

47. Ferrell, *Eisenhower Diaries* (April 1, 1953, entry), 234. Also in Galambos and Chandler, eds., *Papers of Eisenhower* (April 1, 1953), #118, vol. 14, pg. 136–37.

48. *PPP, Eisenhower,* 1953, 24.

49. Ambrose, *Eisenhower: The President,* 63–65.; Gary May, *China Scapegoat: The Diplomatic Ordeal of John Carter Vincent* (Long Grove, Illinois,

1982), 273–78; *NYT* (April 12, 1953). This act replaced Truman's Loyalty Review Board set up through Executive Order 9835.

50. Robert Griffith, "Dwight D. Eisenhower and the Corporate Commonwealth," *American Historical Review* (Feb. 1982), 112–13. On Oppenheimer, see Ferrell, *Eisenhower Diaries* (Dec. 2, 1953, entry), 258–59; and *Congress and the Nation*, 1647–49, 1739; Eisenhower diary (Dec. 2, 1953), Diary Series, Papers as President, Ann Whitman File, EP, DDEL; Galambos and Chandler, eds., *Papers of Eisenhower* (Dec. 2, 1953), #578, vol. 15, pg. 716.

51. Ambrose, *Eisenhower: the President*, 56–61; Richard Fried, *Men Against McCarthy* (New York, 1976), 259.

52. Eisenhower to Hazlett (July 21, 1953) in Robert Griffith, ed., *Ike's Letters to a Friend* (Lawrence, Kansas, 1984), 110.

53. Quoted in Ambrose, *Eisenhower: the President*, 57.

54. Eisenhower to Lucius Clay (Feb. 25, 1954), Diary Series, Papers of President, Ann Whitman File, EP, DDEL.

55. Eisenhower to William Robinson (July 27, 1953), Columnists and Authors File, Robinson Papers, DDEL.

56. Those included Wilton Persons, Bernard Stanley, and Republican National Committee Chairman Leonard W. Hall. There were advisors who encouraged the president to confront McCarthy, particularly Emmet John Hughes and C. C. Jackson. See Fried, *Men Against McCarthy*, 255.

57. Ambrose, *Eisenhower: the President*, 59; Fred I. Greenstein, *The Hidden-Hand Presidency: Eisenhower as Leader* (Baltimore, 1982), 203.

58. Rowland Evans and Robert Novak, *Lyndon B. Johnson: The Exercise of Power* (New York, 1966), 84–85; Hardeman and Bacon, *Rayburn*, 381–82. "Acheson" refers to Dean Acheson, Truman's secretary of state and a favorite target of McCarthy. "White" refers to Harry Dexter White, the assistant secretary of the treasury in the Truman administration and another McCarthy target. In 1948, White died of a heart attack following an intense interrogation by the House Committee on Un-American Activities (HUAC).

59. *NYT* (Feb. 11, 1954). Reston does not mention McCarthy here, but this is just days after McCarthy began his speaking tour.

60. Ibid., (Feb. 14, 1954).

61. Ibid., (Feb. 4, 11, 1954).

62. David Oshinsky, *A Conspiracy So Immense: The World of Joe McCarthy* (New York, 1983), 349–56.

63. Reedy to Johnson (n.d., 1954), Senate Papers, LBJP, LBJL.

64. *NYT* (Nov. 5, 1954).

65. *New Republic* (May 12, 1952).

66. Gillon, *Politics and Vision*, 94, 98; Carl Solberg, *Hubert Humphrey: A Biography* (St. Paul, 1984), 174; Rudy Abramson, *Spanning the Century: The Life of W. Averell Harriman, 1891–1986* (New York, 1992), 536.

67. Dewey Grantham, *The South in Modern America: A Region at Odds* (New York, 1994), 121.

68. David A. Nichols, *A Matter of Justice: Eisenhower and the Beginnings of the Civil Rights Revolution* (New York, 2007), 204; Robert Frederick Burk, *The Eisenhower Administration and Black Civil Rights* (Knoxville, Tennessee, 1984), 5; Steven F. Lawson, *Running for Freedom: Civil Rights and Black Politics in America Since 1941* (New York, 1991), 34. A good source on this topic is Mary Dudziak, *Cold War Civil Rights: Race and the Image of American Democracy* (Princeton, NJ, 2000), passim.

69. *Time* (July 29, 1957).

70. John Emmet Hughes, *The Ordeal of Power* (New York, 1962), 201.

71. Eisenhower announced his plans to desegregate the nation's capital and federal-run public schools in his State of the Union message in January 1953. *PPP, Eisenhower,* 1953, 30. Several schools jointly operated by the federal government were also desegregated in the 1955–56 school year. By the end of 1953, hotels, theaters, and restaurants in Washington were desegregated. See Burk, *Eisenhower and Civil Rights,* 31–2, and 50–52. Truman had issued Executive Order 9981 to end desegregation in the military by June 1954. See *Congress and the Nation,* 1617. By the summer of 1953, the U.S. Army reported all but eight all-black units had been desegregated, and 95 percent of all black troops were in desegregated units. The United States Air Force and Marines had desegregated by 1952. The U.S. Navy lagged behind the other services. See Burk, *Eisenhower and Civil Rights,* 28–33; Dwight D. Eisenhower, *Waging Peace, 1956–1961* (Garden City, NY, 1965) 234–36. Nichols, *A Matter of Justice,* 49–50.

72. Ambrose, *Eisenhower: the President,* 125

73. Steven F. Lawson, *Black Ballots: Voting Rights in the South, 1944–1969* (New York, 1976), 139.

74. *NYT* (July 18, 1957); *PPP, Eisenhower,* 1957, 547.

75. Diary entry (Aug. 14, 1956), Diary Series, Ann Whitman Files, Papers as President, EP, DDEL.

76. *PPP, Eisenhower,* 1954, 491–92.

77. Neuman V. Bartley, *The Rise of Massive Resistance: Race and Politics in the South in the 1950s* (Baton Rouge, Louisiana, 1970), 82–107. By other accounts, Eisenhower felt a need to support civil rights, but believed it was not the place of the federal government to intervene in state and local issues. On this point, see particularly, Nichols, *A Matter of Justice,* 1–4, 18, 53–55.

78. *NYT* (Aug. 21, 1954).

79. Griffith, "Eisenhower and the Corporate Commonwealth," 102. See also Alice Kessler-Harris, *In Pursuit of Equality: Women, Men, and the Quest for Economic Citizenship in 20th Century America* (New York, 2001), 161.

80. *NYT* (Feb. 8, 1954).

81. *Congress and the Nation,* 486.

82. *PPP, Eisenhower,* 1954, 675.

83. *NYT* (Aug. 21, 1954); *Congress and the Nation,* 697–701.

84. *Congress and the Nation,* 281, 852–55, 1730–31; *PPP, Eisenhower,* 1953, 286–87; Aaron Wildavsky, *Dixon-Yates: A Study in Power Politics* (New Haven, Connecticut, 1962), passim. Caro, *Master of the Senate,* 598, 601, 648.

85. *Congress and the Nation,* 955–61.

86. Miller, *Lyndon,* 217.

87. *NYT* (June 19, 1954); Oshinsky, *A Conspiracy So Immense,* 462–65.

88. McCarthy's approval ratings had fallen to below 30 percent. See Gallup poll references in *NYT* (Mar. 3, and 27, 1954).

89. Ibid., (Aug. 3, 1954). George Reedy insisted that Johnson stacked the committee against McCarthy. "What Johnson was really looking for

[were] conservatives. You couldn't have a liberal on [that] committee."
Reedy, OH, #6.

90. Minutes of the Senate Democratic Party Policy Planning Committee (July 29, 1954), Senate Papers, LBJP, LBJL. See also Reedy to Johnson (n.d., 1954), ibid. Here Reedy tells Johnson, "It's a Republican problem. . . ." Also, Reedy memo (June 15, 1954), Senate Papers, 1941–1961, Reedy's Office Files, LBJP, LBJL. Here Reedy adds, it "is a Republican problem from every standpoint."

91. *NYT* (Aug. 3, 1954).

92. Joseph Rauh, OH, JLOHC.

93. Ferrell, ed., *Diary of James C. Hagerty* (May 28, 1954, entry), 58; (Dec.1, 1954, entry), 120; (Dec. 3, 1954, entry), 125; (Dec. 4, 1954, entry), 126; Brownell, *Advising Ike*, 261; Griffith, ed., *Ike's Letters to a Friend* (April 27, 1954, entry), 126.

94. Broadwater, *Adlai Stevenson*, 142; John Bartlow Martin, *Adlai Stevenson and the World: The Life of Adlai Stevenson* (Garden City, New York, 1977), 105.

95. *NYT* (Mar. 8, 1954).

96. *Congress and the Nation*, 1725.

97. Greenstein, *The Hidden-Hand Presidency: Eisenhower as Leader* 171–73; Brownell, *Advising Ike*, 263; Pach and Richardson, *The Presidency of Dwight Eisenhower*, 70.

98. The best example is Ferrell, ed., *Ike's Letters to a Friend* (July 21, 1953, entry), 110.

99. Several White House advisors, particularly C. D. Jackson and Jack Martin, wrote speeches for the president that denounced McCarthy. The president repeatedly rejected them. See particularly Ambrose, *Eisenhower: The President*, 141.

100. *Congress and the Nation*, 1727; Brownell, *Advising Ike*, 262.

101. Miller, *Lyndon*, 223.

102. *Time* (July 4, 1955); *Congress and the Nation*, 20. For McCarthy's alcoholism, see Richard Rovere, *Senator Joe McCarthy* (New York, 1959), 244–45. Others have refused to accept the analysis that McCarthy was an alcoholic. See particularly, M. Stanton Evans, *Blacklisted by History: The Untold Story of Senator Joe McCarthy and His Fight Against America's Enemies* (New York, 2009), 30–31.

103. The quote is from an article by William S. White, *NYT* (May 7, 1954).

104. Eisenhower to Thomas Dewey (Oct. 8, 1954), Diary Series, Papers as President, Ann Whitman File, EP, DDEL. Galambos and Chandler, eds., *Papers of Eisenhower* (Oct. 8, 1954), #1102, vol. 15, pg. 1337.

105. Eisenhower, *Mandate for Change,* 431–33, 435.

106. Ibid., 434–37. Ambrose, *Nixon,* 356–57; Dallek, *Lone Star Rising,* 641; *NYT* (Feb. 14, 1954).

107. In the Senate the margin was forty-eight Democrats to forty-seven Republicans. Wayne Morse (I-OR) pledged to vote with the Democrats. That made the Democratic majority forty-nine to forty-seven. Morse had switched from the Republicans to the Democrats in 1952. *Time* (Nov. 16, 1954).

108. Griffith, ed., *Ike's Letters to a Friend* (Dec. 8, 1954, entry), 137–38. Galambos and Chandler, eds., *Papers of Eisenhower* (Dec. 8, 1954), #1192, vol. 15, pg. 1435. James Hagerty agreed. See James Hagerty, OH, DDEL.

109. See particularly Knowland's response in *NYT* (Nov. 5, 1954).

110. Hagerty, OH. Eisenhower's popularity ratings were running between about 60 percent and 70 percent through most of 1954.

111. *NYT* (Nov. 7, 1954); Johnson and Rayburn to Eisenhower (Oct. 9, 1954), Senate Papers, LBJP, LBJL.

112. *NYT* (Nov. 5, 1954).

Chapter Four

1. *Time* (Nov. 15, 1954).

2. *NYT* (Nov. 18, 1954).

3. *Time* (Dec. 27, 1954).

4. Miller, *Lyndon,* 226–27; *Time* (Mar. 21, 1955); ibid., (Mar. 28, 1955); Hardeman and Bacon, *Rayburn,* 393–94; *NYT* (Mar. 1, 1955).

5. Evans and Novak, *Lyndon B. Johnson,* 162; *Congress and the Nation,* 976–77. The bill's purpose was to limit oil imports.

6. Evans and Novak, *Lyndon B. Johnson,* 150.

7. Miller, *Lyndon,* 229; Caro, *Master of the Senate,* 606.

8. Miller, *Lyndon*, 229. Evans and Novak, *Lyndon B. Johnson*, 151.

9. Reedy, OH, #8; Caro, *Master of the Senate*, 598–609.

10. Miller, *Lyndon*, 234.

11. Ibid., 235. James Cain, OH, JLOHC.

12. *NYT* (Sept. 30, 1955); Steinberg, *Sam Johnson's Boy*, 442.

13. Reedy was, perhaps, the most insistent. See several memos, Reedy to Johnson (Sept. 1955), Pre-Presidential Memo File, LBJP, LBJL.

14. Perhaps the best account of these events is in Jeff Shesol, *Mutual Contempt: Lyndon Johnson, Robert Kennedy and the Feud that Defined a Decade* (New York, 1997), 32–33. See also Johnson to Joe Kennedy (Aug. 25, 1956), in Lyndon Johnson, *The Vantage Point: Perspectives of the Presidency, 1963–1969* (New York, 1971), 3; Evans and Novak, *Lyndon B. Johnson*, 278; Doris Kearns Goodwin, *The Fitzgeralds and the Kennedys: An American Saga* (New York, 1987) 780–81; Dallek, *Lone Star Rising*, 490–91.

15. Reedy, OH, #8.

16. Ibid., #7.

17. Whitney Speech (Nov. 21, 1955), Speech File, Statements of LBJ, LBJP, LBJL. Randall B. Woods, *LBJ: Architect of American Ambition* (New York, 2006), 229.

18. Baker to Johnson (Oct. 4, 1955), Pre-Presidential Confidential File, ibid. Baker's official position and title was Secretary to the Leader.

19. *NYT* (Sept. 25, 1955). The article was by James Reston and appeared on the front page. See Ambrose, *Nixon*, 373–74; and Ambrose, *Eisenhower: The President*, 273. For Adams's views, see Adams, *Firsthand Report*, 149–68.

20. See particularly *NYT* (Sept. 26, 1955).

21. Eisenhower, *Mandate for Change*, 538; Ambrose, *Eisenhower: The President*, 272; Ambrose, *Nixon*, 374; Clarence G. Lasby, *Eisenhower's Heart Attack: How Ike Beat Heart Disease and Held on to the Presidency* (Lawrence, Kansas, 1997), 80, 127.

22. Ambrose, *Eisenhower: The President*, 273.

23. Ambrose, *Nixon*, 377, 380; Milton Eisenhower, *The President Is Calling* (Garden City, NY, 1974), 315; Ferrell, ed., *Diary of James Hagerty* (Dec. 13, 1955, entry), 241–42.

24. *National Review* (Nov. 5, 1955); John Judas, *William F. Buckley, Jr.: Patron Saint of the Conservatives* (New York, 1988), 128–33; David W. Reinhard, *The Republican Right since 1945* (Lexington, Ky, 1983), 129–30; Lasby, *Eisenhower's Heart Attack,* 149.

25. Eisenhower to Hazlett (Dec. 24, 1953), Diary Series, Papers as President, Ann Whitman File, EP, DDEL. Also in Griffith, *Ike's Letters to a Friend* (Dec. 24, 1953, entry), 117; and in Galambos and Chandler, eds., *Papers of Eisenhower* (Dec. 24, 1953), #640, vol. 15, pg. 792. See also Dwight Eisenhower to Milton Eisenhower (Dec. 11, 1953), Diary Series, Papers as President, Ann Whitman File, EP, DDEL. And Galambos and Chandler, eds., *Papers of Eisenhower* (Dec. 11, 1953), #606, vol. 15, pg. 760.

26. *Time* (Sept. 19, 1955).

27. Sherman Adams, OH, DDEL.

28. Adams, *Firsthand Report,* 181.

29. *NYT* (Dec. 6, 1954); Steinberg, *Sam Johnson's Boy,* 392–94.

30. *NYT* (Dec. 23, 1954).

31. Evans and Novak, *Lyndon B. Johnson,* 153. In another incident, Connecticut senator Prescott Bush rejected a bribe from an oil and gas lobbyist and then reported that his son (George H. W. Bush) was denied a large volume of business. See Eisenhower's own report of this in Ferrell, *Eisenhower Diaries* (Feb. 11, 1956, entry), 316. And in Eisenhower diary (Feb. 11, 1956), Diary Series, Papers as President, Ann Whitman File, EP, DDEL. Also in Galambos and Chandler, eds., *Papers of Eisenhower* (Feb. 11, 1956), #1748, vol. 16, pg. 2116.

32. Steinburg, *Sam Johnson's Boy,* 433.

33. Ferrell, ed., *Eisenhower Diaries* (Feb. 11, 1956, entry), 316; Galambos and Chandler, eds., *Papers of Eisenhower* (Feb. 11, 1956), #1748, vol. 16, pg. 2116; Hardeman and Bacon, *Rayburn,* 393–94.

34. Eisenhower, *Mandate for Change,* 548. For Eisenhower's thoughts on the Transcontinental Motor Convoy of 1919 (which also, apparently, influenced his interest in a national highway system) see Dwight D. Eisenhower, *At Ease: Stories I Tell Friends* (Garden City, NY, 1967), 157–67.

35. Smith, *Lucius Clay,* 618–19; Kenneth Jackson, *Crabgrass Frontier: The Suburbanization of the United States* (New York, 1985), 249.

36. Mark Rose, *Interstate: Express Highway Politics, 1939–1989* (Knoxville, Tennessee, 1979), 78–79. There was also a conflict with organized labor.

Union organizers wanted to control the wages of workers on the highway projects. Johnson, who did not want to cast a vote in the Senate against organized labor, scheduled a medical physical at the Mayo Clinic in Minnesota to avoid the vote. See Caro, *Master of the Senate*, 678.

37. Rose, *Interstate*, 90; *Congress and the Nation*, 419.

38. Smith, *Lucius Clay*, 620; Jackson, *Crabgrass Frontier*, 249–50.

39. *NYT* (Mar. 2, 1956); *PPP, Eisenhower*, 1956, 263–66; Reinhard, *Republican Right*, 130.

40. Arthur Schlesinger, Jr., "The Political Problem: 1956" (Sept. 9, 1955), strategy memo, 1956 Presidential Campaign Series, Stevenson Papers, Mudd Library, Princeton; *Time* (June 30, 1955).

41. *Time* (July 16, 1956). Stevenson apparently said this often. See similar comments to Newton Minow in Miller, *Lyndon*, 249.

42. *Time* (June 20, 1955).

43. Stevenson to Arthur Schlesinger, Jr. (Sept. 16, 1955), 1956 Presidential Campaign Series, Stevenson Papers, Mudd Library, Princeton.

44. Strategy memo by Arthur Schlesinger, Jr., "The Political Problem: 1956," (Sept. 6, 1955), ibid.

45. Ibid.

46. *Time* (July 16, 1956); Stevenson Campaign Announcement Speech (Dec. 15, 1955), 1956 Presidential Campaign Series, Stevenson Papers, Mudd Library, Princeton.

47. Eisenhower to George Whitney (Mar. 13, 1956), Name Series, Papers as President, Ann Whitman File, EP, DDEL. Galambos and Chandler, eds., *Papers of Eisenhower* (Mar. 12, 1956), #1782, vol. 16, pg. 2063–64. For the suggestion of secretary of defense, see Earl Mazo, *Richard Nixon: A Political and Personal Portrait* (New York, 1959), 147.

48. Eisenhower to Hazlett (Mar. 2, 1956) Diary Series, Papers as President, Ann Whitman File, EP, DDEL. Also in Griffith, *Ike's Letters to a Friend* (March 2, 1956, entry), 160.

49. Eisenhower diary (Mar. 13, 1956), Diary Series, Papers as President, Ann Whitman File, EP, DDEL.

50. Eisenhower diary (Mar. 13, 1956), ibid.

51. *PPP, Eisenhower*, 1956, 302–3.

52. Eisenhower diary (April 26, 1956, entry), Diary Series, Papers as President, Ann Whitman File, EP, DDEL. Much of this is also quoted in Richard Nixon, *RN: The Memoirs of Richard Nixon* (New York, 1978), 172; and Ambrose, *Nixon*, 397–99; *NYT* (April 27, 1956).

53. Arthur Minnich, Minutes, Cabinet Meeting (March 9, 1956), Cabinet Series, White House Office Files, EP, DDEL; Brownell *Advising Ike*, 218. Sumner was one of the leaders of the Reconstruction era's Radical Republicans who punished the defeated South through a series of Reconstruction acts and civil rights acts.

54. Reedy, OH, #8.

55. The "Manifesto" was officially titled "Declaration of Constitutional Principles." Perhaps the most accessible source for the entire document is Brownell, *Advising Ike*, Appendix C, 359–63. A good explanation of how the "Southern Manifesto" was conceived is Richard Russell to M. Haynes Mizell (April 30, 1962) Series I, Dictation, box 18, Richard Russell Papers, University of Georgia, Athens, Georgia.

56. James H. Rowe, OH, #1, JLOHC.

57. Fite, *Richard Russell*, 333–34. *NYT* (April 10, 1956); *Time* (March 26, 1956), 25. See also, Reedy, OH, #8.

58. Reedy, OH, #8 and #10. See also, Fite, *Richard Russell*, 333–36.

59. Miller, *Lyndon*, 242.

60. Harry McPherson, *A Political Education* (Boston, 1972), 153; Harry McPherson, OH, JLOHC; Goodwin, *Lyndon Johnson*, 174–79.

61. Goodwin, *Johnson*, 241–42; Woods, *LBJ*, 304. Years later, Johnson claimed that he was proud that he had not signed the Southern Manifesto.

62. *NYT* (Nov. 17, 1955).

63. Press Release on Minnesota Primary Results (n.d., March 20–22), 1956 Campaign Series, Stevenson Papers, Mudd Library, Princeton. This press release claims that 125,000 Minnesota Republicans crossed over in an effort to stop Stevenson; in some precincts (according to the memo) the Democratic voter turnout was 300 percent over 1952. Polls showed that Kefauver's numbers were on the rise, while Stevenson's numbers were declining rapidly. *Time* (April 23, 1956).

64. *NYT* (Aug. 12, 1956); *Time* (June 18, 1956); McKeever, *Adlai Stevenson*, 375–76; Miller, *Lyndon*, 252.

65. Evans and Novak, *Lyndon B. Johnson,* 88–92; Hardeman and Bacon, *Rayburn,* 395–97. See Johnson's press release (n.d.) at Johnson for President Committee, Senate Political Files, 1949–1961, LBJP, LBJL. Here he announces that John Nance Garner will be his honorary chairman.

66. *NYT* (Aug. 12, 1956).

67. *NYT* (Aug. 12, 1956); *Time* (Aug. 20, 1956). Truman had concluded that Stevenson was a conservative. See also Abramson, *Spanning the Century,* 540.

68. *NYT* (Aug. 12, 1956).

69. Reedy to Johnson (n.d., Aug.?, 1956), Pre-Presidential Memo File, LBJP, LBJL. Reedy was never certain if Johnson ever wanted to run, see Reedy, OH, #9; and *Time* (Aug. 20, 1956).

70. Fite, *Russell,* 312–13. See Russell's endorsement of Johnson at *NYT* (Aug. 14, 1956).

71. Liz Carpenter, OH, JLOHC.

72. Rowe to Johnson (Aug. 11, 1956), Select Names File, Rowe, LBJA, LBJL.

73. See particularly Abramson, *Spanning the Century,* 540; *Time* (July 16, 1956).

74. On several of these points, see Woods, *LBJ,* 309.

75. Dallek, *Lone Star Rising,* 502. It is often argued that Johnson told Stevenson he would accept a vice presidential nomination. See Evans and Novak, *Lyndon B. Johnson,* 253–55; Hardeman and Bacon, *Rayburn,* 405–6; Johnson, *Vantage Point,* 3.

76. John Sparkman to Robert Kendall (July 17, 1956), 1956 Presidential Campaign Series, Stevenson Papers, Mudd Library, Princeton. Among those delegates was a young Eugene "Bull" Conner of Birmingham, who some nine years later would defend that city against Martin Luther King's marches; and a young George Wallace, then a judge from Clayton, Alabama.

77. *NYT* (Aug. 13, 1956).

78. Ibid. (Aug. 13, 1956). See also Joseph P. Lash, *Eleanor: The Years Alone* (New York, 1972), 241. Harriman, however, insisted on an endorsement of the *Brown* decision.

79. Reedy, OH, #9. There is evidence that it was Kennedy who pushed Stevenson to throw open the convention to choose the vice presidential

nominee. Kennedy may have believed that Stevenson would not choose him, so he hoped to win with delegate votes. See *Time* (Aug. 27, 1956).

80. Kenneth P. O'Donnell and David F. Powers, *"Johnny We Hardly Knew Ye:" Memories of John Fitzgerald Kennedy* (Boston, 2nd ed., 1973), 135–36. As early as July 1, Kennedy had said on the television news program *Face the Nation* that he was not a candidate for vice president. Transcript of *Face the Nation* (July 1, 1956), Pre-Presidential Papers, Kennedy Library, Boston.

81. *Time* (Aug. 15, 1956); Herbert Parmet, *Jack: The Struggles of John F. Kennedy* (New York, 1980), 361–62; Hardeman and Bacon, *Rayburn*, 403–5.

82. *NYT* (Aug. 12, 1956).

83. *Time* (Aug. 13, 1956).

84. Eisenhower to Hazlett (Nov. 2, 1956), Diary Series, Papers as President, 1953–1961, Ann Whitman File, EP, DDEL. See also Ferrell, *Ike's Letters to a Friend* (Nov. 2, 1956, entry), 173.

85. Minutes of Meeting (July 25, 1956), Diary Series, Papers as President, Ann Whitman File, EP, DDEL. Here the president insists that motorcades do "not [keep] with the dignity of the office."

86. "Memorandum for the Record," (Mar. 31, 1956), Diary Series, Papers as President, Ann Whitman File, Diary Series, EP, DDEL.

87. Lodge to Eisenhower (Oct. 15, 1956), ibid.

88. This strategy is spelled out in *Time* (June 18, 1956).

89. *Washington Post* (Aug. 20, 1956); *NYT* (Mar. 29, 1956).

90. *Time* (Sept. 17, 1956). A Gallup poll, cited here, gave Eisenhower-Nixon 52 percent and Stevenson-Kefauver 41 percent.

91. Ibid. (Oct. 15, 1956).

92. "The Text of Bulganin's Letter to Eisenhower," *NYT* (Oct. 21, 1956). Nixon's comments were released the day before. See ibid. (Oct. 20, 1956).

93. John S. D. Eisenhower, *Strictly Personal: A Memoir* (New York, 1974), 189.

94. Eisenhower to Hazlett (Nov. 2, 1956), Diary Series, Papers as President, Ann Whitman File, EP, DDEL. Also in Ferrell, *Ike's Letters to a Friend* (Nov. 2, 1956, entry), 173. Galambos and Chandler, eds., *Papers of Eisenhower* (Nov. 2, 1956), #2063, vol. 17, pg. 2353–57.

95. *Time* (Nov. 12, 1956).

96. Hagerty, OH.

97. *Newsweek* (April 9, 1956).

98. *NYT* (Oct. 13, 1956)

99. Lawson, *Black Ballots*, 162.

100. The nation's African Americans, however, had not done well during Eisenhower's first term. Their income declined (in relation to white income) for the first time since the Great Depression.

101. Stevenson insisted that he would never run again. See "Statements by Adlai Stevenson Concerning the 1960 Presidential Nomination," Sorensen Papers, Kennedy Library, Boston. There is evidence, however, that he would have taken the nomination in 1960 had it been offered. See Donaldson, *First Modern Campaign*, 73–77.

102. Miller, *Lyndon*, 259.

103. Ibid., 260.

104. Evans and Novak, *Lyndon B. Johnson,* 161. The emphasis is Lehman's.

Chapter Five

1. Arthur Larson, *A Republican Looks at His Party* (New York, 1956), 10–19. Larsen was dean of the University of Pittsburgh Law School and a former Rhodes Scholar. He has been described as Eisenhower's "egghead," and a Republican theoretician.

2. *Time* (Aug. 20, 1956). Larson's book is discussed here. See also, David L. Stebenne, *Modern Republican: Arthur Larson and the Eisenhower Years* (Bloomington, Indiana, 2006), 158–59.

3. Larson, *A Republican Looks at His Party*, 2.

4. Ibid., 2–3, 8–9; Stebenne, *Modern Republican*, 158.

5. *Time* (Nov. 15, 1956). Also in "Eisenhower Statements to Reporters," (Nov. 14, 1956), Papers as President, Office Files, EP, DDEL; *PPP, Eisenhower,* 1956, 298.

6. Nixon, *Memoirs*, 180–81.

7. Reinhard, *Republican Right*, 137.

8. Dirksen interview (Sept. 16, 1957), "Reporters' Roundup," Mutual Broadcasting System, Transcript, Dirksen Center, Pekin Illinois.

9. William F. Buckley, Jr., spent much of his book *Up From Liberalism* (New York, 1959) criticizing Larson and his concept of "Modern Republicanism." Barry Goldwater, in his *The Conscience of a Conservative* (Shephardsville, Kentucky, 1960), accused Larson of liberalism, and statism leading to absolutism. See pages 1, 15–16, 19–20. A contemporary criticism is William Shannon, "More of the Same," *Commonweal* (Dec. 21, 1956), 306–7.

10. *PPP, Eisenhower,* 1957, 6–16; *NYT* (Jan. 6, 1957).

11. *NYT* (Jan. 2, 1957). These statements were made to the press following the meeting.

12. Ibid.

13. Ambrose, *Eisenhower: The President,* 383.

14. Evans and Novak, *Lyndon B. Johnson,* 176–77; Ambrose, *Eisenhower: the President,* 388. Salim Yaqub, *Containing Arab Nationalism: The Eisenhower Doctrine and the Middle East* (Chapel Hill, NC, 2006), 93–97, 111.

15. *NYT* (Feb. 11, 24, 1957). Israel withdrew from Gaza in March, 1957, apparently under pressure from the Eisenhower administration. Dallek, *Lone Star Rising,* 513.

16. *NYT* (Feb. 24, 1957).

17. Carl Solberg, *Hubert Humphrey,* 178–79.

18. By most accounts, this drop in popularity had to do with the Soviet launch of *Sputnik* and the confrontation at Little Rock—and the administration's handling of those incidences.

19. *Time* (Jan. 27, 1958).

20. *NYT* (Jan. 17, 1957); Steinberg, *Sam Johnson's Boy,* 474–76. Eisenhower defended Humphrey by saying that the treasury secretary meant that there would be a depression if spending continued for the long term. He added, however, that he did not approve of the statement or the words Humphrey used. *NYT* (Jan 24, 1957); and *PPP, Eisenhower,* 1957, 99.

21. *Time* (May 20, 1957).

22. *PPP, Eisenhower,* 1957, 99; *NYT* (Jan. 24, 1957).

23. *PPP, Eisenhower,* 1957, 354–55.

24. Most of that was finally restored.

25. *PPP, Eisenhower,* 1957, 341–52. By May, Humphrey had left the cabinet, he said for personal reasons, but by most accounts he was forced out.

26. Ibid., 354–55; *Time* (May 27 and June 3, 1957). Eisenhower delivered a radio speech afterward that was received more favorably.

27. Larson had been undersecretary in the Department of Labor and then a speechwriter in the White House before being named to head the USIA in 1956.

28. *Congress and the Nation,* 215; *NYT* (April 17, 1957, May 9, 1957, and Oct. 17, 1957); Steinberg, *Sam Johnson's Boy,* 476–77.

29. *Time* (April 22, 1957).

30. *Cong. Rec.,* 85th Cong., 1st sess., 5258–65. Much of this speech can also be found in *Time* (April 22, 1957). See also, ibid. (May 20, 1957); and *NYT* (April 19, 1957); Robert Alan Goldberg, *Barry Goldwater* (New Haven, 1995), 119–120.

31. The group was known as "The Committee of One Hundred" and continued to exist up to the 1960 Republican convention. See Goldberg, *Barry Goldwater,* 142.

32. "Pre-press Conference Briefing" (April 10, 1957), Diary Series, Papers as President, Ann Whitman File, EP, DDEL.

33. Memorandum, Jack Z. Anderson to Ann Whitman (April 13, 1957), in ibid.

34. *PPP, Eisenhower,* 1956, 25; *NYT* (Jan. 6, 1956). Nichols, *A Matter of Justice,* 66–67.

35. Brownell, *Advising Ike,* 219; Eisenhower, *Waging Peace,* 13–54; *Congress and the Nation,* 1620.

36. Brownell, *Advising Ike,* 218–19; *Congress and the Nation,* 1622; *Time* (May 6, 1957). Nichols, *A Matter of Justice,* 143–68.

37. *Time* (Aug. 6, 1956).

38. Ibid. (Jan. 14, 1957).

39. Miller, *Lyndon,* 264; *Time* (July 1, 1957); Dallek, *Lone Star Rising,* 521; Woods, *LBJ,* 320; *Congress and the Nation,* 1621; Nichols, *A Matter of Justice,* 151–53.

40. Kearns, *Lyndon Johnson,* 156-57; Dallek, *Lone Star Rising,* 521; *Time* (July 1, 1957); Evans and Novak, *Lyndon B. Johnson,* 138–43; Steinberg, *Sam Johnson's Boy,* 468–69. The Senators were Wayne Morse (I-OR), Warren Magnusen (D-WA), Jim Murray (D-MT), and Mike Mansfield

(D-MT). When the Hell's Canyon bill came before the Senate, Russell, Eastland, Johnson, Sam Ervin (D-SC), Russell Long (D-LA), and George Smathers (D-FL) voted for the bill. *Congress and the Nation*, 946–54.

41. *Time* (Aug. 5, 1957).

42. Rowe to Johnson (July 3, 1957), Select Names, James Rowe, LBJA, LBJL.

43. Evans and Novak, *Lyndon B. Johnson*, 137–40; Reedy, *Johnson*, 112–14; Dallek, *Lone Star Rising*, 512; Ambrose, *Eisenhower: The President*, 407–7; *Congress and the Nation*, 1621–24. Fite, *Richard Russell*, 339.

44. *NYT* (July 3, 4, 1957).

45. *PPP, Eisenhower*, 1957, 520–21; *NYT* (July 4, 1957); *Time* (July 15, 1957). *Congress and the Nation*, 1623. Transcript of Press Conference (July 2, 1957), Legislative Meeting Series, Papers as President, Ann Whitman File, EP, DDEL.

46. Clinton Anderson, *Outsider in the Senate: Senator Clinton Anderson's Memoirs* (New York, 1970), 146–47. *NYT* (July 9, 1957).

47. Brownell, *Advising Ike*, 225; *Congress and the Nation*, 225.

48. Fite, *Richard Russell*, 338–39.

49. *Congress and the Nation*, 1623; *NYT* (July 25, 1957).

50. Humphrey, OH. Humphrey said that "it was perfectly obvious that a number of juries in the South were just rigged. They [Southern whites] just would not give them [Southern blacks] a fair shake." Reconstruction-era civil rights acts had allowed for jury trials in criminal contempt cases.

51. *NYT* (Aug. 2, 1957); Evans and Novak, *Lyndon B. Johnson*, 151–3; Dallek, *Lone Star Rising*, 526.

52. Johnson to Stevenson (Aug. 12, 1957), Famous Names, A. Stevenson, LBJA, LBJL.

53. *Congress and the Nation*, 1623; Reedy, OH, #1.

54. *Time* (Aug. 12, 1957).

55. *Congress and the Nation*, 1621–22; Reedy, OH, #1; Nadine Cohodas, *Strom Thurmond and the Politics of Southern Change* (New York, 1993), 294–97.

56. Arthur Minnich, Legislative Leadership Committee (Aug. 13, 1957), Proceedings, DDEL.

57. The Wilkins quote is in Taylor Branch, *Parting the Waters: America in the King Years, 1954–1963* (New York, 1988), 221. Wilkins is, however, quoted as opposing the bill in Miller, *Lyndon,* 269.

58. Branch, *Parting the Waters,* 221; Eisenhower, *Waging Peace,* 160; Steinberg, *Sam Johnson's Boy,* 474.

59. Miller, *Lyndon,* 273. Johnson makes the point in his memoirs, see Johnson, *Vantage Point,* 156

60. *PPP, Eisenhower,* 1957, 546; *NYT* (July 18, 1957).

61. Nichols, *A Matter of Justice,* 170–76. See also Hughes, *Ordeal of Power,* 242.

62. Brownell, *Advising, Ike,* 207; Burk, *Eisenhower and Black Civil Rights,* 178; *NYT* (Sept. 5, 15, 1957); Nichols, A *Matter of Justice,* 170–73.

63. Ibid., 172, 317n; Brownell, *Advising Ike,* 208.

64. *NYT* (Sept. 5, 1957).

65. Faubus to Eisenhower (Sept. 5, 1957) and Eisenhower to Faubus (Sept. 5, 1957), both in Central Files, Official Files, EP, DDEL; *PPP, Eisenhower,* 1957, 659; *NYT* (Sept. 15, 1957).

66. Ibid. (Sept. 25, 1957).

67. Adams, *Firsthand Report,* 268–69; Brownell disagreed with this strategy. See Brownell, *Advising Ike,* 208–09.

68. Eisenhower diary (Oct. 8, 1957), Diary Series, Papers as President, Ann Whitman File, EP, DDEL; Eisenhower, *Waging Peace,* 166; *NYT* (Sept. 15, 1957); Ferrell, *Eisenhower Diaries* (October 8, 1957, entry), 347–48. Also Galambos and Chandler, eds., *Papers of Eisenhower* (Oct. 8, 1957), #374, vol. 18, pg. 481.

69. Brownell, *Advising Ike,* 210. See also, Adams, *Firsthand Report,* 351.

70. Eisenhower, *Waging Peace,* 170; Brownell, *Advising Ike,* 211, 365–82.

71. Eisenhower to Adams, telephone call (Sept. 11, 1957), Diary Series, Papers as President, Ann Whitman File, EP, DDEL.

72. *NYT* (Sept. 25, 1957).

73. Ambrose, *Eisenhower: The President,* 420–21; Fite, *Richard Russell,* 344–45; Robert Mann, *The Walls of Jericho: Lyndon Johnson, Hubert Humphrey, Richard Russell, and the Struggle for Civil Rights* (New York,

1996), 227–28; *U.S. News and World Report* (Oct. 4, 1957), 58; *NYT* (Sept. 25, 27, 1957).

74. Eisenhower often made this point in private. See Arthur Larson, *Eisenhower: The President Nobody Knew* (New York, 1968), 124–25, 127.

75. *PPP, Eisenhower, 1957*, 689–94. There are several articles in the *New York Times*. See particularly, "Red Press Gloats over Little Rock" (Sept. 26, 1957), and "Editorials in France and Italy Chide U.S." (Sept. 26, 1957). This point is covered in Burk, *Eisenhower and Black Civil Rights*, 6–12.

76. Reedy to Johnson (Oct. 17, 1957), Senate Office Files, LBJP, LBJL.

77. *PPP, Eisenhower, 1957*, 719–35.

78. *Time* (Oct. 21, 1957).

79. *NYT* (Oct. 6, 1957).

80. Ibid. (Oct. 9, 1957).

81. This quote is from Adams's memoir, *Firsthand Report*, 302. His statement to the press can be found at *NYT* (Oct. 20, 1957).

82. *NYT* (Oct. 8, 1957).

83. Both quotes can be found in ibid. (Oct. 9, 1957).

84. Ibid. (Oct. 8, 1957).

85. *Time* (Oct. 28, 1957). Eisenhower's rating, however, only dropped to 57 percent, still impressive for a second-term president.

86. Ibid. (Nov 11, 1957); *NYT* (Nov 4, 1957).

87. *PPP, Eisenhower, 1957*, 789–99 and 807–16.

88. *NYT* (Oct. 6, 1957).

89. Ambrose, *Eisenhower: The President*, 430; James Olson, *Stuart Symington: A Life* (Columbia, Mo., 2003), 330–31.

90. Reedy to Johnson (Oct. 17, 1957), Senate Office Files, LBJP, LBJL. Reedy always claimed that he coined the phrase "missile gap."

91. Robert A. Divine, *The Sputnik Challenge: Eisenhower's Response to the Soviet Satellite* (New York, 1993), 63.

92. Ibid., 63.

93. Ibid., 68–70, 76.

94. The president wanted the space program housed in the Defense Department. Arthur Minnich, Legislative Leadership Meeting (Feb. 4, 1958), Proceedings, EP, DDEL.

95. *Congress and the Nation*, 300–1; *Time* (April 14, 1958); Robert A. Divine, "Lyndon Johnson and the Politics of Space," in Robert A. Divine, ed., *The Johnson Years: Vietnam, the Environment, and Science* (Lawrence, Kansas, 1987), 226–27; Reedy, *Lyndon Johnson*, 13; Divine, *Sputnik Challenge*, 111–12, 145–54; Reedy, OH, #11; Evans and Novak, *Lyndon B. Johnson*, 206–09.

96. *Time* (Feb. 10, 1958, and Feb. 26, 1958); *Life* (Feb. 10, 1958); Eisenhower, *Waging Peace*, 257.

97. *Newsweek* (Dec. 29, 1958).

98. Hagerty, OH, #2.

99. *NYT* (Sept. 23, 1958). Adams, *Firsthand Report*, 313. Adams also arranged for Goldfine's son to be readmitted to Dartmouth after he had flunked out his junior year. Adams was on the Dartmouth board of directors. Hagerty, OH, #2.

100. Adams, *Firsthand Report*, 316–17.

101. *Time* (June 23, 1958). *Time* also pointed out that had this happened to a senator or a congressman, there would have been no concern for a representative looking out for a constituent.

102. *PPP, Eisenhower*, 1958, 479–80; *Time* (June 30, 1958).

103. *NYT* (Sept. 23, 1958).

104. *Time* (Feb. 24, 1958 and Mar. 17, 1958); Iwan W. Morgan, *Eisenhower Versus the Spenders* (New York, 1990), 99–100.

105. *Time* (Mar. 31, 1958).

106. Ferrell, *Eisenhower Diaries* (Mar. 17, 1958 entry), 352–53. Also, Galambos and Chandler, *Papers of Eisenhower* (Mar. 17, 1958) #610, vol. 19, pg 779.

107. *Time* (Mar. 17, 1958, May 12, 1958, April 24, 1958, and April 28, 1958).

108. Ibid. (Mar 17, 1958).

109. Ibid. (April 28, 1958); *NYT* (Mar. 13, 1958). *Congress and the Nation*, 420–22, 705–6, 858, 1299; Steinberg, *Sam Johnson's Boy*, 484.

110. *Time* (Feb. 24, 1958).

111. Ibid. (Feb. 24, 1958).

112. Ibid. (Mar. 24, 1958). See also Eisenhower to Hazlett (Feb. 26, 1958), Name Series, Ann Whitman File, EP, DDEL. Also in Griffith, *Ike's Letters to a Friend* (Feb. 26, 1958, entry), 200. Galambos and Chandler, eds., *Papers of Eisenhower* (Feb. 26, 1958) #580, vol. 19, pg. 736.

113. One of the most vocal detractors to Eisenhower's message was James Carey, the president of the International Electrical Workers. See *Time* (June 2, 1958).

114. *Newsweek* (Oct. 20, 1958).

115. "Democratic Party Platform," Famous Names, LBJA, LBJL. Also in *Democratic Digest* (Sept., 1958), 4.

116. *Time* (Sept. 12, 1958).

117. *Congress and the Nation*, 29.

118. *Time* (Sept. 12, 1958).

119. *Congress and the Nation*, 28.

120. Evans and Novak, *Lyndon B. Johnson*, 196.

121. *Congress and the Nation*, 29–30.

122. Rockefeller was immediately perceived as a contender for the 1960 nomination. See *Time* (Nov. 17, 1958).

123. Morgan, *Eisenhower Versus the Spenders*, 125.

124. Ibid., 126.

Chapter Six

1. James Hagerty, OH, #6, COHC.

2. Rowe to Johnson (Nov. 20, 1958), Select Names, LBJA, LBJL.

3. Evans and Novak, *Lyndon B. Johnson*, 199. Others involved included Paul Douglas (D-IL), Pat McNamara (D-MI), John Carroll (D-CO), and Humphrey (D-MN). This exchange was eventually leaked to the press.

4. Ibid., 200; *Time* (Mar. 16 and April 20, 1959). Proxmier explained the "one-man rule" of Lyndon Johnson on *Meet the Press* (Mar. 1, 1959), transcripts, Library of Congress. Charlie McCarthy was the name of ventriloquist Edgar Bergen's dummy.

5. *Time* (April 20, 1959).

6. Ibid. (Nov. 17, 1958).

7. Ibid. (June 8, 1959). *Eisenhower, Mandate for Change,* 442.

8. *PPP, Eisenhower,* 1959, 12–14, 20–21; *Time* (Feb. 16, 1959); Eisenhower, *Waging Peace,* 461–62.

9. Ambrose, *Eisenhower: the President,* 496; Pach and Richardson, *Eisenhower,* 176–77.

10. *Time* (Feb. 16, 1959).

11. Ibid. (Feb. 2, 1959).

12. Morgan, *Eisenhower Versus the Spenders,* 182; *Congress and the Nation,* 492.

13. *Time* (Jan. 5, 1959). See also conservative criticism of Nixon and his "liberal" fiscal policies in an article by Brent Bozell, *National Review* (June 18, 1960), 388.

14. *Time* (Feb. 2, 1959). For additional denials, see ibid. (Nov. 24, 1958).

15. *NYT* (Nov. 18, 1958).

16. Ibid. (Nov. 24, 1958).

17. *Time* (Feb. 23, 1959).

18. Reedy, *Lyndon Johnson,* 127–28. Caro, *Master of the Senate,* 812.

19. Reedy, *Lyndon Johnson,* 127.

20. Stewart Alsop, "Lyndon Johnson: How Does He Do It?" *Saturday Evening Post* (Jan. 24, 1959), 43–44.

21. Miller, *Lyndon,* 501–2; Caro, *Master of the Senate,* 812.

22. *PPP, Eisenhower,* 1953, 6.

23. *Congress and the Nation,* 571–72.

24. Eisenhower, *Mandate for Change,* 90.

25. Ferrell, *Eisenhower Diaries* (Dec. 11, 1953, entry), 264.

26. *PPP, Eisenhower,* 1955, 7–30; ibid., 1956, 1–27; *Congress and the Nation,* 596–97.

27. *Congress and the Nation,* 599, 604.

28. Ibid., 607. Robert Dallek, *An Unfinished Life: John F. Kennedy, 1917–1963* (Boston, 2003), 220.

29. *PPP, Eisenhower,* 1959, 567–70.

30. Melvyn Dubofsky, *The State and Labor in Modern America* (Chapel Hill, North Carolinia, 1994), 220–22.

31. *Congress and the Nation,* 31–32, 283–84, 609–10.

32. Ralph B. Levering, *The Cold War: 1945–1987* (Arlington Heights, Illinois, 2nd ed., 1988), 77.

33. Numerous reports of Castro's eleven-day visit to the United States can be found in the *New York Times* (April 16–23, 1959). See also, Ambrose, *Nixon,* 515–16. And Herbert S. Parmet, *Richard Nixon and His America* (Boston, 1990), 375–77.

34. A very good source on Eisenhower and Latin America in this period is Ambrose, *Eisenhower: the President,* 109–12 and 129–30 (on Mossedegh and the revolution in Iran), 192–96 (on Arbenz and the revolution in Guatemala), and 555–58 (on Castro and the revolution in Cuba).

35. Stephen Ambrose, *Ike's Spies: Eisenhower and the Espionage Establishment* (Garden City, New York, 1981), 309–310; Dallek, *An Unfinished Life,* 359–72.

36. Ambrose, *Ike's Spies,* on Oppenheimer, 284. Kai Bird and Martin J. Sherwin, *American Prometheus: The Triumph and Tragedy of J. Robert Oppenheimer* (New York, 2006), 480–84.

37. Ambrose, *Ike's Spies,* 109; Dallek, *Lone Star Rising,* 557; Caro, *Master of the Senate,* 1033.

38. Steinburg, *Sam Johnson's Boy,* 503–05; Evans and Novak, *Lyndon B. Johnson,* 228–31; Dallek, *Lone Star Rising,* 558; Ambrose, *Eisenhower: the President,* 530–31.

39. *Congress and the Nation,* 31–32; Dallek, *An Unfinished Life,* 279.

40. On the Nixon-Eisenhower relationship, see Ambrose, *Nixon,* 547–48; Ambrose, *Eisenhower: the President,* 559, 596–97.

41. Eisenhower to Hazlett (Mar. 2, 1956), Diary Series, Papers as President, Ann Whitman File, EP, DDEP. Also in Ferrell, *Ike's Letters to a Friend* (March 2, 1956, entry), 160. Galambos and Chandler, eds., *Papers of Eisenhower* (Mar. 2, 1956) #1766, vol. 16, pg. 2042.

42. Milton Eisenhower OH, COHC.

43. *PPP, Eisenhower,* 1960, 144, 147.

44. Mazo, *Richard Nixon*, 243.

45. *Newsweek* (Jan. 25, 1960).

46. *NYT* (July 25 and 27, 1959); *Time* (Aug. 10, 1959); *Newsweek* (Aug. 3, 1959); *Life* (Aug. 10, 1959). A good account of this is Milton Eisenhower, *The President Is Calling*, 328–32. Milton Eisenhower accompanied Nixon to the Soviet Union and was with Nixon in the "Kitchen" during the debates.

47. Joseph Persico, *The Imperial Rockefeller: A Biography of Nelson A. Rockefeller* (New York, 1982), 39.

48 Summary of telephone call, Eisenhower to Rockefeller (June 11, 1960), Eisenhower Diary Series, Papers as President, Ann Whitman File, EP, DDEL. The analysis is from Whitman's notes.

49. Goldberg, *Barry Goldwater*, 142–44.

50. Martin, *Adlai Stevenson*, 521.

51. *NYT* (April 9, 1960); *Time* (July 18, 1960); *Congress and the Nation*, 1627–30.

52. O'Donnell and Powers, *"Johnny, We Hardly Knew Ye,"* 207.

53. *Time* (July 25, 1960).

54. Ibid. (July 25, 1960). See also *Newsweek* (July 25, 1960). See Schlesinger's own recollections in Arthur Schlesinger, Jr., *A Thousand Days: John Kennedy in the White House* (Boston, 1965), 45–50.

55. *Newsweek* (Aug. 8, 1960); Barry Goldwater, *Goldwater* (New York, 1988), 256.

56. See Henry Cabot Lodge, *The Storm has Many Eyes* (New York, 1973), 183–84. It was a common belief that Eisenhower's insistence that Lodge be placed on the Republican ticket in 1960 was a reward for heading the draft-Eisenhower group in 1952.

57. *Congress and the Nation*, 37.

58. Nixon, *Memoirs*, 222. *Time* speculated after the election that Nixon would have won had the president entered the campaign earlier. *Time* (Nov. 14, 1960). See also, Donaldson, *First Modern Campaign,* 140.

59. *Congress and the Nation,* 37.

60. Christopher Mathews, *Kennedy and Nixon: The Rivalry that Shaped Postwar America* (New York, 1996), 148; Theodore C. Sorensen, *Kennedy* (New York, 1965), 198. One of best accounts of the Kennedy-Nixon debates is Don Hewitt, *Tell Me a Story: Fifty Years and 60 Minutes in Television* (New York, 2001), 67–70.

61. Donaldson, *First Modern Campaign,* 122–25.

62. *Congress and the Nation,* 39; Donaldson, *First Modern Campaign,* 149–61.

Chapter Seven

1. Lubell, *Revolt of the Moderates,* 265.

2. Louis Harris, *Is there a Republican Majority? Political Trends, 1952–1956* (New York, 1954), 199.

3. NYT (Nov. 23, 1960). Had African Americans cast their votes in 1960 the same as they had in 1956, Kennedy would most likely have lost Illinois, New Jersey, Michigan, South Carolina, and Delaware. See Theodore White, *Making of the President, 1960,* 424.

4. See *The Taft Story,* n.d., campaign pamphlet; and Bill McAdams to Clarence Brown, "Confidential Memo," titled "Outline of Public Relations and Publicity Program, n.d. (fall1947?), Political Files, Taft Papers, LC. See also Patterson, *Mr. Republican,* 396–99.

5. Rosser Reeves, "To Guarantee an Eisenhower Victory," n.d. (1952?), The :30 Second Candidate, Rosser Reeves Collection, State Historical Society of Wisconsin, Madison, Wisconsin. Reeves is best known for his breakthrough advertising campaigns for M&M's, Anacin, and Minute Maid Orange Juice, among others.

6. Broadwater, *Adlai Stevenson,* 121.

7. Halberstam, *The Fifties,* 225–32.

Bibliography

Abramson, Rudy. *Spanning the Century: The Life of W. Averell Harriman, 1891–1986.* New York: William Morrow, 1992.

Adams, Sherman. *Firsthand Report: The Story of the Eisenhower Administration.* New York: Harper, 1961.

Alsop, Stewart. "Lyndon Johnson: How Does He Do It?" *Saturday Evening Post* (Jan. 24, 1959), 43–44.

Ambrose, Stephen. *Eisenhower: The President.* New York: Simon and Schuster, 1984.

Ambrose, Stephen. *Eisenhower: Soldier, General of the Army, President-Elect: 1890–1952.* New York: Simon and Schuster, 1983.

Ambrose, Stephen. *Nixon: The Education of a Politician, 1913–1962,* Vol. 1. New York: Simon and Schuster, 1987.

Anderson, Clinton. *Outsider in the Senate: Senator Clinton Anderson's Memoirs.* New York: World Publishing, 1970.

Ball, George W. *The Past Has Another Pattern: Memoirs.* New York: Norton, 1982.

Bartley, Neuman V. *The Rise of Massive Resistance: Race and Politics in the South During the 1950s.* Baton Rouge: LSU Press, 1970.

Bird, Kai, and Martin J. Sherwin. *American Prometheus: The Triumph and Tragedy of J. Robert Oppenheimer.* New York, Alfred Knopf, 2005.

Blum, John Morton, ed. *The Price of Vision: The Diary of Henry A. Wallace, 1942–1946.* Boston: Houghton Mifflin, 1973.

Blutcher, Harry C. *My Three Years with Eisenhower: The Personal Diary of Captain Harry C. Blutcher, USNR.* New York: Simon and Schuster, 1946.

Bradley, Omar. *A Soldier's Story.* New York: Henry Holt, 1951.

Branch, Taylor. *Parting the Waters: America in the King Years, 1954–1963.* New York: Simon and Schuster, 1988.

Broadwater, Jeff. *Adlai Stevenson: The Odyssey of a Cold War Liberal.* New York: Twayne, 1994.

Brownell, Herbert. *Advising Ike: The Memoirs of Attorney General Herbert Brownell.* Lawrence: University of Kansas Press, 1993.

Buckley, William F. Jr. *Up From Liberalism.* New York: Arlington House, 1959.

Burk, Robert Frederick. *The Eisenhower Administration and Black Civil Rights.* Knoxville: University of Tennessee Press, 1984.

Cohodas, Nadine. *Strom Thurmond and the Politics of Change.* New York: Simon and Schuster, 1993.

Congress and the Nation, 1945–1964, A Review of Government and Politics in the Postwar Years. Washington, D.C.: U.S. Government Printing Office, 1965.

Dallek, Robert. *Lone Star Rising: Lyndon Johnson and His Times, 1908–1960.* New York: Oxford, 1991.

Divine, Robert A. "Lyndon Johnson and the Politics of Space," in Robert A. Divine, ed., *The Johnson Years, II: Vietnam, the Environment, and Science.* Lawrence: University of Kansas Press, 1987.

Divine, Robert A. *The Sputnik Challenge: Eisenhower's Response to the Soviet Satellite.* New York: Oxford University Press, 1993.

Donaldson, Gary. *The First Modern Campaign: Kennedy, Nixon and the Election of 1960.* Lanham: Roman and Littlefield, 2007.

Donaldson, Gary. *Liberalism's Last Hurrah: The Presidential Campaign of 1964.* Armonk, NY: M.E. Sharpe, 2003.

Donaldson, Gary. *Truman Defeats Dewey.* Lexington: University of Kentucky Press, 1999.

Dubofsky, Melvyn. *The State and Labor in Modern America*. Chapel Hill: University of North Carolina Press, 1994.

Dudziak, Mary I. *Cold War Civil Rights: Race and the Image of American Democracy*. Princeton: Princeton University Press, 2000.

Eisenhower, Dwight D. *Crusade in Europe*. Garden City: Doubleday, 1948.

Eisenhower, Dwight D. *Mandate for Change: 1953–1956*. Garden City: Doubleday, 1963.

Eisenhower, Dwight D. *Waging Peace, 1956–1961*. Garden City: Doubleday, 1965.

Eisenhower, John S.D. *Strictly Personal: A Memoir*. Garden City: Doubleday, 1974.

Eisenhower, Milton. *The President is Calling*. Garden City: Doubleday, 1974.

Evans, Rowland, and Robert Novak. *Lyndon B. Johnson: The Exercise of Power*. New York: New American Library, 1966.

Ewald, William Bragg. *Eisenhower the President: The Crucial Days, 1951– 1960*. Englewood Cliffs: Prentice Hall, 1981.

Ferrell, Robert H., ed. *The Diary of James C. Hagerty: Eisenhower in Mid-course, 1954–1955*. Bloomington: Indiana University Press, 1983.

Ferrell, Robert H., ed. *The Eisenhower Diaries*. New York: Norton, 1981.

Ferrell, Robert H., ed. *Off the Record: The Private Papers of Harry S. Truman*. New York: Penguin, 1980.

Ferrell, Robert H. *Harry S. Truman: A Life*. Columbia: University of Missouri Press, 1996.

Ferrell, Robert H., and Francis H. Heller. "Plain Faking?" *American Heritage*. 46 (May/June, 1995), 14–16.

Fite, Gilbert C. *Richard B. Russell: Senator from Georgia*. Chapel Hill: University of North Carolina Press, 1991.

Fried, Richard M. *Men Against McCarthy*. New York: Columbia University Press, 1976.

Galambos, Louis, and Alfred D. Chandler, eds., *The Papers of Dwight D. Eisenhower*, 21 vols. Baltimore: Johns Hopkins University Press, 1970–2001.

Galbraith, John Kenneth. *A Life in Our Times*. New York: Ballantine, 1982.

Gillon, Steven M. *Politics and Vision: The ADA and American Liberalism, 1947–1985*. New York: Oxford, 1987.

Goldberg, Robert Alan. *Barry Goldwater*. New Haven: Yale University Press, 1995.

Goldwater, Barry. *The Conscience of a Conservative*. Shephardsville: Victor Publishing, 1960.

Goldwater, Barry. *Goldwater*. New York: St. Martins, 1989.

Goodwin, Doris Kearns. *The Fitzgeralds and the Kennedys: An American Saga*. New York: Simon and Schuster, 1987.

Goodwin, Doris Kearns. *Lyndon Johnson and the American Dream*. New York: St. Martin's, 1976.

Grantham, Dewey. *The South in Modern America: A Region at Odds*. New York: Harper Collins, 1994.

Greenstein Fred I. *The Hidden-Hand Presidency: Eisenhower as Leader*. Baltimore: Johns Hopkins University Press, 1982.

Griffith, Robert. "Dwight D. Eisenhower and the Corporate Commonwealth," *The American Historical Review* (Feb., 1982), 87–122.

Griffith, Robert. *Ike's Letters to a Friend: 1941–1958*. Lawrence: University of Kansas Press, 1984.

Gunther, John. *Eisenhower: The Man and the Symbol*. New York: Harper Collins, 1952.

Hardeman, D. B., and Donald C. Bacon. *Rayburn: A Biography*. Lanham: Madison, 1987.

Hewett, Don. *Tell Me a Story: Fifty Years and 60 Minutes in Television*. New York: Public Affairs Press, 2001.

Hughes, John Emmet. *The Ordeal of Power: A Political Memoir of the Eisenhower Years*. New York: Antheneum, 1963.

Humphrey, Hubert. *Education of a Public Man: My Life in Politics*. Minneapolis: University of Minnesota Press, 1991.

Jackson, Kenneth. *Crabgrass Frontier: The Suburbanization of the United States*. New York: Oxford, 1985.

Jilson, Cal. *American Government: Political Change and Institutional Development.* 4th ed., New York: Routledge, 2008.

Johnson, Lyndon B. *The Vantage Point: Perspectives of the Presidency, 1963–1969.* New York: Holt, Rinehart and Winston, 1971.

Johnson, Walter, ed., *The Papers of Adlai E. Stevenson, Governor of Illinois, 1949–1953.* Boston: Little Brown, 1973.

Johnson, Walter, ed., *The Papers of Adlai E. Stevenson, Washington to Springfield, 1941–1948.* Boston: Little Brown, 1973.

Judas, John. *William F. Buckley, Jr.: Patron Saint of the Conservatives.* New York: Simon and Schuster, 1988.

Kessler-Harris, Alice. *In Pursuit of Equality: Women, Men, and the Quest for Economic Citizenship in 20th Century America.* New York: Oxford, 2001.

Larson, Arthur. *A Republican Looks at His Party.* New York: Harper, 1956.

Larson, Arthur. *Eisenhower: The President Nobody Knew.* New York: Scribner's, 1968.

Lash, Joseph P. *Eleanor: The Years Alone.* New York: Smithmark, 1972.

Lawson, Steven F. *Black Ballots: Voting Rights in the South, 1944–1969.* New York: Columbia University Press, 1976.

Lawson, Steven F. *Running For Freedom: Civil Rights and Black Politics since 1951.* New York: McGraw-Hill, 1996.

Leuctenburg, William. *Troubled Feast: American Society since 1945.* New York: Harper Collins, 1983.

Lodge, Henry Cabot. *The Storm Has Many Eyes: A Personal Narrative.* New York: W.W. Norton, 1973.

Lubell, Samuel. *Revolt of the Moderates.* New York: Harper, 1956.

Lyon, Peter. *Eisenhower: Portrait of a Hero.* Boston: Little Brown, 1974.

Manchester William. *The Glory and the Dream: A Narrative History of America, 1932–1972.* Boston: Little Brown, 1973.

Mann, Robert. *The Walls of Jericho: Lyndon Johnson, Hubert Humphrey, Richard Russell, and the Struggle for Civil Rights.* New York: Harcourt Brace, 1996.

Martin, John Bartlow. *Adlai Stevenson of Illinois.* Garden City Doubleday, 1976.

Mathews, Christopher. *Kennedy and Nixon: The Rivalry that Shaped Postwar America.* New York: Simon and Schuster, 1996.

May, Gary. *China Scapegoat: The Diplomatic Ordeal of John Carter Vincent.* Long Grove: Waveland Press, 1982.

Mazo, Earl. *Richard Nixon: A Political and Personal Portrait.* New York: Avon, 2nd edition, 1960.

McKeever, Porter. *Adlai Stevenson: His Life and Legacy.* New York: William Morrow, 1989.

Miller, Merle. *Lyndon: An Oral Biography.* New York: Ballantine, 1980.

Miller, Merle. *Plain Speaking: An Oral Biography of Harry S. Truman.* New York: Berkeley Publishing, 1973.

Millis, Walter, ed. *The Forrestal Diaries.* New York: Viking, 1951.

Morgan, Iwan W. *Eisenhower Versus the Spenders.* New York: St. Martin Press, 1990.

Morgan, Kay Summersby. *Fast Forgetting: My Love Affair with Dwight D. Eisenhower.* New York: Simon and Schuster, 1976.

Neal, Steve. *Harry and Ike*: *The Partnership that Remade the Postwar World.* New York: Scribner, 2001.

Nichols, David A. *A Matter of Justice: Eisenhower and the Beginning of the Civil Rights Revolution.* New York: Simon and Schuster, 2007.

Nixon, Richard. *RN: The Memoirs of Richard Nixon.* New York: Grosset and Dunlap, 1978.

Nixon, Richard. *Six Crises.* Garden City: Doubleday, 1962.

O'Donnell, Kenneth P., and David F. Powers. *"Johnny We Hardly Knew Ye:" Memories of John Fitzgerald Kennedy.* Boston: Pocket Books, 2nd ed., 1973.

Olson, James. *Stuart Symington: A Life.* Columbia: University of Missouri Press, 2003.

Oshinsky, David. *A Conspiracy So Immense: The World of Joe McCarthy.* New York: Oxford, 1983.

Pach, Chester, and Elmo Richardson. *The Presidency of Dwight D. Eisenhower.* Lawrence: University of Kansas Press, 1991.

Parmet, Herbert S. *Jack: The Struggles of John F. Kennedy.* New York: Dial, 1980.

Parmet, Herbert S. *Richard Nixon and His America.* Boston: Little Brown, 1990.

Patterson, James T. *Mr. Republican: A Biography of Robert A. Taft.* Boston: Houghton Mifflin, 1972.

Persico, Joseph. *The Imperial Rockefeller: A Biography of Nelson A. Rockefeller.* New York: Simon and Schuster, 1982.

Pickett, William B. *Eisenhower Decides to Run: Presidential Politics and Cold War Strategy.* Chicago: Ivan Dee, 2000.

Public Papers of the Presidents of the United States: Containing the Public Messages, Speeches, and Statements of the President. Dwight D. Eisenhower, 8 vols., Jan. 1953 to Jan. 1960, Washington: United States Government Printing Office, 1960–1961.

Reedy, George. *Lyndon B. Johnson: A Memoir.* New York: Andrews and Mc Meel, 1982.

Reinhard, David W. *The Republican Right since 1945.* Lexington: University of Kentucky Press, 1983.

Rose, Mark H. *Interstate: Express Highway Politics, 1939–1989.* Knoxville: University of Tennessee Press, 1979.

Schlesinger, Jr., Arthur M. *A Thousand Days: John F. Kennedy in the White House.* Boston: Houghton Mifflin, 1965.

Shannon, William. "More of the Same," *Commonweal* (Dec. 21, 1956), 306–7.

Shesol, Jeff. *Mutual Contempt: Lyndon Johnson, Robert Kennedy, and the Feud That Defined a Decade.* New York: Norton, 1997.

Smith, Jean Edward. *Lucius D. Clay: An American Life.* New York: Henry Holt, 1990.

Solberg Carl. *Hubert Humphrey: A Biography.* St. Paul, MN: Borealis,1984.

Sorensen, Theodore C. *Kennedy.* New York: Harper and Row, 1965.

Stebenne, David L. *Modern Republican: Arthur Larson and the Eisenhower Years.* Bloomington: Indiana University Press, 2006.

Steinberg, Alfred. *Sam Johnson's Boy: A Close-up of the President from Texas.* New York: MacMillan, 1968.

Tananbaum, Duane. *The Bricker Amendment Controversy: A Test of Eisenhower's Political Leadership*. Ithaca: Cornell University Press, 1988.

Truman, Harry S. *Memoirs: Years of Trial and Hope*. New York: New American Library, 1965, first published in 1956.

Wagner, Steven. *Eisenhower Republicanism: Pursuing the Middle Way*. DeKalb: Northern Illinois University Press, 2006.

Wildavsky, Aaron. *Dixon-Yates: A Study in Power Politics*. New Haven: Yale University Press, 1962.

Woods, Randall. *LBJ: Architect of American Ambition*. New York: Free Press, 2006.

Yaqub, Salim. *Containing Arab Nationalism: The Eisenhower Doctrine and the Middle East*. Chapel Hill: University of North Carolina Press, 2006.

Zieger, Robert H. *American Workers, American Unions: The Twentieth Century*. Baltimore: Johns Hopkins University Press, 2002.

NEWSPAPERS AND PERIODICALS

Fortune
Life
Newsweek
New York Times
Public Opinion Quarterly
Saturday Evening Post
Time
U.S. News and World Report
Washington Post

ORAL HISTORIES

Sherman Adams, Eisenhower Library Oral History Collection
James Cain, Johnson Library Oral History Collection
Liz Carpenter, Johnson Library Oral History Collection
Milton Eisenhower, Columbia University Oral History Collection
James Hagerty, Columbia University Oral History Collection
James Hagerty, Eisenhower Library Oral History Collection
Hubert Humphrey, Johnson Library Oral History Collection

James McPherson, Johnson Library Oral History Collection
Joseph Rauh, Johnson Library Oral History Collection
George Reedy, Johnson Library Oral History Collection
James Rowe, Johnson Library Oral History Collection
William S. White, Johnson Library Oral History Collection

PAPERS, DOCUMENTS, AND MANUSCRIPTS

Americans for Democratic Action, Papers, Wisconsin State Historical
    Society, Madison, Wisconsin
Everett M. Dirksen Papers, Dirksen Congressional Center, Pekin, Illinois
Dwight D. Eisenhower Papers, Dwight D. Eisenhower Library, Abilene,
    Kansas
Face the Nation, transcripts, John F. Kennedy Library, Boston,
    Massachusetts
Lyndon B. Johnson Archives, Lyndon B. Johnson Library, Austin, Texas
Lyndon B. Johnson Papers, Lyndon B. Johnson Library, Austin, Texas
Meet the Press, transcripts, Lawrence Spivak Papers, Library of Congress,
    Washington, DC
William D. Robinson Papers, Dwight D. Eisenhower Library, Abilene,
    Kansas
Richard B. Russell Papers, Richard B. Russell Library for Political Research
    and Studies, University of Georgia Libraries, Athens, Georgia
Theodore Sorensen Papers, John F. Kennedy Library, Boston, Massachusetts
Adlai E. Stevenson Papers, Seeley G. Mudd Library, Princeton University,
    Princeton, New Jersey
Robert A. Taft Papers, Library of Congress, Washington, DC

ABBREVIATIONS

ADA Americans for Democratic Action
COHC Columbia (University) Oral History Collection
DDEL Dwight David Eisenhower Library
EP Eisenhower Papers
JLOHC Johnson Library Oral History Collection
LC Library of Congress

LBJA Lyndon B. Johnson Archives
LBJL Lyndon B. Johnson Library
LBJP Lyndon B. Johnson Papers
NYT New York Times
OH Oral History
PPP Public Papers of the Presidents

Index

Note: Page numbers with photographs are in *italics*.